Software Testing Foundations

About the Authors

Andreas Spillner is emeritus professor of computer science at the University of Applied Sciences Bremen. During the 1990s and early 2000s he spent 10 years as spokesman for the *TAV* (Test, Analysis, and Verification) group at the Gesellschaft für Informatik (German Computer Science Society) that he also helped to found. He is a founder member of the *German Testing Board* and was made an honorary member in 2009. He was made a fellow of the *Gesellschaft für Informatik* in 2007. His software specialty areas are technology, quality assurance, and testing.

Tilo Linz is co-founder and a board member of imbus AG, a leading software testing solution provider. He has been deeply involved in software testing and quality assurance for more than 25 years. As a founding member and chairman of the *German Testing Board* and a founding member of the *International Software Testing Qualifications Board*, he has played a major role in shaping and advancing education and training in this specialist area both nationally and internationally. Tilo is the author of *Testing in Scrum* (published by Rocky Nook), which covers testing in agile projects based on the foundations presented in this book.

Andreas Spillner · Tilo Linz

Software Testing Foundations

A Study Guide for the Certified Tester Exam

- **Foundation Level**
- **ISTQB® Compliant**

5th, revised and updated Edition

dpunkt.verlag

Andreas Spillner · *andreas.spillner@hs-bremen.de*
Tilo Linz · *tilo.linz@imbus.de*

Editor: Dr. Michael Barabas / Christa Preisendanz
Translation and Copyediting: Jeremy Cloot
Layout and Type: Josef Hegele
Production Editor: Stefanie Weidner
Cover Design: Helmut Kraus, *www.exclam.de*
Printing and Binding: mediaprint solutions GmbH, 33100 Paderborn, and Lightning Source®, Ingram Content Group.

Bibliographic information published by the Deutsche Nationalbibliothek (DNB)
The Deutsche Nationalbibliothek lists this publication in the Deutsche Nationalbibliografie; detailed bibliographic data can be found on the Internet at *http://dnb.dnb.de*.

ISBN dpunkt.verlag:
Print   978-3-86490-834-7
PDF   978-3-96910-298-5
ePUB   978-3-96910-299-2
mobi   978-3-96910-300-5

ISBN Rocky Nook:
Print   978-1-68198-853-5
PDF   978-1-68198-854-2
ePUB   978-1-68198-855-9
mobi   978-1-68198-856-6

5th, revised and updated edition 2021 Copyright © 2021 dpunkt.verlag GmbH
Wieblinger Weg 17
69123 Heidelberg

Title of the German Original: Basiswissen Softwaretest
Aus- und Weiterbildung zum Certified Tester – Foundation Level nach ISTQB®-Standard
6., überarbeitete und aktualisierte Auflage 2019
ISBN 978-3-86490-583-4

Distributed in the UK and Europe by Publishers Group UK and dpunkt.verlag GmbH.
Distributed in the U.S. and all other territories by Ingram Publisher Services and Rocky Nook, Inc.

Many of the designations in this book used by manufacturers and sellers to distinguish their products are claimed as trademarks of their respective companies. Where those designations appear in this book, and dpunkt.verlag was aware of a trademark claim, the designations have been printed in caps or initial caps. They are used in editorial fashion only and for the benefit of such companies, they are not intended to convey endorsement or other affiliation with this book.
No part of the material protected by this copyright notice may be reproduced or utilized in any form, electronic or mechanical, including photocopying, recording, or by any information storage and retrieval system, without written permission of the copyright owner. While reasonable care has been exercised in the preparation of this book, the publisher and author assume no responsibility for errors or omissions, or for damages resulting from the use of the information contained herein.
This book is printed on acid-free paper.
Printed in Germany and in the United States.

5 4 3 2 1 0

Preface to the 5th Edition

The first edition of the book was published in German at the end of 2002. Since then, *Basiswissen Softwaretest* has been the best-selling book on software testing in the German-speaking world.

Bestseller

This 5th edition in English has been comprehensively revised and updated. It is based on the latest (6th) edition of the German-language book and the current 2018 *ISTQB® Certified Tester – Foundation Level* syllabus.

The *Certified Tester* qualification scheme is extremely successful and is widely recognized and accepted within the IT industry. It has become the de facto global standard for software testing and quality assurance education. By the end of 2020 there were over 955,000 exams taken and more than 721,000 certifications issued in 129 countries around the world [URL: ISTQB]. Many IT employment ads for beginners and experienced workers reflect this, and certified training is often an obligatory requirement. The *Certified Tester* scheme is also part of the curriculum at many universities and technical colleges.

The Certified Tester training scheme

In spite of this rapid development, there is a lot of the grass-roots knowledge in the field of computer science that doesn't change very much over the years. We take the *Foundations* part of our book title seriously and don't discuss topics that have yet to be proven in everyday practice. Specialist topics such as web app or embedded system testing are not part of these foundations.

Grass-roots knowledge required in the IT world

This 5th edition of *Software Testing Foundations* has been comprehensively revised and extended, and its content brought completely up to date.

What's new!

The latest revision of the ISTQB® syllabus has seen some test techniques shifted to higher training levels, so these are no longer part of the *Foundations* syllabus. However, we have kept the corresponding sections in the book and have highlighted them as **side notes**. If you are using the book exclusively for exam preparation you can simply skip the **side note** sections.

Side notes are not part of the official syllabus

New test techniques included

Many readers have told us that they use the book for reference in their everyday work scenarios. This is why we have included a number of additional test techniques that do not appear in the *Foundations* syllabus. These include techniques such as pair-wise testing that weren't covered in previous editions.

The case study that illustrates the implementation of the test techniques has been adapted and comprehensively updated.

We have revised the lists of standards to reflect the changes made by the introduction of ISO 29119, and all the URLs referenced in the text have been updated too.

Online resources

Any future changes to the syllabus and the glossary that affect the book text can be found on our website [URL: Softwaretest Knowledge], where you will also find exercises that relate to the individual chapters in the book. Any necessary corrections or additions to the book text are also made available at the website.

For a book like this, success is rarely down to the authors alone, and we would like to thank all our colleagues at the German Testing Board and the *International Software Testing Qualifications Board*, without whom the *Certified Tester* program would never have achieved the global success

Thanks

that it enjoys. Many thanks also to Hans Schaefer, our co-author of the previous four editions of the book, for his constructive cooperation.

We would further like to thank our readers for their many comments and reviews, which have encouraged us during our work and motivated us to keep getting better. Heartfelt thanks also go to our editor Christa Preisendanz and the entire team at dpunkt.verlag for years of successful cooperation.

We wish all our readers success in the practical implementation of the testing approaches described in the book and—if you are using the book to prepare for the *Certified Tester Foundation Level* exam—we wish you every success in answering the exam questions.

Andreas Spillner and *Tilo Linz*
May 2021

Foreword by Yaron Tsubery

The software systems industry continues to grow rapidly and, especially over the last two decades, exponentially. Market requirements and a growing appetite for exciting new challenges have fuelled the development of new software technologies. These new opportunities affect almost everyone on our planet and reach us primarily via the internet and, subsequently, via smart devices and technologies.

The need for software that is easy to create and maintain has caused many key industries—such as health, automotive, defense, and finance—to open up and become visible to the world via applications and/or web interfaces. Alongside these traditional domains, new types of services (such as social media and e-commerce) have appeared and thrived on the global market. The rapid growth and enormous demands involved in introducing new software-based products that greatly impact our lifestyles and our wellbeing require new and faster ways of producing software solutions.

This situation has created a market in which multiple companies compete for market share with extremely similar products. Such competition is beneficial to consumers (i.e., software users) and, as a result, software-based products have started to become commoditized. Software manufacturers have begun to think more economically, generating increased revenues using fewer resources (i.e., doing more with less). Continual introduction of new products into our daily lives has given rise to the "agile" design and production ethos—driving a cultural change in the tradition software development life cycle, as well as pushing forward the necessity of more and early automatic tests (e.g. as driven by the DevOps movement)—that is increasingly commonplace in today's software industry, while the business leaders behind software-based products have understood that the world is becoming smaller and that competition is getting fiercer all the time. An increasingly short time to market is essential not only for generating revenue, but also simply to survive in today's market. Successful and innovative companies understand that they need to put the customer first if they want to maintain product quality, generate brand loyalty, and increase their market share. In other words, the software industry has understood the importance of the customer to the overall product life cycle.

We in the software testing business have always known the importance of quality to the customer, because part of our job is to represent the customer's point of view. The challenges we face have grown with the complexity of software products, and we sometimes still find ourselves having to justify the necessity for software testing, even if it has become a largely standard practice within the software industry. Recently, the rise of software-based artificial intelligence (AI)—such as software enhancement in robots and autonomous devices—has created a whole new set of challenges.

Software testing is an extremely important factor in the industry. Alongside controlling costs and quality, the main issue is customer focus. Preserving a healthy balance between cost and quality is an essential customer requirement, making it critical to have well-trained and highly professional people assigned to quality and software testing roles. Recruiting skilled professionals is the key to success. The primary factors we look for when recruiting are related to a person's knowledge and skills. We look at the degree to which a person is aligned with the software testing profession, and with the required technology and industry domain (such as web, mobile, medical devices, finance, automotive, and so on). We also have to ask ourselves whether a person is suited to work in the product domain itself (for example, when candidates come from competitors). Communications and soft skills that fit in with the team/group/company are important too. In the case of industry newcomers, we have to consider how much potential a person has. This book teaches the fundamentals of software testing and provides a solid basis for enhancing your knowledge and experience through constant learning from external sources, your own personal experience, and from others.

When reading an educational book, I expect it to be sequentially structured and easy to understand. This book is based on the *Certified Tester Foundation Level (CTFL)* syllabus, which is part of the ISTQB® (International Software Testing Qualifications Board) education program. The ISTQB® has created a well-organized and systematic training program that is designed to teach and qualify software testers in a variety of roles and domains. One of the primary objectives of the ISTQB® program is to create professional and internationally accepted terminology based on knowledge and experience. The chapters in the book are designed to take you on that journey and provide you with the established and cutting-edge fundamentals necessary to becoming a successful tester. They combine comprehensive theory with detailed practical examples and side notes that will enhance and broaden your view of software systems and how to test them. This book provides a great way to learn more about software testing for anyone who is studying the subject, thinking about joining the software testing profession, or for newcomers to the field.

For those who already have a role in software testing, the practical examples provided (based on a case study and corresponding side notes) are sure to help you learn. They provide a great basis for comparison with and application to your own real-world projects. This book contains a wealth of great ideas that will help you to build and improve your own software testing skills. The new, revised edition is based on the latest (2018) ISTQB® CTFL, which has been updated to cover agile processes and experience gained from changes that have taken place within the industry over the last few years. It also includes references to the other syllabi and professional content upon which it is based, and an updated version of the case study introduced in earlier editions. The case study is based on a multi-layer solution that includes both specific and general technical aspects of software system architecture. The case study in this edition is based on a new-generation version of the system detailed in previous editions, thus enabling you to learn from a practical, project-based viewpoint.

The world is changing fast every day. Some of the technologies that we use today will become obsolete within a few years and the products we build will probably become obsolete even sooner. Software is an integral and essential part of virtually all the technology that surrounds us. Along with growth and expansion in the artificial intelligence (AI) arena and other new technologies that have yet to be introduced, this continual change offers new and exciting opportunities for the software testing profession. We are sure to find ourselves tuning our knowledge and experience in various ways, and we may even find ourselves teaching and coaching not only humans but also machines and systems that test products for us.

The fundamental knowledge, grass-roots experience, and practical examples provided by this book will prepare you for the ever-changing world and will shape your knowledge to enable you to test better and, in the future, perhaps pass on your knowledge to others.

I wish you satisfying and fruitful reading.

Yaron Tsubery
Former ISTQB® President
President ITCB®

Overview

1	Introduction	1
2	Software Testing Basics	7
3	Testing Throughout the Software Development Lifecycle	49
4	Static Testing	95
5	Dynamic Testing	121
6	Test Management	201
7	Test Tools	251

Appendices 277

A	Important Notes on the Syllabus and the Certified Tester Exam	279
B	Glossary	281
C	References	309
	Index	317

Contents

1	**Introduction**		**1**
2	**Software Testing Basics**		**7**
	2.1	Concepts and Motivations	7
		2.1.1 Defect and Fault Terminology	9
		2.1.2 Testing Terminology	12
		2.1.3 Test Artifacts and the Relationships Between Them	14
		2.1.4 Testing Effort	16
		2.1.5 Applying Testing Skills Early Ensures Success.	19
		2.1.6 The Basic Principles of Testing	20
	2.2	Software Quality.	22
		2.2.1 Software Quality according to ISO 25010	22
		2.2.2 Quality Management and Quality Assurance	26
	2.3	The Testing Process.	27
		2.3.1 Test Planning	29
		2.3.2 Test Monitoring and Control	30
		2.3.3 Test Analysis	31
		2.3.4 Test Design	34
		2.3.5 Test Implementation	36
		2.3.6 Test Execution	37
		2.3.7 Test Completion	40
		2.3.8 Traceability	41
		2.3.9 The Influence of Context on the Test Process	42
	2.4	The Effects of Human Psychology on Testing	43
		2.4.1 How Testers and Developers Think.	46
	2.5	Summary.	47

Contents

3 Testing Throughout the Software Development Lifecycle — **49**

3.1 Sequential Development Models 49
  3.1.1 The Waterfall Model 50
  3.1.2 The V-Model 51
3.2 Iterative and Incremental Development Models 54
3.3 Software Development in Project and Product Contexts 56
3.4 Testing Levels 58
  3.4.1 Component Testing 58
  3.4.2 Integration Testing 66
  3.4.3 System Testing 74
  3.4.4 Acceptance Testing 76
3.5 Test Types 80
  3.5.1 Functional Tests 80
  3.5.2 Non-Functional Tests 83
  3.5.3 Requirements-Based and Structure-Based Testing 85
3.6 Testing New Product Versions 86
  3.6.1 Testing Following Software Maintenance 88
  3.6.2 Testing Following Release Development 90
  3.6.3 Regression Testing 91
3.7 Summary 93

4 Static Testing — **95**

4.1 What Can We Analyze and Test? 96
4.2 Static Test Techniques 97
4.3 The Review Process 98
  4.3.1 Review Process Activities 99
  4.3.2 Different Individual Review Techniques 102
  4.3.3 Roles and Responsibilities within the Review Process 106
4.4 Types of Review 108
4.5 Critical Factors, Benefits, and Limits 114
4.6 The Differences Between Static and Dynamic Testing 117
4.7 Summary 119

5	**Dynamic Testing**			**121**
	5.1	Black-Box Test Techniques		126
		5.1.1	Equivalence Partitioning	126
		5.1.2	Boundary Value Analysis	137
		5.1.3	State Transition Testing	145
		5.1.4	Decision Table Testing	153
		5.1.5	Pair-Wise Testing	159
		5.1.6	Use-Case Testing	168
		5.1.7	Evaluation of Black-Box Testing	171
	5.2	White-Box Test Techniques		172
		5.2.1	Statement Testing and Coverage	173
		5.2.2	Decision Testing and Coverage	175
		5.2.3	Testing Conditions	179
		5.2.4	Evaluation of White-Box Testing	188
	5.3	Experience-Based Test Techniques		189
	5.4	Selecting the Right Technique		195
	5.5	Summary		199
6	**Test Management**			**201**
	6.1	Test Organization		201
		6.1.1	Independent Testing	201
		6.1.2	Roles, Tasks, and Qualifications	205
	6.2	Testing Strategies		210
		6.2.1	Test Planning	210
		6.2.2	Selecting a Testing Strategy	213
		6.2.3	Concrete Strategies	215
		6.2.4	Testing and Risk	217
		6.2.5	Testing Effort and Costs	220
		6.2.6	Estimating Testing Effort	222
		6.2.7	The Cost of Testing vs. The Cost of Defects	223
	6.3	Test Planning, Control, and Monitoring		225
		6.3.1	Test Execution Planning	226
		6.3.2	Test Control	232
		6.3.3	Test Cycle Monitoring	232
		6.3.4	Test Reports	233

	6.4	Defect Management.	235
		6.4.1 Evaluating Test Reports	236
		6.4.2 Creating a Defect Report	238
		6.4.3 Classifying Failures and Defects	241
		6.4.4 Defect Status Tracking	242
		6.4.5 Evaluation and Reporting	245
	6.5	Configuration Management	246
	6.6	Relevant Standards and Norms	248
	6.7	Summary.	249
7	**Test Tools**		**251**
	7.1	Types of Test Tools	252
		7.1.1 Test Management Tools	252
		7.1.2 Test Specification Tools	256
		7.1.3 Static Test Tools.	257
		7.1.4 Tools for Automating Dynamic Tests.	260
		7.1.5 Load and Performance Testing Tools.	266
		7.1.6 Tool-Based Support for Other Kinds of Tests	267
	7.2	Benefits and Risks of Test Automation	268
	7.3	Using Test Tools Effectively	271
		7.3.1 Basic Considerations and Principles	271
		7.3.2 Tool Selection.	272
		7.3.3 Pilot Project.	273
		7.3.4 Success Factors During Rollout and Use.	274
	7.4	Summary.	275

Appendices		**277**
A	**Important Notes on the Syllabus and the Certified Tester Exam**	**279**
B	**Glossary**	**281**
C	**References**	**309**
C.1	Literature	309
C.2	Norms and Standards	311
C.3	URLs	313
Index		**317**

1 Introduction

Software is everywhere! Nowadays there are virtually no devices, machines, or systems that are not partially or entirely controlled by software. Important functionality in cars—such as engine or gear control—have long been software-based, and these are now being complemented by increasingly smart software-based driver assist systems, anti-lock brake systems, parking aids, lane departure systems and, perhaps most importantly, autonomous driving systems. Software and software quality therefore not only govern how large parts of our lives function, they are also increasingly important factors in our everyday safety and wellbeing.

Equally, the smooth running of countless companies today relies largely on the reliability of the software systems that control major processes or individual activities. Software therefore determines future competitiveness. For example, the speed at which an insurance company can introduce a new product, or even just a new tariff, depends on the speed at which the corresponding IT systems can be adapted or expanded.

Quality has therefore become a crucial factor for the success of products and companies in the fields of both technical and commercial software.

High dependency on reliable software

Most companies have recognized their dependence on software, whether relying on the functionality of existing systems or the introduction of new and better ones. Companies therefore constantly invest in their own development skills and improved system quality. One way to achieve these objectives is to introduce systematic software evaluation and testing procedures. Some companies already have comprehensive and strict testing procedures in place, but many projects still suffer from a lack of basic knowledge regarding the capacity and usefulness of software testing procedures.

This book aims to provide the basic knowledge necessary to set up structured, systematic software evaluation and testing techniques that will help you improve overall software quality.

Grass-roots knowledge of structured evaluation and testing

This book does not presume previous knowledge of software quality assurance. It is designed for reference but can also be used for self-study.

The text includes a single, continuous case study that provides explanations and practical solutions for each of the topics covered.

This book is aimed at all software testers in all types of companies who want to develop a solid foundation for their work. It is also for programmers and developers who have taken over (or are about to take over) existing test scenarios, and it is also aimed at project managers who are responsible for budgeting and overall procedural improvement. Additionally, it offers support for career changers in IT-related fields and people involved in application approval, implementation, and development.

Especially in IT, lifelong learning is essential, and software testing courses are offered by a broad range of companies and individuals. Universities, too, are increasingly offering testing courses, and this book is aimed at teachers and students alike.

Certification program for software testers

The ISTQB® *Certified Tester* program is today seen as the worldwide standard for software testing and quality assurance training. The ISTQB® (*International Software Testing Qualifications Board*) [URL: ISTQB] coordinates qualification activities in individual countries and ensures the global consistency and comparability of the syllabi and exam papers. National *Testing Boards* are responsible for publishing and maintaining local content as well as the organization and supervision of exams. They also approve courses and offer accreditation for training providers. Testing Boards therefore guarantee that courses are of a consistently high standard and that participants end up with an internationally recognized certificate. Members of the Testing Boards include training providers, testing experts from industrial and consulting firms, and university lecturers. They also include representatives from trade associations.

Three-stage training scheme

The *Certified Tester* training scheme is made up of units with three levels of qualification. For more details, see the ISTQB® [URL: ISTQB] website. The basics of software testing are described in the *Foundation Level* syllabus. You can then move on to take the *Advanced Level* exam, which offers a deeper understanding of evaluation and testing skills. The *Expert Level* certificate is aimed at experienced software testing professionals, and consists of a set of modules that cover various advanced topics (see also section 6.1.2). In addition, there are syllabi for agile software development (foundation and advanced level) as well as special topics from the testing area (for example, Security Tester, Model-Based Tester, Automotive Software Tester).

This book covers the contents of the *Foundation Level* syllabus. You can use the book for self-study or in conjunction with an approved course.

The topics covered in this book and the basic content of the *Foundation Certificate* course are as follows:

Chapter overview

Chapter 2 discusses the basics of software testing. Alongside the concepts of when to test, the objectives to aim for, and the required testing thoroughness, it also addresses the basic concepts of testing processes. We also talk about the psychological difficulties that can arise when you are looking for errors in your own work.

Software testing basics

Chapter 3 introduces common development lifecycle models (sequential, iterative, incremental, agile) and explains the role that testing plays in each. The various test types and test levels are explained, and we investigate the difference between functional and non-functional testing. We also look at regression testing.

Lifecycle testing

Static testing (i.e., tests during which the test object is not executed) are introduced in Chapter 4. Reviews and static tests are used successfully by many organizations, and we go into detail on the various approaches you can take.

Static testing

Chapter 5 addresses testing in a stricter sense and discusses "black-box" and "white-box" dynamic testing techniques. Various test techniques and methods are explained in detail for both. We wrap up this chapter by looking at when it makes sense to augment common testing techniques using experience-based or intuitive testing techniques.

Dynamic testing

Chapter 6 discusses the organizational skills and tasks that you need to consider when managing test processes. We also look at the requirements for defect and configuration management, and wind up with a look at the economics of testing.

Test management

Testing software without the use of dedicated tools is time-consuming and extremely costly. Chapter 7 introduces various types of testing tools and discusses how to choose and implement the right tools for the job you are doing.

Test tools

Most of the processes described in this book are illustrated using a case study based on the following scenario:

Case Study: VirtualShowRoom VSR-II

A car manufacturer has been running an electronic sales system called *VirtualShowRoom (VSR)* for over a decade. The system runs at all the company's dealers worldwide:

- Customers can configure their own vehicle (model, color, extras, and so on) on a computer, either alone or assisted by a salesperson. The system displays the available options and immediately calculates the corresponding price. This functionality is performed by the *DreamCar* module.

- Once the customer has selected a configuration, he can then select optimal financing using the *EasyFinance* module, order the vehicle using the *JustInTime* module, and select appropriate insurance using the *NoRisk* module. The *FactBook* module manages all customer and contract data.

The manufacturer's sales and marketing department has decided to update the system and has defined the following objectives:

- *VSR* is a traditional client-server system. The new *VSR-II* system is to be web-based and needs to be accessible via a browser window on any type of device (desktop, tablet, or smartphone).
- The *DreamCar*, *EasyFinance*, *FactBook*, *JustInTime*, and *NoRisk* modules will be ported to the new technology base and, during the process, will be expanded to varying degrees.
- The new *ConnectedCar* module is to be integrated into the system. This module collects and manages status data for all vehicles sold, and communicates data relating to scheduled maintenance and repairs to the driver as well as to the dealership and/or service partner. It also provides the driver with various additional bookable services, such as a helpdesk and emergency services. Vehicle software can be updated and activated "over the air".
- Each of the five existing modules will be ported and developed by a dedicated team. An additional team will develop the new *ConnectedCar* module. The project employs a total of 60 developers and other specialists from internal company departments as well as a number of external software companies.
- The teams will work using the *Scrum* principles of agile development. This agile approach requires each module to be tested during each iteration. The system is to be delivered incrementally.
- In order to avoid complex repeat data comparisons between the old and new systems, *VSR-II* will only go live once it is able to duplicate the functionality provided by the original *VSR* system.

Within the scope of the project and the agile approach, most project participants will be confronted or entrusted with test tasks to varying degrees. This book provides the basic knowledge of the test techniques and processes required to perform these tasks. Figure 1-1 shows an overview of the planned *VSR-II* system.

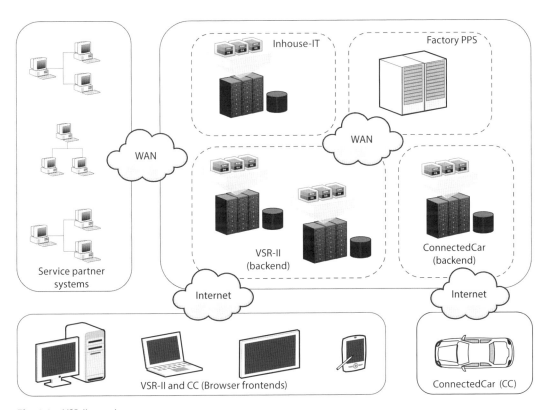

Fig. 1-1 *VSR-II overview*

The appendices at the end of the book include references to the syllabus and *Certified Tester* exam, a glossary, and a bibliography. Sections of the text that go beyond the scope of the syllabus are marked as side notes.

Certified Tester syllabus and exam

The book's website [URL: Softwaretest Knowledge] includes sample exam questions relating to each chapter, updates and addenda to the text, and references to other books by authors whose work supports the *Certified Tester* training scheme.

The book's website

We have put a free implementation of *VSR-II* as a test object online for training purposes[1]. It reproduces the *VSR-II* examples included in the book on a realistic, executable system, so you can "test" live to find the software bugs hidden in *VSR-II* by applying the test techniques presented in the book. It takes just a few mouse clicks to get started:

Web-based Training System vsr.testbench.com

1. Open your browser and load *vsr.testbench.com*
2. Create your personal *VSR-II* training workspace
3. Log into your *VSR-II* workspace and start

Fig. 1-2 *VSR-II Training System Login-Screen*

Also included in your registration for a *VSR-II* training workspace is a free basic license for the test management system *TestBench CS*, which includes the *VSR-II* test specification as a demo project and several of the *VSR-II* test cases presented in the book.

You can use *TestBench CS* not only for learning and training, but also for efficient testing of your own "real" software. A description of all features can be found at [URL: TestBench CS].

Many thanks to our colleagues at imbus Academy, imbus JumpStart and imbus TestBench CS Development Team for this awesome implementation of the VSR-II Case Study as a web-based training system.

2 Software Testing Basics

This introductory chapter explains the basic concepts of software testing that are applied in the chapters that follow. Important concepts included in the syllabus are illustrated throughout the book using our practical VSR-II case study. The seven fundamental principles of software testing are introduced, and the bulk of the chapter is dedicated to explaining the details of the testing process and the various activities it involves. To conclude, we will discuss the psychological issues involved in testing, and how to avoid or work around them.

2.1 Concepts and Motivations

Industrially manufactured products are usually spot-checked to make sure they fulfill the planned requirements and perform the required task. Different products have varying quality requirements and, if the final product is flawed or faulty, the production process or the design has to be modified to remedy this. *Quality requirements*

What is generally true for industrial production processes is also true for the development of software. However, checking parts of the product or the finished product can be tricky because the product itself isn't actually tangible, making "hands-on" testing impossible. Visual checks are limited and can only be performed by careful scrutiny of the development documentation. *Software is intangible*

Software that is unreliable or that simply doesn't perform the required task can be highly problematic. Bad software costs time and money and can ruin a company's reputation. It can even endanger human life—for example, when the "autopilot" software in a partially autonomous vehicle reacts erroneously or too late. *Faulty software is a serious problem*

It is therefore extremely important to check the quality of a software product to minimize the risk of failures or crashes. Testing monitors software quality and reduces risk by revealing faults at the development stage. Software testing is therefore an essential but also highly complex task. *Testing helps to assess software quality*

Case Study:
The risks of using
faulty software

Every release of the *VSR-II* system has to be suitably tested before it is delivered and rolled out. This aims to identify and remedy faults before they can do any damage. For example, if the system executes an order in a faulty way, this can cause serious financial problems for the customer, the dealer and the manufacturer, as well as damaging the manufacturer's image. Undiscovered faults like this increase the risk involved in running the software.

Testing involves taking a spot-check approach

Testing is often understood as spot-check execution[1] of the software in question (the test object) on a computer. The test object is fed with test data covering various test cases and is then executed. The evaluation that follows checks whether the test object fulfills its planned requirements.[2]

Testing involves more than just executing tests on a computer

However, testing involves much more than just performing a series of test cases. The test process involves a range of separate activities, and performing tests and checking the results are just two of these. Other testing activities include test planning, test analysis, and the design and implementation of test cases. Additional activities include writing reports on test progress and results, and risk analysis. Test activities are organized differently depending on the stage in a product's lifecycle. Test activities and documentation are often contractually regulated between the customer and the supplier, or are based on the company's own internal guidelines. Detailed descriptions of the individual activities involved in software testing are included in sections 2.3 and 6.3.

Static and dynamic testing

Alongside the dynamic tests that are performed on a computer (see Chapter 5), documents such as requirement specifications, user stories, and source code also need to be tested as early as possible in the development process. These are known as static tests (see Chapter 4). The sooner faults in the documentation are discovered and remedied, the better it is for the future development process, as you will no longer be working with flawed source material.

Verification and validation

Testing isn't just about checking that a system fulfills its requirements, user stories, or other specifications; it is also about ensuring that the product fulfills the wishes and expectations of its users in a real-world environment. In other words, checking whether it is possible to use the system as intended and making sure it fulfills its planned purpose. Testing therefore also involves validation (see Principle #7 in section 2.1.6—*"Absence-of-errors is a fallacy"*).

---

1. Here, we are referring to the dynamic testing processes discussed in Chapter 5. Static testing (see Chapter 4) doesn't require the software to be executed.
2. Testing alone cannot prove that all requirements have been fulfilled (see below).

There is currently no such thing as a fault-free software system, and this situation is unlikely to change for systems above a given degree of complexity or those with a large number of lines of code. Many faults are caused by a failure to identify or test for exceptions during code development—things like failing to account for leap years, or not considering constraints when it comes to timing or resource allocation. It is therefore common—and sometimes unavoidable—that software systems go live, even though faults still occur for certain combinations of input data. However, other systems work perfectly day in day out in all manner of industries.

No large system is fault-free

With the exception of very small programs, even if every test you perform returns zero defects, you cannot be sure that additional tests won't reveal previously undiscovered faults. It is impossible to prove complete freedom from faults by testing.

Freedom from faults cannot be achieved through testing

2.1.1 Defect and Fault Terminology

A situation can only be classed as faulty if you define in advance what exactly is supposed to happen in that situation. In order to make such a definition, you need to know the requirements made of the (sub)system you are testing as well as other additional information. In this context, we talk about the test basis against which tests are performed and that serves as the basis for deciding whether a specific function is faulty.

The test basis as a starting point for testing

A defect is therefore defined as a failure to fulfill a predefined requirement, or a discrepancy between the actual behavior (at run time or while testing) and the expected behavior (as defined in the specifications, the requirements, or the user stories). In other words, when does the system's behavior fail to conform to its actual requirements?

What counts as a defect?

Unlike physical systems, software systems don't fail due to age or wear. Every defect that occurs is present from the moment the software is coded, but only becomes apparent when the system is running.

System failures result from faults and only become apparent to the tester or the user during testing or at run-time. For example, when the system produces erroneous output or crashes.

Faults cause failures

We need to distinguish between the effects of a fault and its causes. A system failure is caused by a fault in the software, and the resulting condition is considered to be a defect. The word "bug" is also used to describe defects that result from coding errors, such as an incorrectly programmed or forgotten instruction in the code.

Defect masking

It is possible that a fault can be offset by one or more other faults in other parts of the program. Under these circumstances, the fault in question only becomes apparent when the others have been remedied. In other words, correcting a fault in one place can lead to unexpected side effects in others.

Not all faults cause system failures, and some failures occur never, once, or constantly for all users. Some failures occur a long way from where they are caused.

A fault is always the result of an error or a mistake made by a person—for example, due to a programming error at the development stage.

People make errors

Errors occur for various reasons. Some typical (root) causes are:

- All humans make errors!
- Time pressure is often present in software projects and is a regular source of errors.
- The complexity of the task at hand, the system architecture, the system design, or the source code.
- Misunderstandings between participants in the project—often in the form of differing interpretations of the requirements or other documents.
- Misunderstandings relating to system interaction via internal and external interfaces. Large systems often have a huge number of interfaces.
- The complexity of the technology in use, or of new technologies previously unknown to project participants that are introduced during the project.
- Project participants are not sufficiently experienced or do not have appropriate training.

A human error causes a fault in part of the code, which then causes some kind of visible system failure that, ideally, is revealed during testing (see figure 2-1: Debugging, see below). Static tests (see Chapter 4) can directly detect faults in the source code.

System failures can also be caused by environmental issues such as radiation and magnetism, or by physical pollution that causes hardware and firmware failures. We will not be addressing these types of failures here.

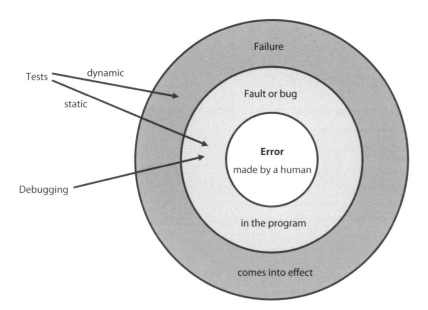

Fig. 2-1
The relationships between, errors, faults, and failures

Not every unexpected test result equates to a failure. Often, a test will indicate a failure even though the underlying fault (or its cause) isn't part of the test object. Such a result is known as a "false positive". The opposite effect can also occur—i.e., a failure doesn't occur even though testing should reveal its presence. This type of result is known as a "false negative". You have to bear both of these situations in mind when evaluating your test results. Your result can also be a "correct positive" (failure revealed by testing) or a "correct negative" (expected behavior confirmed by testing). For more detail on these situations, see section 6.4.1.

False positive and false negative results

If faults and the errors or mistakes that cause them are revealed by testing it is worth taking a closer look at the causes in order to learn how to avoid making the same (or similar) errors or mistakes in future. The knowledge you gain this way can help you optimize your processes and reduce or prevent the occurrence of additional faults.

Learning from your mistakes

Case Study: Vague requirements as a cause of software faults

Customers can use the *VSR EasyFinance* module to calculate various vehicle-financing options. The interest rate the system uses is stored in a table, although the purchase of vehicles involved in promotions and special offers can be subject to differing interest rates.

VSR-II is to include the following additional requirement:

REQ: If the customer agrees to and passes an online credit check, the *EasyFinance* module applies an interest rate from a special bonus interest rate table.

The author of this requirement unfortunately forgot to clarify that a reduction in the interest rate is not permissible for vehicles sold as part of a special offer. This resulted in this special case not being tested in the first release. In turn, this meant that customers were offered low interest rates online but were charged higher rates when billed, resulting in complaints.

2.1.2 Testing Terminology

Testing is not debugging

In order to remedy a software fault it has to be located. To start with, we only know the effect of the fault, but not its location within the code. The process of finding and correcting faults is called debugging and is the responsibility of the developer. Debugging is often confused with testing, although these are two distinct and very different tasks. While debugging pinpoints software faults, testing is used to reveal the effect a fault causes (see figure 2-1).

Confirmation testing

Correcting a fault improves the quality of the product (assuming the correction doesn't cause additional, new faults). Tests used to check that a fault has been successfully remedied are called confirmation tests. Testers are often responsible for confirmation testing, whereas developers are more likely to be responsible for component testing (and debugging). However, these roles can change in an agile development environment or for other software lifecycle models.

Unfortunately, in real-world situations fault correction often leads to the creation of new faults that are only revealed when completely new input scenarios are used. Such unpredictable side effects make testing trickier. Once a fault has been corrected you need to repeat your previous tests to make sure the targeted failure has been remedied, and you also need to write new tests that check for unwanted side effects of the correction process.

Static and dynamic tests are designed to achieve various objectives:

Objectives of testing

- A qualitative evaluation of work products related to the requirements, the specifications, user stories, program design, and code
- Prove that all specific requirements have been completely implemented and that the test object functions as expected for the users and other stakeholders
- Provide information that enables stakeholders to make a solid estimate of the test object's quality and thus generate confidence in the quality provided[3]
- The level of quality-related risk can be reduced through identification and correction of software failures. The system will then contain fewer undiscovered faults.
- Analysis of the program and its documentation in order to avoid unwanted faults, and to document and remedy known ones
- Analyze and execute the program in order to reproduce known failures
- Receive information about the test object in order to decide whether the component in question can be committed for integration with other components
- Demonstrate that the test object adheres and/or conforms to the necessary contractual, legal and regulatory requirements and standards

Test objectives can vary depending on the context. Furthermore, they can vary according to the development model you use (agile or otherwise) and the level of test you are performing—i.e., component, integration, system, or acceptance tests (see section 3.4).

Objectives depend on context

When you are testing a component, your main objective should be to reveal as many failures as possible and to identify (i.e., debug) and remedy the underlying faults as soon as possible. Another primary objective can be to select tests that achieve the maximum possible level of code coverage (see section 2.3.1).

One objective of acceptance testing is to confirm that the system works and can be used as planned, and thus fulfills all of its functional and non-functional requirements. Another is to provide information that enables stakeholders to evaluate risk and make an informed decision about whether (or not) to go live.

---

3. If comprehensive testing reveals few (or no) failures, this increases stakeholder confidence in the product.

Side Note:
Scheme for naming different types of testing

> The various names used for different types of tests can be confusing. To understand the naming of tests it is useful to differentiate between the following naming categories:
>
> 1. **Test objective**
>   The naming of a test type is based on the test objective (for example, a "load test").
>
> 2. **Test method/technique**
>   A test is named according to the method or technique used to specify and/or perform the test (i.e., "state transition testing", as described in section 5.1.3)
>
> 3. **Test object**
>   A test is named according to the type of object to be tested (for example, "GUI test" or "database test")
>
> 4. **Test level**
>   A test is named according to the corresponding level of the development model being used (for example, a "system test")
>
> 5. **Test person**
>   A test is named after the person or group who perform the test (for example, "developer test", "user test")
>
> 6. **Test scope**
>   A test is named according to its scope (for example, a "partial regression test")
>
> As you can see, not all of these terms define a distinct type of test. Instead, the different names highlight different aspects of a test that are important or in focus in a particular context or with regard to a particular testing objective.

2.1.3 Test Artifacts and the Relationships Between Them

The previous sections have already described some types of test artifacts. The following sections provide an overview of the types of artifacts necessary to perform dynamic testing.

Test basis

The test basis is the cornerstone of the testing process. As previously noted, the test basis comprises all documents that help us to decide whether a failure has occurred during testing. In other words, the test basis defines the expected behavior of the test object. Common sense and specialist knowledge can also be seen as part of the test basis and can be used to reach a decision. In most cases a requirements document, a specification, or a user story is available, which serves as a test basis.

Test cases and test runs

The test basis is used to define test cases, and a test run takes place when the test object is fed with appropriate test data and executed on a computer. The results of the test run are checked and the team decides whether a failure has occurred—i.e., whether there is a discrepancy between the test object's expected and actual behaviors. Usually, certain preconditions have to be met in order to run a test case—for example, the corresponding database has to be available and filled with suitable data.

An individual test cannot be used to test the entire test basis, so it has to focus on a specific aspect. Test conditions are therefore extrapolated from the test basis in order to pursue specific test objectives (see above). A test condition can be checked using one or more tests and can be a function, a transaction, a quality attribute, or a structural element of a component or system. Examples of test conditions in our case study *VSR-II* system are vehicle configuration permutations (see section 5.1.5), the look and feel of the user interface, or the system's response time. *Test conditions*

By the same token, a test object can rarely be tested as a complete object in its own right. Usually, we need to identify separate items that are then tested using individual test cases. For example, the test item for *VSR-II*'s price calculation test condition is the `calculate_price()` method (see section 5.1.1). The corresponding test cases are specified using appropriate testing techniques (see Chapter 5). *Test item*

It makes little sense to perform test cases individually. Test cases are usually combined in test suites that are executed in a test cycle. The timing of test cycles is defined in the test execution schedule. *Test suites and test execution schedules*

Test suites are automated using scripts that contain the test sequence and all of the actions required to create the necessary preconditions for testing, and to clean up once testing is completed. If you execute tests manually, the same information has to be made available for the manual tester. *Test scripts*

Test runs are logged and recorded in a test summary report. *Test logs*

For every test object, you need to create a test plan that defines everything you need to conduct your tests (see section 6.2.1). This includes your choice of test objects and testing techniques, the definition of the test objectives and reporting scheme, and the coordination of all test-related activities. *Test plan*

Figure 2-2 shows the relationships between the various artifacts involved. Defining the individual activities involved in the testing process (see section 2.3) helps to clarify when each artifact is created.

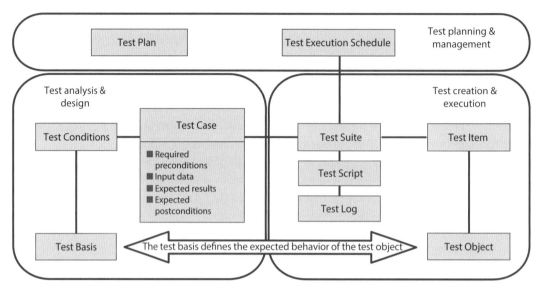

Fig. 2-2   *The relationships between test artifacts*

2.1.4 Testing Effort

Testing effort depends on the project (environment)

Testing takes up a large portion of the development effort, even if only a part of all conceivable tests—or, more precisely, all conceivable test cases—can be considered. It is difficult to say just how much effort you should spend testing, as this depends very much on the nature of the project at hand.[4]

The importance of testing—and thus the amount of effort required for testing—is often made clear by the ratio of testers to developers. In practice, the following ratios can be found: from one tester for every ten developers to three testers per developer. Testing effort and budget vary massively in real-world situations.

Case Study: Testing effort and vehicle variants

VSR-II enables potential customers to configure their own vehicle on a computer screen. The extras available for specific models and the possible combinations of options and preconfigured models are subject to a complex set of rules. The old *VSR* System allowed customers to select combinations that were not actually deliverable. As a consequence of the *VSR-II* QA/Test planning requirement *Functional suitability/DreamCar = high* (see below) customers should no longer be able to select non-deliverable combinations.

---

4.   Section 6.2.5 goes into more detail on this topic.

2.1 Concepts and Motivations

The product owner responsible for the *DreamCar* module wants to know how much testing effort will be required to test this aspect of the module as comprehensively as possible. To do this, he makes an estimate of the maximum number of vehicle configuration options available. The results are as follows:

There are 10 vehicle models, each with 5 different engine options; 10 types of wheel rims with summer or winter tires; 10 colors, each with matt, glossy, or pearl effect options; and 5 different entertainment systems. These options result in 10×5×10×2×10×3×5=150.000 different variants, so testing one variant every second would take a total of 1.7 days.

A further 50 extras (each of which is selectable or not) produce a total of 150.000×2^{50} = 168.884.986.026.393.600.000 variations.

The product owner intuitively knows that he doesn't have to test for every possible combination, but rather for the rules that define which combinations of options are not deliverable. Nevertheless, possible software faults create the risk that the *DreamCar* module wrongly classifies some configurations as deliverable (or permissible combinations as non-deliverable).

How much testing effort is required here and how much can it effectively cost? The product owner decides to ask the QA/testing lead for advice. One possible solution to the issue is to use pairwise testing (see the side note in section 5.1.5).

Side Note:
When is increased testing effort justifiable?

Is a high testing effort affordable and justifiable? Jerry Weinberg's response to this question is: "Compared with what?" [DeMarco 93]. This response points out the risks of using a faulty software system. Risk is calculated from the likelihood of a certain situation arising and the expected costs when it does. Potential faults that are not discovered during testing can later generate significant costs.

Example:
The cost of failure

In March 2016, a concatenation of software faults destroyed the space telescope *Hitomi*, which was built at a cost of several hundred million dollars. The satellite's software wrongly assumed that it was rotating too slowly and tried to compensate using countermeasures. The signals from the redundant control systems were then wrongly interpreted and the speed of rotation increased continuously until the centrifugal force became too much and Hitomi disintegrated (from [URL: Error Costs]).

In 2018 and 2019 two Boeing 737 MAX 8 airplanes crashed due to design flaws in the airplane's MCAS flight control software [URL: MAX-groundings]. Here too, the software—misdirected by incorrect sensor information—generated fatal countermeasures.

> Testing effort has to remain in reasonable proportion to the results testing can achieve. "Testing makes economic sense as long as the cost of finding and remedying faults is lower than the costs produced by the corresponding failure occurring when the system is live."[5] [Pol 00]. Reasonable testing effort therefore always depends on the degree of risk involved in failure and an evaluation of the danger this incurs. The price of the destroyed space telescope Hitomi could have paid for an awful lot of testing.

Case Study: Risks and losses when failures occur

The *DreamCar* module constantly updates and displays the price of the current configuration. Registered customers with validated ID can order a vehicle online.

Once a customer clicks the *Order* button and enters their PIN, the vehicle is ordered and the purchase committed. Once the statutory revocation deadline has passed, the chosen configuration is automatically passed on to the production management system that initiates the build process.

Because the online purchase process is binding, if the system calculates and displays an incorrect price the customer has the right to insist on the paying that price. This means that wrongly calculated prices could lead to the manufacturer selling thousands of cars at prices that are too low. Depending on the degree of miscalculation, this could lead to millions of dollars in losses. Having each purchase order checked manually is not an option, as the whole point of the *VSR-II* system is that vehicles can be ordered completely automatically online.

Defining test thoroughness and scope depending on risk factors

Systems or system parts with a high risk have to be tested more extensively than those that do not cause major damage in case of failure.[6] Risk assessment has to be carried out for the individual system parts or even for individual failure modes. If there is a high risk of a system or subsystem malfunctioning, the test requires more effort than for less critical (sub) systems. These procedures are defined through international standards for the production of safety-critical systems. For example, the [RTC-DO 178B] Airborne Systems and Equipment Certification standard prescribes complex testing procedures for aviation systems.

Although there are no material risks involved, a computer game that saves scores incorrectly can be costly for its manufacturer, as such faults affect the public acceptance of a game and its parent company's other products, and can lead to lost sales and damage to the company's reputation.

---

5. These costs include not only software repair, renewed testing, and replacement of the faulty software, but also immaterial costs such as bad publicity and legal issues.
6. Section 6.2.4 goes into detail on this topic.

2.1.5 Applying Testing Skills Early Ensures Success

In software projects, it is never too early to begin preparing your tests. The following examples illustrate the benefits of involving testers with appropriate test knowledge in individual activities within the software development life cycle:

Testing is an important factor in any success story

- If testers are involved in checking the requirements (for example, using reviews, detailed in section 4.2) or refining user stories, they can use their specialist knowledge to find and remedy ambiguities and faults very early in the work product. The identification and correction of flawed requirements reduces the risk of producing inappropriate or non-testable functionality.

Close cooperation between developers and testers throughout the development process

- Close cooperation between testers and systems designers at the design stage helps all those involved to better understand the system's design and the corresponding tests. This increased awareness can reduce the risk of producing fundamental construction faults and makes it easier to design appropriate tests—for example, to test interfaces during integration testing (see section 3.4.2).

- Developers and testers who work together at the coding stage have a better understanding of the code itself and the tests it requires. This reduces the risk of producing faulty code and of designing inappropriate tests (see *false negatives* in section 6.4.1).

- If testers verify and validate software before release, they are sure to identify and remedy additional faults that would otherwise remain undiscovered. This increases the probability that the product fulfills its requirements and satisfies all of its stakeholders.

In addition to these examples, achieving the previously defined test objectives will also aid successful software development and maintenance.

2.1.6 The Basic Principles of Testing

The previous sections addressed software testing, whereas the following section summarize the basics of testing in general. These are guidelines that have developed over decades of testing experience.

1. **Principle #1:**
   Testing shows the presence of defects, not their absence
   Testing establishes the presence of defects and reveals the faults that cause them. Depending on the effort made and the thoroughness of the tests involved, testing reduces the probability of leaving undiscovered faults in the test object. However, testing does not enable us to prove that a test object contains no faults. Even if an object doesn't fail during testing, this is no proof of freedom from faults or overall correctness.

2. **Principle #2:**
   Exhaustive testing is impossible
   With the exception of extremely simple or trivial test objects, it is impossible to design and perform a complete test suite that covers all possible combinations of input data and their preconditions. Tests are always samples, and the effort allocated to them depends on the risks they cover and the priority assigned to them.

3. **Principle #3:**
   Early testing saves time and money
   Dynamic and static testing activities should be defined and begun as early as possible in the system's lifecycle. The term "shift left" implies early testing. Early testing reveals faults at an early stage of the development process. In a software context, this helps to avoid (or at least reduce) the increasingly costly repair of faults later in the development lifecycle.

4. **Principle #4:**
   Defects cluster together
   Generally speaking, defects are not evenly distributed throughout a system. Most defects can usually be found in a small number of modules, and this (estimated or observed) clustering effect can be used to help analyze risk. Testing effort can then be concentrated on the most relevant parts of the system (see also principle #2 above).

5. **Principle #5:**
   Beware the pesticide paradox
   Over time, tests become less effective the same way insects develop resistance to pesticides. If you repeat tests on an unchanged system, they won't reveal any new failures. In order for your tests to remain effective you need to check your test cases regularly and, if necessary, modify them or add new ones. This ensures that you test previously unchecked components and previously untested input data, thus revealing any failures that these produces. The pesticide paradox can have a positive effect too. For example, if an automated regression test reveals a low number of failures, this may not be the result of high software quality but rather due to the ineffectiveness of the (possibly outdated) test cases in use.

6. **Principle #6:**
   Testing is context-dependent
   Tests need to be adapted to the proposed purpose and the surrounding environment of the system in question. No two systems can be effectively tested the same way. Testing thoroughness, exit criteria, and other parameters need to be defined uniquely according to the system's working environment. An embedded system requires different tests than, for example, an e-commerce system. Testing in an agile project will be very different from that in a project based on a sequential life-cycle model.

7. **Principle #7:**
   Absence-of-errors is a fallacy
   Even if you test all requirements comprehensively and correct all the faults you find, it is still possible to develop a system that is difficult to use, that doesn't fulfill the user's expectations, or that is simply of poor quality compared with other, similar systems (or earlier versions of the same system). Prototyping and early involvement of a system's users are preventive measures used to avoid this problem.

2.2 Software Quality

Side Note

Software testing serves to identify and remedy failures and increase software quality. Test cases should be chosen to mirror the subsequent real-world use that the system is designed for. The quality that testing verifies should then equate to the quality of the user experience.

However, software quality is about more than just correcting the faults found during testing.

2.2.1 Software Quality according to ISO 25010

ISO 25010: Quality in Use and Product Quality models

According to the ISO 25010 standard [ISO 25010], software quality can be classified in two major ways[7]:

- The *Quality in Use Model*, and
- The *Product Quality Model*

The *quality in use* model comprises the following five characteristics:

- Effectiveness
- Efficiency
- Satisfaction
- Freedom from risk
- Context coverage

The product quality model comprises eight characteristics:

- Functional suitability
- Performance efficiency
- Compatibility
- Usability
- Reliability
- Security
- Maintainability
- Portability

The product quality model has the most similarities with the previous ISO 9126 standard. Details of the *Data Quality Model* can be found in the ISO 25012 standard [ISO 25012].

In order to effectively judge the quality of a software system, all of these characteristics and quality criteria need to be considered during testing. The level of quality that each characteristic of the test object is intended to fulfill has to be defined in advance in the quality requirements. The fulfillment of these requirements and their criteria then has to be checked using appropriate tests.

→

---

7. ISO 25010 is not part of the curriculum material for the *Certified Tester Foundation Level* course. To help our readers to familiarize themselves with the general concepts of "software quality", we have included this introduction to ISO 25010 as a side note.

ISO 25010 breaks down the 13 quality characteristics listed above into a total of 40 further sub-characteristics. It is beyond the scope of this text to go into detail on all 40 sub-characteristics of the *quality in use* and *product quality* models. More details are available online at [ISO 25010]. Some of the more important characteristics are summarized below:

Forty (sub-)characteristics

The *functional suitability* (or, more simply, functionality) of the product quality model covers all the characteristics involved in describing the planned functionality of the system.

Functional suitability/ functionality

A quality characteristic is divided into three sub-characteristics:

- **Functional completeness**
  Does the function set cover all specified tasks and user objectives?
- **Functional correctness**
  Does the product/system deliver correct results with the required degree of accuracy?
- **Functional appropriateness**
  To what degree do the available functions fulfill the required tasks and specified objectives?

Appropriate tests can be used to check whether specified and implicit requirements are mirrored in the available functionality, thus answering the questions posed above.

Functionality is usually described in terms of specified input/output behavior and/or a specific system reaction to specified input. Tests are designed to demonstrate that each required functionality has been implemented in such a way that the specified input/output behavior or system behavior is complied with.

The reliability aspect of the product quality model describes a system's ability to perform at a specific level under specified circumstances for a specified period of time.

Reliability

This *quality* characteristic has four sub-characteristics:

- **Maturity**
  To what degree does a system, product, or component provide the required reliability under normal operating conditions?
- **Availability**
  Is the system, product, or component always ready for use, and how easily is it available when it is required?
- **Fault tolerance**
  How well does the system, product, or component function in spite of the presence of known hard- or software faults?
- **Recoverability**
  How long does it take to recover specific data and normal service following a system or product failure or crash?

The *satisfaction* aspect of the *quality in use model* addresses the degree to which user needs are fulfilled when the product or system is used under specified circumstances.

Satisfaction

→

This *quality* characteristic has four sub-characteristics:

- **Usefulness**
  How happy is the user with the perceived fulfillment of pragmatic objectives, including the results and consequences of using the system?
- **Trust**
  How certain is the user (or other stakeholder) that the product or system will behave as intended?
- **Pleasure**
  How much pleasure does the user experience when using the system to fulfill his/her personal requirements?
- **Comfort**
  How comfortable does the user find the system—also in terms of physical well-being?

Most of the characteristics of the *quality in use model* have a strong personal element and can only be objectively viewed and precisely evaluated under exceptional circumstances. In order to test this quality characteristic you will need to refer to multiple users (or user groups) in order to obtain usable test results.

A software system cannot fulfill all quality characteristics to the same degree. Fulfilling one characteristic often means not fulfilling another. A highly efficient software system is not easily portable, as its developers will have designed it to utilize specific attributes of the platform it runs on.

Prioritizing quality characteristics

It is therefore necessary to prioritize these characteristics. The resulting priorities will also act as a guideline for the testing thoroughness for each characteristic.

Case Study: Applying ISO 25010 to VSR-II

The *VSR-II* testing/QA lead suggests using the product quality model described in ISO 25010 to the project steering committee. The committee agrees and asks the testing/QA lead to prepare a concept paper on how to apply the standard in the context of the *VSR-II* project. The core of the draft is a matrix that illustrates the relevance of each quality attribute to each product component and which interpretations to apply. The initial draft of the matrix looks like this:

Quality Characteristic	Dream Car	Easy Finance	Fact Book	Just In Time	No Risk	Connected Car
Functional suitability	high	high	high	high	high	high
Performance efficiency	high	mid	high	mid	mid	high
Compatibility	VSR	VSR	VSR	VSR	VSR	–
Usability	high	mid	–	mid	mid	high
Reliability	mid	mid	high	high	mid	high
Security	mid	mid	high	high	mid	high
Maintainability	high	mid	mid	mid	mid	high
Portability	low	low	–	low	low	mid

Table 2-1
Classifying quality characteristics

These risk classifications are to be interpreted relative to one another and are justified by the testing/QA lead for each quality characteristic, e.g.:

- **Functional suitability/all modules**
  Every module serves large numbers of users and processes a lot of data, so functional failures have the potential to produce considerable costs. The requirement is therefore classified as "high" for all modules.

- **Compatibility/*ConnectedCar***
  There are no requirements, as this module is to be built from scratch.

- **Usability/*FactBook***
  There are no requirements, as this is a back-end module and the API already exists.

- **Portability/*DreamCar***
  This characteristic is classified as "low" because the framework in use covers it without the application of additional measures.

Which checks and tests are required will be established during QA/test planning for each module. This top-level classification can be used to establish basic parameters—for example, automated continuous integration tests (see section 3.2) are required for a "high" attribute, a single round of acceptance testing is sufficient for "mid" attributes, while a written design guideline on how the team approaches an issue is sufficient for "low" attributes. The QA/test lead is sure to have to go through a number of assessment rounds with the teams to arrive at an agreement on these high-level rules.

2.2.2 Quality Management and Quality Assurance

QM   Quality management (QM) covers all organizational activities and measures that serve to control quality. Quality management is usually responsible for defining quality policies, quality objectives, quality planning, quality assurance, and quality improvement. This makes quality management a core management activity. Quality management is mandatory in industries such as aviation, automotive, and healthcare.

ISO 9000   The ISO 9000 family of quality management standards [ISO 9000] is widely used, and the ISO/IEC 90003 *Software Engineering standard* [ISO 90003] stipulates how the ISO 9001 [ISO 9001] general guidelines are applied to computer software.

QA   Quality assurance (QA) usually concentrates on measures which aim to ensure that specified procedures are applied and defined processes are adhered to. It is assumed, if a company sticks to its predefined processes, that it will fulfill the required quality characteristics and therefore achieve the specified quality levels. Under these circumstances, the results will usually show increased quality, which in turn helps to avoid failures in the work products and the corresponding documentation.

QA and testing   The term "quality assurance" is often used when referring to testing processes or even as a synonym for testing. QA and testing processes are closely related but are definitely not the same. QA generates confidence in the fulfillment of quality requirements, which can be achieved by testing. Effective QA also involves analyzing the causes of all kinds of defects, and serves to identify (test) and remedy (debug) them. The results are discussed in meetings called "retrospectives" and can be used to improve the processes involved. Testing therefore serves to demonstrate that the required quality levels are achieved.

Testing activity is part of the overall software development and maintenance process and, because QA is about making sure such processes are implemented and executed correctly, QA also supports effective testing. The following section describes the testing process itself in more detail.

2.3 The Testing Process

Development models

Chapter 3 introduces different types of software development lifecycle models (also referred to more simply as "development models"). These are designed to aid structuring, planning, and management of new or continuing software projects. In order to perform well-structured tests, you will usually need more than just a description of the activities that make up the development model. In addition to positioning testing within the overall development process, you will also need a detailed dedicated testing schedule. In other words, the content of the development task called "testing" needs to be broken down into smaller, more manageable steps.

Testing comprises a sequence of individual activities

There are many widely used and proven test activities, and a test process will be made up of these kinds of activities. You need to put together a suitable test process according to the specified (or inherited) project situation. The specific test activities you choose, and how (and when) you implement them will depend on a number of factors, and will generally be based on a company or project-specific testing strategy (see section 6.2). If you ignore certain test activities you will increase the likelihood of the test process failing to reach its objectives.

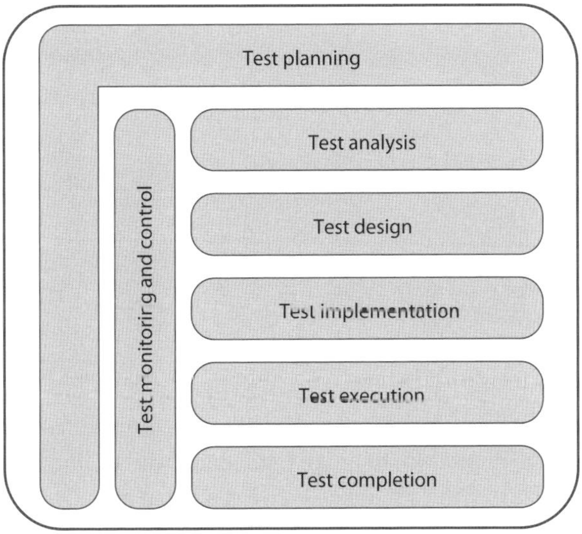

Fig. 2-3
The testing process

- Test planning
  - Test monitoring and control
    - Test analysis
    - Test design
    - Test implementation
    - Test execution
    - Test completion

The main activities

A test process[8] will generally comprise the following activities (see figure 2-3):

- Test planning
- Test monitoring and control
- Test analysis
- Test design
- Test implementation
- Test execution
- Test completion

Each of these activities comprises multiple individual tasks that produce their own output and vary in nature according to the project at hand.

Fig. 2-4
The test process showing time overlap

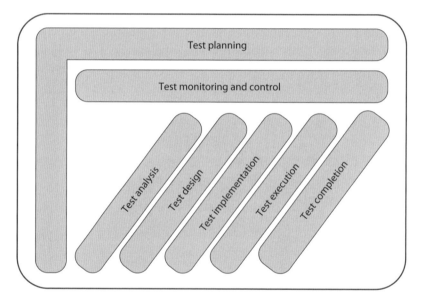

Iterative testing

Even if the individual tasks involved in the test process are defined in a logical sequence, in practice they can (and may) overlap, and are sometimes performed concurrently (see figure 2-4). Even if you intend to perform your test activities in a predefined sequence, a sequential development model (for example, the "waterfall" model) can cause overlap, combination, concurrency, or cancellation of individual activities or parts of activities.

---

8. The ISO 29119-2 standard (see [ISO 29119]) provides more detail on test processes.

Adapting these activities to fit the system and project context (see below) is usually necessary, regardless of which development model you are using.

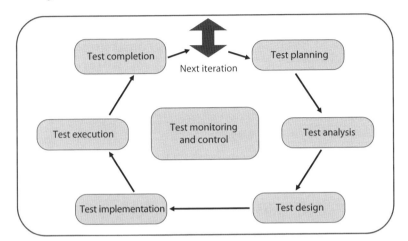

Fig. 2-5
An iterative test process

Software is often developed in small iterative steps—for example, agile development methods use continuous build and test iterations. The corresponding test activities therefore need to take place continuously and iteratively (see figure 2-5).

The following sections provide an overview of the individual test steps and their output. Test management is responsible for the monitoring and execution of most of these activities, which are described in detail in Chapter 6 (see sections 6.2 and 6.3).

2.3.1 Test Planning

Structured handling of a task as extensive as testing will not work without a plan. Test planning begins directly at the start of a software project. Like with any plan, it is necessary to review your testing plan regularly and update or adapt it to fit changing situations and project parameters. Test planning is therefore a repeat activity that is carried out and, if necessary, adjusted throughout the entire product lifecycle.

The main task when planning your testing is the creation of a test plan based on your chosen testing strategy. This test plan defines the test objects, the quality characteristics and the testing objectives, as well as the testing activities you plan to use to verify them. The test plan thus describes your

The test plan:
planning the content

testing technique, the required resources, and the time required to perform the corresponding test activities.

Coverage criteria

The point at which you have performed sufficient testing is determined by the planned coverage and is also part of the test plan. Such criteria are often referred to as "completion criteria" or "exit criteria" or, in the case of agile projects, "definition of done". If coverage criteria are defined for each test level or type, you can evaluate objectively whether the tests you have performed can be seen as sufficient. Coverage criteria can also be used to monitor and control testing, and they also verify when you have reached your testing objectives.

The test plan also contains information about the test basis, which serves as the cornerstone for all your testing considerations. The test plan also needs to include information regarding traceability between the test basis and the results of your test activities. For example, this can help you to determine which changes to the test basis modify which testing activities, thus enabling you to adapt or augment them.

The test plan also defines which tests are to be performed at which test level (see section 3.4). It often makes sense to draft a separate test plan for each test level, and you can use a master test plan to aggregate these into one.

Test planning: scheduling

The test schedule contains a list of all activities, tasks and/or events involved in the test process. This list includes the planned start and end times for every activity. Interdependencies between activities are noted in the test schedule.

The plan also defines deadlines for key activities to support its practical implementation during the project. The test schedule can be part of the test plan.

2.3.2 Test Monitoring and Control

Ensuring traceability

Monitoring and control involve constant observation of the current testing activities compared with the planned activities, reporting any discrepancies, and the execution of the activities required to achieve the planned objectives under the changed circumstances. The update of the plan must also be based on the changed situation.

Are the exit criteria fulfilled?

Test monitoring and control activities are based on the exit criteria for each activity or task. The evaluation of whether the exit criteria for a test at a particular test level have been fulfilled can include:

- Achievement of the degree of coverage defined in the test plan according to the available test results and logs. If the predefined criteria are fulfilled, the activity can be terminated.
- The required component or system quality is determined based on test results and logs. If the required quality has been achieved, the test activity can be concluded.
- If risk evaluation is part of the test plan and you need to prove that you have sufficient risk coverage, this can also be determined using the test results and logs.

If the required exit criteria have not been fulfilled by the tests you have performed, you need to design and execute additional tests. If this isn't possible for any reason, you need to clarify the situation and evaluate the ensuing risk.

Perform additional tests or take a risk?

Stakeholders expect to receive regular test progress reports on current testing progress compared with the overall plan. Alongside any deviation from the original plan, these reports should also contain information regarding any prematurely terminated tests (see above) or non-fulfillment of the planned exit criteria. Test summary reports are to be provided when project milestones are reached.

Progress and completion reports

All test reports should contain details relevant to their recipients and include a progress report as well as test results. Reports should also answer or preempt management questions, such as the (expected) end time, planned vs. actual use of resources, and the amount of testing effort involved.

Progress monitoring can be based on the reports made by team members or on figures and analysis provided by automated tools.

2.3.3 Test Analysis

Test analysis involves determining what exactly needs to be tested. For this purpose, the test basis is examined to see whether the documents to be used are sufficiently detailed and contain testable features in order to derive test conditions. The degree to which the test conditions need to be checked is determined by measurably defined coverage criteria.

"What" do we need to test?

The following documents and data can be used to analyze the test basis and the planned test level:

Analyzing the test basis	Requirements that specify the planned functional and non-functional system or component behavior. The requirements specifications include technical requirements, functional requirements, system requirements, user stories[9], epics[10], use cases, and similar work products or documentation. For example, if a requirement doesn't specify the predicted result and/or system behavior precisely enough, then test cases cannot be simply derived. A reworking is necessary.
Analyzing documentation	Design or implementation data that gives rise to specific component or system structures. System or software architecture documents, design specifications, call graphs, model diagrams (for example, UML[11] or entity relationship diagrams[12]), interface specifications, and similar materials can be used for the test basis. For example, you will need to analyze how easily interfaces can be addressed (interface openness) and how easily the test object can be divided into smaller sub-units in order to test these separately. You need to consider these aspects at the development stage, and the test object needs to be designed and coded accordingly.
Check the test object	You need to investigate the individual components or the system itself, including the code base, database metadata, database queries, and other interfaces. For example, you need to check that the code is well structured and easy to understand, and that the required code coverage (see section 5.1) is easy to achieve and verify.
Consider risk analysis	Risk analysis reports that cover functional, non-functional, and structural aspects of the system or its components need to be investigated too. If potential software failures create serious risks, testing needs to be correspondingly thorough. Testing can be performed less formally for software that is not mission-critical.
Potential documentation errors	The cornerstone of the entire testing process is the test basis. If the test basis contains defects, you cannot formulate "correct" test conditions and you won't be able to draft "proper" test cases. You therefore need to analyze the test basis for defects too. Check whether it contains ambiguities, or whether there are gaps or omissions in the descriptions of functions.

---

9. User stories describe requirements from the point of view of the various specialist business units, the developers and the testers, and are written jointly by them.
10. An "epic" is a collection of connected features or sub-features that make up a single complex feature (see also [URL: Epic]).
11. [URL: UML]
12. [URL: ERM]

You need to check the documentation for inconsistencies, imprecision, contradictions, and for repeat and/or redundant passages. Any defects or discrepancies you find should be corrected immediately.

The discovery and removal of defects from the test basis is extremely important, especially if the documentation hasn't been reviewed (see section 4.3). Development methodologies such as behavior-driven development (BDD, [URL: BDD]) and acceptance test-driven development (ATDD, [URL: ATDD]) use acceptance criteria and user stories to create test conditions and test cases before coding begins. This approach makes it simpler to identify and remedy defects at a much earlier stage in the development process.

Once the test conditions have been identified and defined, you need to prioritize them. This ensures that the most important and high-stakes test conditions are tested first. In real-world situations, time restrictions often make it impossible to perform all the planned tests.

Prioritizing tests

At the planning stage, you need to ensure that there is unambiguous bi-directional traceability between the test basis and the results of your testing activities (see above). This traceability has to precisely define which test condition checks which requirement and vice versa.

Traceability is important

This is the only way to ensure that you can later determine how thoroughly which requirements need to be tested and—depending on the test conditions—using which test cases.

It is useful to consider which test technique to use (i.e., black-box, white-box, experience-based, see Chapter 5) at the analysis stage. Each technique has its own system for reducing the likelihood of overlooking test conditions and helping to define these precisely. For example, using an equivalence partition (or "equivalence class") test (see section 5.1.1) ensures that the entire input domain is used for the creation of test cases. This prevents you from forgetting or overlooking negative input in your requirements definitions. You can then define your test conditions to cover negative input data.

Choosing test techniques

If you use an experience-based testing technique (see section 5.3), you can use the test conditions defined during analysis as objectives for your test charter. A test charter is a kind of "assignments" that, alongside traditional test objectives, provides potential ideas for additional tests. If the test objectives are traceable back to the test basis, you can evaluate the achieved coverage (for example, for your requirements), even when you are using an experience-based technique.

2.3.4 Test Design

How to test and which test cases to use

When designing tests you determine how you are going to test. At the design stage, test conditions are used to create test cases (or sequences of test cases). Here, you will usually use one of the test techniques detailed in Chapter 5.

Test cases can be specified on two "levels": abstract and concrete (see *Case Study: Abstract and concrete test cases* below).

Abstract and concrete test cases

An abstract (or "high-level") test case doesn't include specific input values or expected results, and is described using logical operators. The advantage of such cases is that they can be used during multiple test cycles and with varying data but can still adequately document the scope of each case. A concrete (or "low-level") test case uses specific input data and expected result values.

When you begin to design a test, you can use abstract as well as concrete test cases. Because only concrete test cases can be executed on a computer, abstract test cases have to be fleshed out with real input and output values. In order to utilize the advantages of abstract test cases (see above), you can derive abstract test cases from concrete cases too.

Test cases involve more than just test data

Preconditions have to be defined for every test case. A test also requires clear constraints that must be adhered to. Furthermore, you need to establish in advance what results or behavior you expect the test to produce. In addition to output data, results include any changes to global (persistent) data and states, as well as any other reactions to the execution of the test case.

The test oracle

You need to use adequate sources to predict test results. In this context, people talk about the "test oracle" that has to be "consulted" regarding the expected results. For example, specifications can serve as an oracle. There are two basic approaches:

- The tester derives the expected output value from the input value based on the test object's requirements and specifications as defined in the test basis.

- If the inverse of a function exists, you can execute the inverse and compare its output with the input value for your original test case. This technique can, for example, be used when testing encryption and decryption algorithms

The following example illustrates the difference between abstract and concrete test cases.

Case Study: Abstract and concrete test cases

A dealership can give its salespeople the option of discounts to apply to the price of a vehicle. For prices below $15,000 there is no discount. For prices up to $20,000, a discount of 5% is appropriate. If the price is below $25,000, a 7% discount is possible. If the price is above $25,000, a discount of 8.5% is to be applied.

The above text enables us to derive the following relationships between price and discount:

Price < 15,000   Discount = 0%
15.000 ≤ Price ≤ 20,000 Discount = 5%
20.000 < Price < 25,000 Discount = 7%
Price ≥ 25,000   Discount = 8.5%

The text itself obviously offers potential for interpretation[13]. In other words, the text can be misunderstood, whereas the mathematical formulae derived from it are unambiguous.

Based on the formulae, we can define the following test cases (see table 2-2):

Abstract Test Case	1	2	3	4
Input vale x (price in $)	x<15000	15000≤x ≤20000	20000<x <25000	x≥25000
Predicted result (discount in %)	0	5	7	8.5

Table 2-2 Abstract test cases

In order to execute these tests, the abstract cases have to be converted to concrete cases—i.e., we have to apply specific input values (see table 2-3). Exceptional conditions and boundary cases are not covered here.

Concrete Test Case	1	2	3	4
Input value x (price in $)	14500	16500	24750	31800
Predicted result (discount in $)	0	825	1732.50	2703

Table 2-3 Concrete test cases

The values shown here serve only to illustrate the difference between abstract and concrete test cases. We didn't use a specific test technique to design these tests, and the cases shown aren't meant to test the discount component exhaustively. For example, there is no test case that covers false input (such as a negative price). You will find more detail on the systematic creation of test cases using a specific test technique in Chapter 5.

---

13. The text only says which discounts apply if the price is below or above $ 25,000, but doesn't actually stipulate the discount for a price of exactly $ 25,000.

In addition to specifying abstract and concrete test cases, test design also includes prioritizing your test cases and providing appropriate testing infrastructure:

Priorities and traceability

- Test analysis has already prioritized the test conditions. These same priorities can be used and fine-tuned for your test cases (or sets of test cases). This way, you can assign different priorities to the individual tests within a set that are designed to verify a single test condition. High-priority tests are executed first.

  The same principle applies to the traceability of test conditions, which can be broken down to cover individual test cases or sets of cases.

Testing infrastructure and environment

- The required testing infrastructure has to be evaluated and implemented. Test infrastructure consists of all the organizational elements required for testing. These include the test environment, testing tools, and appropriately equipped workstations. A test environment is required in order to run the test object on a computer and verify the specified test cases (see below). This environment comprises hardware, any necessary simulation equipment and software tools, and other supporting materials. In order to avoid delays while testing, the test infrastructure should be up and running (and tested) before testing begins.

Following on from the test analysis, the test design stage can reveal further defects in the test basis. Likewise, test conditions that were defined at the analysis stage can be fine-tuned at the design stage.

2.3.5 Test Implementation

Is everything ready to begin testing?

The task of test implementation is the final preparation of all necessary activities so that the test cases can be executed in the next step. Test design and test implementation activities are often combined.

Firm up the testing infrastructure

One of main tasks during implementation is the creation and integration of all testware, with special attention being paid to the details of the testing infrastructure. The test framework[14] has to be programmed and installed in the test environment. Checking the environment is extremely important, as faults in the testing environment can cause system failures. In order to ensure that there are no delays or obstacles to testing, you also need to check that all additional tools (such as service

---

14. The function and structure of a test framework are described in detail in Chapter 5.

virtualization, simulators, and other infrastructure elements) are in place and working.

To ensure that your concrete test cases can be utilized without further changes or amendments, all test data have to be correctly transferred to the test environment. Abstract test cases have to be fed with specific test data.

Firm up your test cases

As well as firming up your test cases, you need to define the test procedure itself—i.e., the planned tests have to be put into a logical sequence. This takes place according to the priorities you have defined (see section 6.2).

To keep a test cycle effective and to retain a logical structure, test cases are grouped into test suites. A test suite consists of multiple tests grouped according to the planned sequence of execution. The sequence has to planned so that the postconditions of a test case serve as the preconditions for the following test case. This simplifies the test procedure, as it obviates the need for dedicated pre- and postconditions for every test case. A test suite also includes the cleanup activities required once execution is complete.

Test suite, test procedure, test script

Automating test procedures using scripts saves a lot of time compared with manual testing.

The most efficient way to plan the execution of test cases, test suites, and test procedures is defined in a test execution schedule (see section 6.3.1).

The traceability of your test cases to the requirements and/or test conditions needs to be checked and, if necessary, updated. Test suites and procedures also have to be taken into account when checking traceability.

2.3.6 Test Execution

It makes sense to begin by checking that all the components you want to test and the corresponding testware are available. This involves installing the test object in the test environment and checking that it can be started and run. If this check reveals no obstacles, testing can begin.

Completeness check

- Test execution should begin by checking the test object's main function (see the "smoke test" section in the *Other Techniques* side note in section 5.1.6). If this reveals failures or deviations from the expected results, you need to remedy the corresponding defect(s) before continuing with testing.

Our Tip
Check the test object's main functions

Tests without logs are worthless

The test execution process—whether manual or automated according to the test execution schedule—has to be precisely and completely logged. You need to log each test result (i.e., pass, fail, blocked[15]) so that they are comprehensible to people who are not directly involved with the test process (for example, the customer). Logs also serve to verify that the overall testing strategy (see section 6.2) has been performed as planned. Logs should show which parts were tested, when, by whom, how intensively and with what results. If a planned test case or test sequence is left out for any reason, this needs to be logged too.

The importance of clarity and reproducibility

Alongside the test object (or test item), a whole raft of documents and other information are involved in test execution. These include: the test framework, input data, logs, and so on. The data and other information that relate to a test case or test run have to be managed so that the test can easily be repeated later using the same data and constraints. The IDs and/or version numbers of the tools used should be noted and recorded by configuration management (see section 6.5).

Is there really a failure?

If there is a difference between the expected and actual result, evaluating the test logs will help you to decide whether this really is due to a failure. If you do discover a failure, make sure you document it before you begin to look for its causes. It may be necessary to specify and execute supplementary test cases. You should also report the defect. See section 6.4.1 for more on test logging, section 6.3.4 for more on the defect report, and section 6.4 for a general discussion of defect management.

Retesting

Once you have corrected a fault, you need to check that the corresponding failure has also been resolved and that no new failures have been caused by the correction process. You may need to specify new test cases to verify the modified code.

Our Tip

Check whether a defect is actually due to the test object itself

■ You will need to check carefully whether a failure really is due to the test object. There is nothing worse for a tester's reputation than a reported failure whose cause is actually a flawed test case. At the same time, you have to take care not to be over-wary of such cases, and you mustn't be scared to report potential failures, even if you are not sure of their cause. Both these situations are bad for the project.

---

15. A planned test case is considered "blocked" if the preconditions for its execution are not fulfilled.

2.3 The Testing Process

- Ideally, you will correct faults individually and retest to make sure that your corrections don't unintentionally influence each other. However, this approach is simply not practical in the real world. If a test is executed by an independent tester rather than the developer, individual corrections won't be possible. Reporting every fault to the developer and waiting for these to be remedied before retesting is not a justifiable effort. The usual approach is to correct bunches of faults and then set up a new version of the software for testing.

Individual fault correction is not practical

In addition to logging the differences between the expected and actual results, you need to evaluate coverage and—if necessary—log the run time of the tests. There are specialized tools available for these kinds of tasks (see Chapter 7).

Bi-directional traceability is an important part of all the testing activities we have looked at so far. Here too, you need to check traceability and, if necessary, update the system so that the relationships between the test basis and the test conditions, cases, test runs, and results are up to date. Once a test sequence is completed, you can use its inbuilt traceability to evaluate whether every item in the test basis has been covered by a corresponding test process.

Traceability is important here too

This way, you can check which requirements have passed planned and executed tests and which requirements couldn't be verified due to failed tests or failures that were registered during testing. You may find that some requirements have not yet been verified because the corresponding tests have not yet been performed. Information of this kind enables you to verify whether the planned coverage criteria have been fulfilled and therefore whether the test can be viewed as successfully completed.

Test objectives fulfilled?

Effective coverage criteria and traceability enable you to document your test results so that they are easily comprehensible for all the project's stakeholders.

Other common exit criteria are discussed in section 6.3.1.

2.3.7 Test Completion

The right time for test completion

Test completion is the final activity in the testing process and involves collating all the data collected by the completed test activities in order to evaluate the test experience and consolidate the testware and its associated materials. The correct moment for test completion varies according to the development model you use. It can be:

- When the system goes live
- The end (or discontinuation) of the test project
- The completion of an agile project iteration
  (for example, as part of a retrospective or a review meeting)
- The completion of testing activities for a specific test level
- The completion of test activities for a maintenance release

At completion time, you also need to make sure that all planned activities have been completed and that the defect reports are complete. Open or unresolved failures (i.e., unresolved deviations from an existing requirement) remain open and are carried over to the next iteration or release. In agile environments, such unresolved cases are classed as new *product backlog* items for inclusion in the next iteration.

Change requests and modified requirements that stem from the evaluation of test results are handled similarly.

Test summary report

The test summary report (see section 6.3.4) aggregates all your testing activities and results, and includes an overall evaluation of the tests you have performed compared with your predefined exit criteria. The summary report is distributed to all stakeholders.

Archiving testware

Software systems are generally utilized over a long period of time, during which failures will turn up that weren't discovered during testing. During its lifetime, a system will also be subject to change requests from its users (or customers). Both of these situations mean that the system has to be reprogrammed and the modified code has to be tested anew. A large portion of the testing effort involved in this kind of maintenance can be avoided if the testware you originally used (test cases, logs, infrastructure, tools, and so on) are still available and can be handed over to the maintenance department. This means that the existing testware only have to be adapted rather than set up from scratch when it comes to performing system maintenance. Testware can also be profitably adapted for use in similar projects. For some industries, the law requires proof of testing, and this can only be provided if all the testware are properly archived.

- Conserving testware after testing can be extremely laborious, so testers often capture an image of the test environment or use the Docker freeware to create a so-called *Container*—an easily transportable and reusable file that contains all the related resources and that can be installed and run as an independent test environment.

Our Tip
Create an image or use a Container

The experience you gather when testing can be analyzed and used in future projects. Deviations between your plans and the actual activities you perform are just as interesting as looking for their causes. You should use your findings to unleash your potential for improvement and make changes to the activities you undertake for future iterations, releases, and projects. These kinds of changes help the overall test process to mature.

Learning from experience

2.3.8 Traceability

When we talk about testing activities, we often mention the importance of traceability. The following sections summarize the traceability between the test basis and test results and detail other advantages of effective traceability.

Traceability between the test basis and test results

Traceability is essential to effective test monitoring and control that spans the entire test process. It establishes the relationships between each item in the test basis and the various test results. Traceability helps you to assess the degree of coverage you achieve—for example, checking whether all requirements have been covered by at least one test case. Such traceability data helps you control the overall progress of the test process.

Over and above checking coverage, effective traceability also supports the following aspects:

- Traceability helps to assess the impact of changes by analyzing which changes to the requirements affect which test conditions, test runs, test cases, and test items

- Traceability enables you to elevate your results to a "higher" abstract level, thus making the testing process more easily comprehensible to non-specialists. Considering only the executed test cases doesn't provide information on how thorough or broad-based the testing process was. It is only when you include traceability information that the output becomes intelligible to all relevant groups of stakeholders. It also helps to fulfill abstract IT governance criteria.

Higher, abstract level

- The same argument is valid for test progress and test summary reports—i.e., effective traceability makes them easier to understand. The status of each item in the test basis should be included in reports. One of the following statements can be made for each individual requirement:
  - Tests were passed
  - Tests failed, failures occurred
  - Planned tests have not yet been executed

- Traceability also enables us to make technical aspects of testing comprehensible to all stakeholders. Using company objectives as a yardstick, it enables them to evaluate product quality, procedural capacity, and project progress.

Tool-based support   In order to best utilize the advantages of traceability, some companies build dedicated management systems that organize test results in a way that automatically delivers traceability data. There are various test management tools available that inherently implement traceability.

2.3.9 The Influence of Context on the Test Process

The context of the testing process   The following are some of the factors that influence the testing process within an organization (see also section 6.2.5):

- The choice and usage of test activities depends on the software development lifecycle model you use. Most agile models don't include detailed directions for testing and its associated activities.

- Depending on the chosen and implemented system architecture the system may be divided into subsystems. This affects test levels (component, integration, system, and acceptance testing—see section 3.4) and the corresponding technique used to derive or select test cases (see *Test Techniques* in Chapter 5).

- The test type also influences the testing process. A test type is a group of test activities designed to test a component or a system for interrelated quality characteristics. A test type is often focused on a single quality characteristic—for example, load testing (see section 3.5).

- In the case of significant product or project risk, the test process needs to be designed to address the maximum number of risks through test cases, and thus minimize them (see section 6.2.4).

- The context in which a software system is used also has an effect on the testing process. For example, software used exclusively for company-internal vacation planning will be subject to less thorough testing than a custom system built to control a client's industrial facility.

- Company guidelines and best practices can also have an effect on the testing process and the rules that govern it. The advantage here is that the factors influencing the process do not have to be discussed and redefined for each project. Required internal and external standards have the same effect.

Operational limitations also affect the structure and implementation of test processes. Such limitations include:

Operational limitations

- Budget and other resources (for example, specialist staff) that are usually in short supply for testing purposes
- Extended deadlines that leave less time than planned for testing
- The complexity of the system to be tested. Complex systems are not easy to test! The test process must be designed to reflect the complexity of the system.
- Contractual and regulatory requirements. These can have a direct effect on the scope of the testing process, and therefore on that of the individual activities involved.

2.4 The Effects of Human Psychology on Testing

Everyone makes mistakes, but nobody likes to admit it! The main objective of software testing is to reveal deviations from the specifications and/or the customer's requirements. All failures found must be communicated to the developers. The following sections address how to deal with the psychological issues that can result.

Errare humanum est

Software development is often seen as a constructive activity while testing the product and checking the documentation are more often seen as destructive. This view often results in the people involved in a project having very different attitudes to their work. However, this assumption is not at all justifiable as, according to [Myers 12, p. 13, Software testing principle #10]: "Testing is an extremely creative and intellectually challenging task." Furthermore, testing plays a significant role in the success of a project and the quality of the resulting product (see section 2.1).

Disclosing errors

Failures found must be communicated to the author of the faulty document or source code. Management, too, needs to know about which (or at least how many) defects have been revealed by testing. The way this communicated can be beneficial to the relationships among analysts, product owners, designers, developers, and testers, but can also have a negative effect on these important lines of communication. Admitting (or proving) errors is not an easy thing to do and requires a great deal of sensitivity.

Discovering failures can be construed as criticism of a product or its author, and can occur as a result of static or dynamic tests. Examples of such situations are:

- A review meeting in which a requirements document is discussed
- A meeting at which user stories are fleshed out and fine-tuned
- During dynamic test execution

Always take confirmation bias into account

"Confirmation bias"[16] is a psychological term that describes the tendency to search for, interpret, favor, and recall information in a way that confirms or strengthens your prior personal beliefs or hypotheses. This tendency plays a significant role in the communication of software faults. Software developers generally assume that their code is fault-free, and confirmation bias makes it difficult for them to admit that their work might be flawed. Other cognitive preconceptions, too, can make it tricky for those involved to understand or accept the results of software tests.

Recognized defects are a positive thing

Another thoroughly human trait is the tendency to "shoot the messenger" who brings bad news. Test results are often seen as bad news, even though the opposite is often true: recognized defects can be remedied and the quality of the test object improved. Software failures that are out in the open are actually a positive thing!

Soft skills required

In order to avoid (or at least reduce) the potential for this kind of conflict, testers and test managers need well-developed soft skills. Only then can everyone involved effectively discuss faults, failures, test results, test progress, and risk. Mutual respect always creates a positive working environment and engenders good relationships between all the people involved in the project.

---

16. *See* https://en.wikipedia.org/wiki/Confirmation_bias.

2.4 The Effects of Human Psychology on Testing

Examples of positive communication:

- Arguments or simply "getting loud" are never good for cooperation in the workplace. To make sure work progresses amicably, it often helps to remind everyone of their mutual objectives and the high product quality they are aiming for.

    Examples of positive communication

- As already mentioned, you can never repeat enough that discovering a defect and rectifying it is a positive thing. Other positive aspects are:
    - Error recognition can help developers to improve their work and therefore their results too. A lot of developers are not aware that test results can help them hone their own skills.
    - Discovered and rectified faults are best framed to management as a means to save time and money, and as a way to reduce the risk of poor product quality.

- Documentation style also plays a role in communication. Test results and other findings need to be documented neutrally and should stick to the facts. If a document is flawed, don't criticize its author. Always write objective, fact-based defect reports and review findings.

    Keep documentation neutral and factual

- Always consider the other person's point of view. This makes it easier to understand why someone perhaps reacts negatively to something you wrote or said.

- Misunderstandings in general and talking at cross-purposes never engender constructive communication. If you find yourself in such a situation (or expect one to arise), always ask how what you said was understood and confirm what was actually said. This works in both directions.

Section 2.1.2 lists typical testing objectives. Clearly defined objectives also have a distinct psychological effect. People often like to align their behavior to clearly defined objectives. As well as testing objectives, you can orient yourself toward team objectives, management objectives, or other stakeholders' objectives. The important thing is that testers pursue and stick to these objectives as impartially as possible.

2.4.1 How Testers and Developers Think

Different mindsets

Because they pursue very different objectives, developers and testers usually think quite differently. Developers design and produce a product, while testers verify and validate the product with a view to discovering faults and failures. It is possible to improve product quality by combining these two different mindsets.

Assumptions and preferred decision-making techniques are reflected in the way most people think. Alongside curiosity, a tester's mindset will usually include a healthy level of professional pessimism combined with a critical view of the test object. Interest in detail and the will to communicate positively with everyone involved are other characteristics that are useful in testers. Testers develop their soft skills through years of hands-on experience.

A developer's main interest is in designing and implementing a solution to a problem, so he won't be keen on considering which aspects of the solution are flawed or buggy. Although some aspects of a developer's mindset are similar to those of a tester, the confirmation bias described above always makes it more difficult for developers to recognize errors in their own work (see also section 6.1.1).

Side Note

Can a developer change his mindset and test his own software? There is no simple answer to this question, and someone who both develops and tests a product requires a rare degree of critical distance to their own work. After all, who likes to investigate and confirm their own mistakes? Generally speaking, developers prefer to find as few faults as possible in their own code.

Developer tests

The greatest weakness of "developer tests" (see section 3.4.1) is that every developer who tests his own code will always view his work with too much optimism. It is highly likely that he will overlook meaningful test cases or, because he is more interested in programming than testing, he won't test thoroughly enough.

Blind to your own mistakes

If a developer misunderstands the assignment and designs a program with a fundamental flaw, an appropriate test case simply won't occur to him and he won't find the flaw. One way to reduce this common "blindness to your own mistakes" is to work in pairs and get each developer to test the other's work (see section 6.1, model #1).

On the other hand, inside knowledge of your own test object can be an advantage, as you don't need to spend time getting to know the code. It is up to management to decide when the advantage of knowing your own work outweighs the disadvantages caused by blindness to your own mistakes. This decision is based on the importance of the test object and the level of risk involved if it fails.

→

> In order to design meaningful test cases, a tester has to learn about the test object, which takes time. On the other hand, a tester has specialist skills that a developer would have to learn in order to test effectively—a learning process for which there is usually no time to spare.
>
> It is a great aid to cooperation and understanding between developers and testers if both acquire some knowledge to the other's skills. Developers should always know some testing basics, and testers should always have some development experience.

Developers require testing skills, testers require development skills.

2.5 Summary

- Testing terminology is only loosely defined and similar terms are often used to mean different things—a cause of frequent misunderstandings. This is why consistent use of terminology is an important part of the *Certified Tester* course. The glossary at the end of this book provides an overview of all the most important terms.

- Testing takes up a large proportion of a project's development resources. Precisely how much testing effort is required depends on the type of project at hand.

- The testing process—starting with planning and preparation steps—needs to be begun as early as possible in order to generate the maximum testing benefits within the project.

- Always follow the seven basic testing principles.

- Testing is an important part of the quality assurance complex in the context of software development. Appropriate quality models and characteristics are defined by the international ISO 25010 standard [ISO 25010].

Side Note

- It is important to recognize and observe the connections and the boundaries between testing, quality assurance, and quality management.

- The testing process comprises test planning, monitoring and control, analysis, design, implementation, execution, and completion. These activities can overlap and can be performed sequentially or in parallel. The overall testing process has to be adapted to fit the project at hand.

- Bidirectional traceability between the results of the individual testing activities ensures that you can make meaningful statements about the results of the testing process, and to make a reasonable estimate of how much effort will be involved in making changes to the system. Traceability is also critical to effective test monitoring and control.

- All of the many factors that influence testing within an organization have to be considered.
- People make mistakes but don't usually like to admit it! This is why psychological issues play a significant role in the overall testing process.
- The mindsets of testers and developers are very different, but both can benefit by learning from one another.

3 Testing Throughout the Software Development Lifecycle

This chapter offers a brief introduction to common lifecycle models used in software development projects, and explains the role testing plays in each. It discusses the differences between various test levels and test types, and explains where and how these are applied within the development process.

Most software development projects are planned and executed along the lines of a software development lifecycle model that is chosen in advance. Such models are also referred to as software development process models or, more concisely, development models.

Such a model divides a project into separate sections, phases, or iterations and arranges the resulting tasks and activities in a corresponding logical order (see [URL: SW-Dev-Process]). Additionally, the model usually describes the roles that each task is assigned to and which of the project's participants is responsible for each task. The development methods to be used in the individual phases are often described in detail too.

Every development model has its own concepts regarding testing, and these can vary widely in meaning and scope. The following sections detail popular development models from a tester's point of view.

The two basic types of development model in use today are *sequential* and *iterative/incremental*. The following sections include discussion of both types.

Types of lifecycle models

3.1 Sequential Development Models

As the name suggests, a sequential development model arranges the activities involved in the development process in a linear fashion. The assumption here is that development of the product and its feature set is finished when all the phases of the development model have been completed. This model does not envisage overlaps between phases or product iterations.

The planned delivery date for projects run this way can lie months—or even years—in the future.

3.1.1 The Waterfall Model

An early model was the so-called "waterfall model" [Royce 70]. It is impressively simple and, in the past, enjoyed a high degree of popularity. Each development phase can only begin once the previous phase has been completed, hence the model's name[1]. However, the model can produce feedback loops between neighboring phases that require changes to be made in a previous phase. Figure 3-1 shows the phases incorporated in Royce's original model:

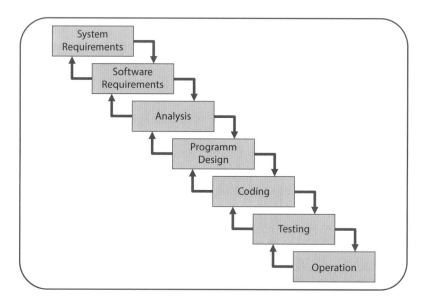

Fig. 3-1
The waterfall model according to Royce

The major shortcoming of this model is that it bundles testing as a single activity at the end of the project. Testing only takes place once all other development activities have been completed, and is thus seen as a kind of "final check" akin to inspecting goods that leave a factory. In this case, testing is not seen as an activity that takes place throughout the development process.

---

1. Royce himself didn't use the term waterfall for his model. He wrote: "Unfortunately, for the process illustrated, the design iterations are never confined to the successive steps."

3.1.2 The V-Model

The V-model is an extension of the waterfall model (see [Boehm 79], [ISO/IEC 12207]). The advent of this model made a huge and lasting difference to the way testing is viewed within the development process. Every tester and every developer should learn the V-model and learn about how it integrates the testing process. Even if a project is based on a different development model, the principles illustrated here can still be applied.

The basic idea is that development and testing are corresponding activities of equal value. In the diagram, they are illustrated by the two branches of the "V"[2]:

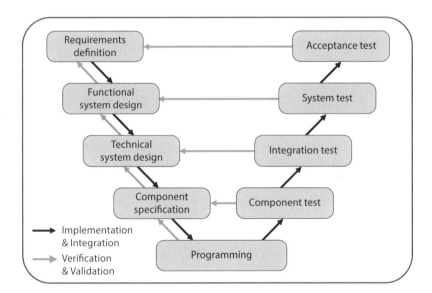

Fig. 3-2

The V-model

The left-hand branch represents the steps that are required to design and develop the system with increasing detail up to the point at which it is actually coded.[2]

The constructional activities in the left-hand branch correspond to the activities outlined in the waterfall model:

---

2. There are many different versions of the V-model in use. The number and names of the individual phases vary according to the sources quoted and the preferences of the organization doing the developing.

- **Definition of requirements**
  This is where the customer and end-user requirements are collected, specified, and approved. The purpose and proposed features of the system are now stipulated.
- **Functional design**
  The requirements are mapped to specific features and dialog flows.
- **Technical design**
  The functional design is mapped to a technical design that includes definition of the required interfaces to the outside world, and divides the system into easily manageable components that can be developed independently (i.e., the system architecture is drafted).
- **Component specification**
  The task, behavior, internal construction, and interfaces to other components are defined for each component.
- **Programming**
  Each specified component is programmed (i.e., implemented as a module, unit, class etc.) using a specific programming language.

Because it is easiest to identify defects at the level of abstraction on which they occur, each of the steps in the left-hand branch is given a corresponding testing step in the right-hand branch. The right-hand branch therefore represents an integration and testing flow during which system components are successively put together (i.e., integrated) to build increasingly large subsystems, that are then tested to ensure that they fulfill their proposed functions. The integration and testing process ends with acceptance testing for the complete system.

- **Component tests** ensure that each individual component fulfills its specified requirements.
- **Integration tests** ensure that groups of components interact as specified by the technical design.
- **System tests** ensure that the system as a whole functions according to its specified requirements.
- **The acceptance test** checks that the system as a whole adheres to the contractually agreed customer and end-user criteria.

These test steps represent a lot more than just a chronological order. Each test level checks the product (and/or specific work products) at a different level of abstraction and follows different testing objectives.

This is why the various test levels involve different testing techniques, different testing tools, and specialized personnel. Section 3.4 presents more details regarding each of these test levels.

In general, each test level can include verification and validation tests:

- **Verification** involves checking that the test object fulfills its specifications completely and correctly. In other words, the test object (i.e., the output of the corresponding development phase) is checked to see whether it was "correctly" developed according to its specifications (the input for the corresponding phase). *Did we build the system right?*

- **Validation** involves checking that the test object is actually usable within its intended context. In other words, the tester checks whether the test object actually solves the problem assigned to it and whether it is suited to its intended use. *Did we build the right system?*

Practically speaking, every test includes both aspects, although the validation share increases with each level of abstraction. Component tests are largely focused on verification, whereas an acceptance test is mainly about validation.

To summarize, the most important characteristics of the V-model are: *The V-model's hallmarks*

- Development and test activities take place separately (indicated by the left and right-hand branches) but are equally important to the success of the project.
- The model's "V" shape helps to visualize the verification/validation aspects of testing.
- It differentiates between collaborative test levels, whereby each level is testing against its corresponding development level.

The V-model creates the impression that testing begins late in the development process, following implementation. This is wrong! The test levels in the right-hand branch of the model represent the distinct phases of test execution. Test preparation (planning, analysis, and design) must begin within the corresponding development step in the left-hand branch. *The principle of early testing*

3.2 Iterative and Incremental Development Models

Iterative development

The basic idea behind iterative development is that the development team can use the experience they gain from previous development stages along with real-world and customer feedback from earlier system versions to improve the product in future iterations. Such improvements can take the form of fault corrections or the alteration, extension or addition of specific features. The primary objective of all these scenarios is to improve the product step by step in order to meet customer expectations increasingly accurately.

Incremental development

The idea behind incremental development is to develop a product in preplanned stages, with each completed stage offering a more full-featured version (increment) of the product. Increments can vary greatly in size—for example from changing a simple web page layout to adding a complete new module with additional functionality. The primary objective of incremental development is to minimize time to market—i.e., to release a simple product version (or a simple version of a feature) to provide the customer as quickly as possible with a working version of the product or feature. Further enhancements will then be offered continually depending on the customer's responses and wishes.

Iterative-incremental development

In practice, the borders between these two methodologies are blurred and they are often referred to together as *iterative-incremental development*. A defining characteristic of both is that each product release enables you to receive regular, early feedback from the customer and/or end-user. This reduces the risk of developing a system that doesn't meet the customer's expectations.

Examples of combined iterative-incremental models are: the *spiral model* [Boehm 86], *Rapid Application Development* (RAD) [Martin 91], *Rational Unified Process* (RUP) [Kruchten 03], and *Evolutionary Development* [Gilb 05].

Agile software development

All forms of agile software development are iterative-incremental development models. The best-known agile models are: *Extreme Programming (XP)* [Beck 04], *Kanban* [URL: Kanban], and *Scrum* [Beedle 02], [URL: Scrum Guide]. In recent years, Scrum has become the most popular of these and is extremely widespread.

3.2 Iterative and Incremental Development Models

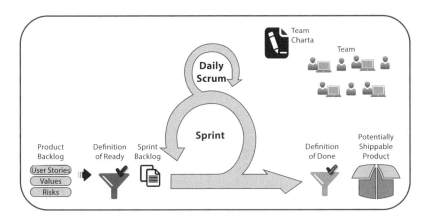

Fig. 3-3
Scrum-based agile development

The pace at which new increments/releases are created varies from model to model. While non-agile iterative-incremental projects tend to foresee releases at intervals of six months to a year, or sometimes even longer, agile models in contrast attempt to reduce the release cycle to a quarterly, monthly, or even weekly rhythm.

Testing to the rhythm of the iterations

Here, testing has to be adapted to fit such short release cycles. For example, this means that every component requires re-usable test cases that can be easily and instantly repeated for each new increment. If this condition is not met, you risk reducing system reliability from increment to increment.

Each increment also requires new test cases that cover any additional functionality, which means the number of test cases you need to maintain and execute (on each release) increases over time. The shorter the release cycle, it remains critical but becomes more difficult for all test cases to be satisfactorily executed within the allotted release timeframe. Therefore test automation is an important tool when adapting your testing to agile development.

Once you have set up a reliable automated test environment that executes your test cases with sufficient speed, you can use it for every new build. When a component is modified, it is integrated into the previous complete build, followed by a fresh automated test run[3]. Any failures that appear should be fixed in the short term. This way, the project always has a fully integrated and tested system running within its test environment. This approach is called "Continuous Integration" (CI).

Continuous Integration and Continuous Deployment

---

3. Or at least the test cases that cover the modified components and its interfaces.

This approach can be augmented using "Continuous Deployment" (CD): If the test run (during CI) is fault-free, the tested system is automatically copied to the production environment and installed there and thus deployed in a ready-to-run state[4].

Continuous Delivery = Continuous Testing

Combining CI and CD results in a process called "Continuous Delivery". These techniques can only be successfully applied if you have a largely automated testing environment at your disposal which enables you to perform "continuous testing".

Continuous testing and other critical agile testing techniques are explained in detail in [Crispin 08] and [Linz 14].

3.3 Software Development in Project and Product Contexts

The requirements for planning and traceability of development and testing vary according to the context. Likewise, the appropriateness of a particular lifecycle model for the development of a specific product also depends on the contexts within which it is developed and used. The following project- and product-based factors play a role in deciding which model to use:

- The company's business priorities, project objectives, and risk profile. For example, if time-to-market is a primary requirement.

- The type of product being developed. A small (perhaps department-internal) system has a less demanding development process than a large project designed for multi-year use by a huge customer base, such as our *VSR-II* case study project. Such large products are often developed using multiple models.

- The market conditions and technical environment in which the product is used. For example, a product family developed for use in the *Internet of Things* (IoT) can consist of multiple types of objects (devices, services, platforms, and so on), each of which is developed using a specific and suitable lifecycle model. Because IoT objects are used for long periods of time in large numbers, it makes sense if their operational usage (distribution, updates, decommissioning, and so on) is mirrored in specific phases or catalogs of tasks within the lifecycle

---

4. This approach is increasingly widespread in the development and maintenance of web-based e-commerce applications.

3.3 Software Development in Project and Product Contexts

model. This makes developing new versions of such a system particularly challenging.

- Identified product risks. For example, the safety aspects involved in designing and implementing a vehicle braking system.
- Organizational and cultural aspects. For example, the difficulties generated by communication within international teams can make iterative or agile development more difficult.

One of the objectives of the *VSR-II* project is to make it "as agile as possible", so the *DreamCar* module and all the browser-based front-end components and subsystems are developed in an agile Scrum environment. However, because they are safety-critical, the *ConnectedCar* components are to be developed using the traditional V-model.

Case Study: Mixing development models in the VSR-II project

Prototyping [URL: Prototyping] is also an option early on in a project and, once the experimental phase is complete, you can switch to an incremental approach for the rest of the project.

A development model can and should be adapted and customized for use within a specific project. This adaptation process is called "tailoring".

Tailoring

Tailoring can involve combining test levels or certain testing activities and organizing them especially to suit the project at hand. For example, when integrating off-the-shelf commercial software into a larger system, interoperability tests at the integration testing stage (for example, when integrating with existing infrastructure or systems) can be performed by the customer rather than the supplier, as can acceptance testing (functional and non-functional operational and customer acceptance tests). For more detail, see section 3.4 and 3.5.

The tailored development model then comprises a view of the required activities, timescales, and objectives that is binding for all project participants. Any detailed planning (schedules, staffing, and infrastructure allocation) can then utilize and build upon the tailored development model.

Regardless of which lifecycle model you choose, your tailoring should support good and effective testing. Your testing approach should include the following attributes:

Attributes of good testing

- Testing and its associated activities are included as early as possible in the lifecycle—for example, drafting test cases and setting up the test environment (see the *principle of early testing* above).

- For every development activity, a corresponding test activity is planned and executed.
- Test activities are planned and managed specifically to suit the objectives of the test level they belong to.
- Test analysis and test design begin within the corresponding development phase.
- As soon as work products (requirements, user stories, design documents, code etc.) exist, testers take part in discussions that refine them. Testers should participate early and continuously in this refinement process.

3.4 Testing Levels

A software system is usually composed of a number of subsystems, which in turn are made up of multiple components often referred to as units or modules. The resulting system structure is also called the systems "software architecture" or "architecture". Designing an architecture that perfectly supports the system's requirements is a critical part of the software development process.

During testing, a system has to be examined and tested on each level of its architecture, from the most elementary component right up to the complete, integrated system. The test activities that relate to a particular level of the architecture are known as a testing "level", and each testing level is a single instance of the test process.

The following sections detail the differences between the various test levels with regard to their different test objects, test objectives, testing techniques, and responsibilities/roles.

3.4.1 Component Testing

Terminology Component testing involves systematically checking the lowest-level components in a system's architecture. Depending on the programming language used to create them, these components have various names, such as "units", "modules" or (in the case of object-oriented programming) "classes". The corresponding tests are therefore called "module tests", "unit tests", or "class tests".

Regardless of which programming language is the used, the resulting software building blocks are the "components" and the corresponding tests are called "component tests".

Components and component testing

The component-specific requirements and the component's design (i.e., its specifications) are to be consulted to form the test basis. In order to design white-box tests or to evaluate code coverage, you must analyze the component's source code and use it as an additional test basis. However, to judge whether a component reacts correctly to a test case, you have to refer to the design or requirements documentation.

The test basis

As detailed above, modules, units, or classes are typical test objects. However, things like shell scripts, database scripts, data conversion and migration procedures, database content, and configuration files can all be test objects too.

Test objects

A component test typically tests only a single component in isolation from the rest of the system. This isolation serves to exclude external influences during testing: If a test reveals a failure, it is then obviously attributable to the component you are testing. It also simplifies design and automation of the test cases, due to their narrowly focused scope.

A component test verifies a component's internal functionality

A component can itself consist of multiple building blocks. The important aspect is that the component test has to check only the internal functionality of the component in question, not its interaction with components external to it. The latter is the subject of integration testing. Component test objects generally arrive "fresh from the programmers hard disk", making this level of testing very closely allied to development work. Component testers therefore require adequate programming skills to do their job properly.

The following example illustrates the point:

According to its specifications, the *VSR-II DreamCar* module calculates a vehicle's price as follows:

Case Study: Testing the calculate_price class

We start with the list price (`baseprice`) minus the dealer discount (`discount`). Special edition markup (`specialprice`) and the price of any additional extras (`extraprice`) are then added.

If three or more extras not included with the special edition are added (`extras`), these extras receive a 10% discount. For five extras or more, the discount increases to 15%.

The dealer discount is subtracted from the list price, while the accessory discount is only applied to the extras. The two discounts cannot be applied together.

The resulting price is calculated using the following C++ method[5]:

```
double calculate_price   (double baseprice, double specialprice,
                          double extraprice, int extras,
                          double discount)
{
double addon_discount; double result;
if (extras ≥ 3)
   addon_discount = 10;
else
   if (extras ≥ 5)
         addon_discount = 15;
   else  addon_discount = 0;
if (discount > addon_discount)
   addon_discount = discount;
result   = baseprice/100.0 * (100-discount) + specialprice
         + extraprice/100.0 *(100-addon_discount);
return result;
}
```

The test environment   In order to test this calculation, the tester uses the corresponding class interface by calling the calculate_price() method and providing it with appropriate test data. The tester then records the component's reaction to this call—i.e., the value returned by the method call is read and logged.

This piece of code is buggy: the code for calculating the discount for ≥ 5 can never be reached. This coding error serves as an example to explain the white-box analysis detailed in Chapter 5.

To do this you need a "test driver". A test driver is a separate program that makes the required interface call and logs the test object's reaction (see also Chapter 5).

---

5. Avoid comparing for equality with floating-point numbers, as rounding errors can distort the result. In our test case, because price values < 12900.00 can be calculated, the absolute value (abs) of the difference between price and 12900.00 has to be evaluated.

3.4 Testing Levels

For the calculate_price() test object, a simple test driver could look like this:

```
bool test_calculate_price() {
double price;
bool test_ok = TRUE;

// testcase 017
price = calculate_price(10000.00,2000.00,1000.00,3,0);
test_ok = test_ok && (abs (price-12900.00) < 0.01);

// testcase 02
price = calculate_price(25500.00,3450.00,6000.00,6,0);
test_ok = test_ok && (abs (price-34050.00) < 0.01);

// testcase ...

// test result return test_ok;

}
```

The test driver in our example is very simple and could, for example, be extended to log the test data and the results with a timestamp, or to input the test data from an external data table.

To write a test driver you need programming skills. You also have to study and understand the test object's code (or at least, that of its interface) in order to program a test driver that correctly calls the test object. In other words, you have to master the programming language involved and you need access to appropriate programming tools. This is why component testing is often performed by the component's developers themselves. Such a test is then often referred to as a "developer test", even though "component testing" is what is actually meant. The disadvantages of developers testing their own code are discussed in section 2.4.

Developer tests

Component tests are often confused with debugging. However, debugging involves eliminating defects, while testing involves systematically checking the system for failures (see section 2.1.2).

Testing vs. debugging

> **Our Tip**
> *Use Component test frameworks*
>
> ■ Using component test frameworks (see [URL: xUnit]) significantly reduces the effort involved in programming test drivers, and creates a consistent component test architecture throughout the project. Using standardized test drivers also makes it easier for other members of the team who aren't familiar with the individual components or the test environment to perform component tests[6]. These kinds of test drivers can be controlled via a command-line interface and provide mechanisms for handling test data, and for logging and evaluating test results. Because all test data and logs are identically structured, it is possible to evaluate the results across multiple (or all) tested components.

Component test objectives

The component testing level is characterized not only by the type of test objects and the test environment, but also by very specific testing objectives.

Testing functionality

The most important task of a component test is checking that the test object fully and correctly implements the functionality defined in its specifications (such tests are also known as "function tests" or "functional tests"). In this case, functionality equates to the test object's input/output behavior. In order to check the completeness and correctness of the implementation, the component is subjected to a series of test cases, with each covering a specific combination of input and output data.

Case Study: Testing VSR-II's price calculations

This kind of testing input/output data combinations is illustrated nicely by the test cases in the example shown above. Each test case inputs a specific price combined with a specific number of extras. The test case then checks whether the test object calculates the correct total price.

For example, test case #2 checks the "discount for five or more extras". When test case #2 is executed, the test object outputs an incorrect total price. Test case #2 produces a failure, indicating that the test object does not fulfill its specified requirements for this input data combination.

Typical failures revealed by component testing are faulty calculations or missing (or badly chosen) program paths (for example, overlooked or wrongly interpreted special cases).

Testing for robustness

At run time, a software component has to interact and swap data with multiple neighboring components, and it cannot be guaranteed that the component won't be accessed and used wrongly (i.e., contrary to its

---

6. Sometimes, developers work in pairs and test each other's components. This practice is often referred to as "buddy testing" or "code swapping".

specification). In such cases, the wrongly addressed component should not simply stop working and crash the system, but should instead react "reasonably" and robustly. Testing for robustness is therefore another important aspect of component testing. The process is very similar to that of an ordinary functional test, but serves the component under test with invalid input data instead of valid data. Such test cases are also referred to as "negative tests" and assume that the component will produce suitable exception handling as output. If adequate exception handling is not built in, the component may produce runtime errors, such as division by zero or null pointer access, that cause the system to crash.

Case Study: Negative tests

For the price calculation example we used previously, a negative test would involve testing with negative input values or a false data type (for example, char instead of int)[7]:

```
// testcase 20
price = calculate_price(-1000.00,0.00,0.00,0,0);
test_ok = test_ok && (ERR_CODE == INVALID_PRICE);
...
// testcase 30
price = calculate_price("abc",0.00,0.00,0,0);
test_ok = test_ok && (ERR_CODE == INVALID_ARGUMENT);
```

Various interesting things come to light:

- Because the number of possible "bad" input values is virtually limitless, it is much easier to design "negative tests" than it is to design "positive tests".
- The test driver has to be extended in order to evaluate the exception handling produced by the test object.
- Exception handling within the test object (evaluating ERR_CODE in our example) requires additional functionality. In practice, you will often find that half of the source code (or sometimes more) is designed to deal with exceptions. Robustness comes at a price.

---

7. The compilers of some programming languages can detect the use of wrong data types at compile time.

Alongside functionality and robustness, component testing can also be used to check other attributes of a component that influence its quality and that can only be tested (if at all) using a lot of additional effort at higher test levels. Examples are the non-functional attributes "efficiency" and "maintainability"[8].

Testing for efficiency

The efficiency attribute indicates how economically a component interacts with the available computing resources. This includes aspects such as memory use, processor use, or the time required to execute functions or algorithms. Unlike most other test objectives, the efficiency of a test object can be evaluated precisely using suitable test criteria, such as kilobytes of memory or response times measured in milliseconds. Efficiency testing is rarely performed for all the components in a system. It is usually restricted to components that have certain efficiency requirements defined in the requirements catalog or the component's specification. For example, if limited hardware resources are available in an embedded system, or for a real-time system that has to guarantee predefined response-time limits.

Testing for maintainability

Maintainability incorporates all of the attributes that influence how easy (or difficult) it is to enhance or extend a program. The critical factor here is the amount of effort that is required for a developer (team) to get a grasp of the existing program and its context. This is just as valid for a developer who needs to modify a system that he programmed years ago as for someone who is taking over code from a colleague.

The main aspects of maintainability that need to be tested are code structure, modularity, code commenting, comprehensibility and up-to-dateness of the documentation, and so on.

Case Study: Code that is difficult to maintain

The sample `calculate_price()` code contains a number of maintainability issues. For example, there are no code comments at all, and numerical constants have not been declared as such and are instead hard-coded. If, for example, such a constant needs to be modified, it isn't clear if and where else in the system it needs to be changed, forcing the developer to make huge efforts figuring this out.

---

8. The opportunity to perform early non-functional testing at component level—rather than later during system testing—is rarely used in real-world situations. Serious efficiency issues are often therefore discovered only shortly before the release date and can only then be corrected (or at least attenuated) by applying huge amounts of resources.

Attributes like maintainability cannot of course be checked using dynamic tests (see Chapter 5). Instead, you will need to analyze the system's specifications and its codebase using static tests and review sessions (see section 4.3). However, because you are checking attributes of individual components, this kind of analysis has to be carried out within the context of component testing.

As already mentioned, component testing is highly development-oriented. The tester usually has access to the source code, supporting a white-box oriented testing technique in component testing. Here, a tester can design test cases using existing knowledge of a component's internal structure, methods, and variables (see section 5.2).

Testing strategies

The availability of the source code is also an advantage during test execution, as you can use appropriate debugging tools (see section 7.1.4) to observe the behavior of variables during testing and see whether the component functions properly or not. A debugger also enables you to manipulate the internal state of a component, so you can deliberately initiate exceptions when you are testing for robustness.

White-box tests

The calculate_price() code includes the following test-worthy statement:

Case Study: Code as test basis

```
if (discount > addon_discount)
    addon_discount = discount;
```

Additional test cases that fulfill the condition (discount > addon_discount) are simple to derive from the code. But the price calculation specification contains no relevant information, and corresponding functionality is not part of the requirements. A code review can reveal a deficiency like this, enabling you to check whether the code is correct and the specification needs to be changed, or whether the code needs to be modified to fit the specification.

However, in many real-world situations, component tests are "only" performed as black-box tests—in other words, test cases are not based on the component's inner structure[9]. Software systems often consist of hundreds or thousands of individual building blocks, so analyzing code is only really practical for selected components.

During integration, individual components are increasingly combined into larger units. These integrated units may already be too large to inspect

---

9. This is a serious omission, as it leaves as much as 60-80% of the code untested, thus providing an ideal "hiding place" for all kinds of faults.

their code thoroughly. Whether component testing is done on the individual components or on larger units (made up of multiple components) is an important decision that has to be made as part of the integration and test planning process.

Test-first

"Test-first" is the state-of-the-art approach to component testing (and, increasingly, on higher testing levels too). The idea is to first design and automate your test cases and to program the code which implements the component as a second step. This approach is strongly iterative: you test your code with the test cases you have already designed, and you then extend and improve your product code in small steps, repeating until the code fulfills your tests. This process is referred to as "test-first programming", or "test-driven development" (often abbreviated to TDD—see also [URL: TDD], [Linz 14]). If you derive your test cases systematically using well founded test design techniques (see Chapter 5), this approach produces even more benefits—for example, negative tests, too, will be drafted before you begin programming and the team is forced to clarify the intended product behavior for these cases.

3.4.2 Integration Testing

Terminology

Integration testing is the next level that follows on from component testing. Integration testing assume that the test objects handed over to this level are already component tested and that any component-internal defects have been corrected as far as possible.

Integration

Developers, testers, and specialized integration teams then assemble groups of these components into larger units. This process is called "integration".

Integration testing

Once assembled, you have to test whether the integrated components interact correctly with each other. This process is known as "integration testing", and is designed to find faults in the interfaces and the interaction between the integrated components.

The test basis

At this level, all the documents that describe the software architecture and the design of the software system, especially interface specifications, workflow and sequence diagrams, and also use case diagrams, are to be consulted as the test basis.

You might ask yourself why integration testing is necessary when all the components have already been individually tested. Our case study illustrates the kinds of problems that have to be solved:

The *VSR-II DreamCar* module is made up of a number of basic components.

Case Study: Integration tests for the VSR-II DreamCar module

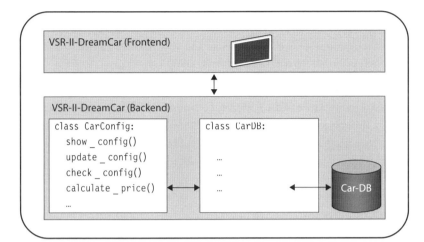

Fig. 3-4
The structure of the VSR-II DreamCar module

One of these components is the CarConfig class, which is responsible for ensuring that a vehicle configuration (base model, special edition, additional extras, and so on) is permissible and for calculating the resulting price. The class includes the calculate_price() and check_config() methods. The class reads the required model options and price data from a database using the CarDB class.

The frontend reads the current vehicle configuration using get_config() and presents the results to the end-user for further tweaking in the graphical user interface. Changes to the current configuration are returned to the backend using update_config(). check_config() then checks that the configuration is permissible and recalculates the price appropriately.

Although component testing revealed no failures in the CarConfig and CarDB classes, their interaction can still be buggy. For example, you may find that check_config() cannot process certain extras provided by the database, or that check_config() requests data that CarDB extracts from the database but that is returned to check_config() in an unsuitable format.

The interaction between the frontend and the backend can be faulty too. For example, if the frontend doesn't correctly display a logically permissible configuration, the user sees this as a fault. Or perhaps because update_config() is called inappropriately—for example, instead of handing over each change individually, the frontend only sends complete reconfigurations as a single data set to update_config(), which can handle this kind of data, but might perform too slowly as a result.

However, with the integration of the *DreamCar* module, integration testing for the *VSR-II* project has only just begun. The components that make up the other

VSR-II modules (see Chapter 2, figure 2-1) have to be integrated too, before the modules themselves are integrated into the overall system: *DreamCar* has to be connected to *ContractBase*, which in turn is connected to the *JustInTime* (ordering), *NoRisk* (insurance), and *EasyFinance* (vehicle financing) subsystems. One of the final integration steps includes connecting *VSR-II* to the external *FactoryPPS* production planning system (see Chapter 1, figure 1-1).

Integration testing is critical

As illustrated by the example above, component testing cannot guarantee that the interfaces between the components are fault-free. This is what makes the integration testing level critical to the overall testing process. Potential interface faults must be discovered there and their causes isolated.

System integration testing

The example above also shows that the interfaces to the external system environment also have to be covered during the integration and integration testing process. When interfaces to external software (or hardware) systems are tested, the process is often referred to as "integration testing in the large" or "system integration testing".

System integration testing can only be performed once system testing is complete. In this situation, the risk lies in the development team only being able to test "their half" of the interface in question. The "other half" is developed externally and can therefore change unexpectedly at any time. Even if system tests are passed, this doesn't guarantee that external interfaces will always work as expected.

Different levels of integration

This means that there are multiple levels of integration testing that cover test objects of varying sizes (interfaces between internal components or subsystems, or between the entire system and external systems such as web services, or between hardware and software). If, for example, business processes are to be tested in the form of a cross-interface workflow made up of multiple systems, it can be extremely difficult to isolate the interface or component that causes the fault.

Integration test objects are made up of multiple components

The integration process assembles individual components to produce larger units and, ideally, every integration step will be followed by an integration test. Every module thus built can serve as the basis for further integration into even larger units. Integration test objects can therefore consist of units (or subsystems) that have been integrated iteratively.

Third-party systems and bought-in components

In practice, software systems are nowadays rarely built from scratch, but are instead the result of the extension, modification, or combination of existing systems (for example, a database, a network, new hardware, and so on). Many system components are standardized products bought on the open market (such as the *DreamCar* database). Component testing doesn't usually include these kinds of existing or standardized objects, whereas integration testing has to cover these components and their interaction with other parts of the system.

The most important integration test objects are the interfaces that connect two or more components. Furthermore, integration testing can also cover configuration programs and files. Depending on the system's architecture, access to databases or other infrastructure components can also be part of the (system) integration testing process.

Integration testing also requires test drivers to provide test objects with data, and to collect and log the results. Because the test objects are compound units that have no interfaces to the outside world that aren't already provided by their component parts, it makes sense to re-use the test drivers created for the individual component tests.

The test environment

If the component testing stage was well organized, you will have access to a generic test driver for all components, or at least a set of test drivers that were designed according to a unified architecture. If this is the case, testers can adapt and use these existing test drivers for integration testing with a minimum of extra effort.

A badly organized component testing process will perhaps provide only a few suitable drivers that have differing operational structures. The downside of this kind of situation is that the test team now has to invest significant time and effort in the creation or improvement of the test environment at a late stage in the project, thus wasting precious integration testing time.

Because interface calls and data traffic via the test driver interfaces need to be tested, integration testing often uses "monitors" as an additional diagnostic tool. A monitor is a program that keeps a check on the movement of data between components and logs what it sees. Commercial software is available for monitoring standard data traffic such as network protocols, whereas you will have to develop custom monitors for use with project-specific component interfaces.

Monitors

The objective of integration testing is clearly to find interface faults. Issues can already occur during the first attempt at integrating two components if their interface formats don't match, if required files are missing, or if the developer has programmed components that don't stick to the specified divisions. Such faults will usually be detected early on by failing compile or build runs.

Test objectives

Difficult-to-find issues are faults that occur at runtime during data exchange (i.e., communication) between components, and detecting such faults requires dynamic testing. The following basic types of communication faults can be distinguished:

- A component transmits no data, syntactically false data, or wrongly coded data that the receiving component cannot process, thus causing an exception or a crash. The root cause is a functional component error, an incompatible interface format, or a protocol error.

- The communication works, but the components involved interpret the transferred data differently, due to the functional failure of a component or a misinterpreted specification.

- Data is transferred correctly, but at the wrong moment (timing or timeout issues) or at intervals that are too short (causing throughput, capacity, or load issues).

Case Study: Integration errors in VSR-II

During *VSR*-II integration testing the following failures of the types described above could occur:

- Selected extras in the *DreamCar* GUI are not handed over to check_config(), thus producing incorrect price and order data.

- In the *DreamCar* module, vehicle colors are represented by codes (for example, 442 means metallic blue). However, the production planning system (*FactoryPPS*, see Chapter 1, figure 1-1) interprets some codes differently (here, 442 means pearl effect red). Such discrepancies mean that an order that is correct from *VSR-II*'s point of view could lead to the wrong product being built and delivered.

- The host system confirms every transferred order. In some cases, checking deliverability takes so long that *VSR*-II assumes that there is a data transfer error and cancels the connection. The result is a customer who cannot order a vehicle that he has spent a lot of time configuring.

Because the failures only occur during interaction between software units, none of these types of faults can be discovered during component testing.

Alongside functional tests, integration testing can involve non-functional tests too. This is useful in cases where non-functional attributes of a component's interface are classed as system-relevant or risky (such as performance, behavior under load, or volume-related behavior).

Is it possible to leave out component testing altogether and start the testing process directly with integration testing? Yes, this is possible and, unfortunately, common practice. However, this approach has potentially serious drawbacks:

Is component testing necessary?

- Most of the failures revealed by this kind of testing will be caused by functional faults inside individual components. In other words, what is actually a component test is executed in an unsuitable environment that complicates access to individual components.
- Because there is no easy access to each individual component, some failures will not be provoked and are thus impossible to find.
- If a failure or crash occurs, it is difficult or impossible to localize the component which caused the failure.

Doing without component testing saves effort only at the price of poor rates of fault discovery and increased diagnostic efforts. Combining component testing with integration testing is far more efficient.

In which sequence should the components be integrated to maximize testing efficiency? Testing efficiency is measured using the relationship between testing costs (staff, tools, and so on) and usefulness (the number and seriousness of discovered failures) for a particular test level. The test manager is responsible for choosing and implementing the optimum testing and integration strategy for the project at hand.

Integration strategies

Individual components are finished at times that can be weeks or months apart. Project managers and test managers won't want to wait until all the relevant components are ready to be integrated in a single run.

Components are ready at different times

A simple ad hoc strategy for dealing with this situation is to integrate the components in the (random) sequence in which they are finished. This involves checking that a freshly arrived component is due for integration with a component or subsystem that already exists. If this check is successful, the new component can be integrated and integration tested.

Work on the central *ContractBase* module in *VSR-II* turns out to be more complex than originally thought, and completion of the module is delayed by several weeks. In order to avoid wasting time, the project manager decides to begin testing for the *DreamCar* and *NoRisk* modules.

These two modules have no mutual interface, but do swap data via *ContractBase*. To calculate the appropriate insurance premium, *NoRisk* requires the vehicle type and other parameters.

*Case Study:
The integration strategy for the VSR-II project*

A stub must be programmed for use as a temporary placeholder for *ContractBase*. This stub receives simple vehicle configurations from *DreamCar*, determines the vehicle's type code and passes it to *NoRisk*. The stub also enables the entry of various other insurance-relevant customer details. *NoRisk* then calculates the premium and displays it in a window for checking and logs it as a test result. The stub thus temporarily fills the gap left by the incomplete *ContractBase* module.

This example emphasizes that, although it might save time, starting integration testing too early generates increased effort creating stubs.

Test management has to choose a testing strategy that optimizes the relationship between time savings and the increased effort involved in maintaining the test environment.

Constraints that influence integration

Which strategy is best (i.e., is most economical and saves most time) depends on constraints that have to be analyzed for every project:

- The **system architecture** determines the number and type of components the system consists of and the dependencies between them.
- The **project schedule** defines when individual components are due for completion, integration, and testing.
- The overall **testing plan** defines how thoroughly which aspects of the system are to be tested and at which testing level.

Agree on an Integration strategy

The test manager has to look at these constraints and use them to develop an integration strategy that suits the current project. Because the delivery time of the individual components is key, it is always a good idea to consult with the project manager at the project planning stage to ensure that components are delivered in a sequence and at times that support testing.

Basic strategies

Test managers can align to one of the following basic integration strategies as a guide to planning:

- **Top-down integration**

    Testing begins with the main component that calls other components, but—apart from the operating system—doesn't get called itself. Subsidiary components are replaced by stubs. Components on lower system layers are then gradually integrated, while the (already tested) layer above serves as the test driver.

    - The upside: Because components that have already been tested make up the bulk of the run-time environment, you will need only rudimentary test drivers, or no test drivers at all.

- The downside: Subsidiary components that have not yet been integrated have to be replaced by stubs, which can involve a lot of extra work.

- **Bottom-up integration**
  Testing begins with the basic components that don't call any others (except for operating system functions). Larger units are built gradually from tested components, which are then integration tested.
  - The upside: No stubs are required.
  - The downside: Higher-level components have to be simulated using test drivers.

- **Ad hoc integration**
  Components are integrated in the (random) order of their completion (see above).
  - The upside: Time savings, as every component is integrated into the environment as early as possible.
  - The downside: Stubs and test drivers are required.

- **Backbone integration**
  A skeleton framework ("backbone") is created, and individual components are successively integrated into it. Continuous integration (CI) (see section 3.1) is a contemporary version of this strategy in which the backbone is made up of existing components to which newly tested ones are added.
  - The upside: Components can be integrated in any sequence.
  - The downside: A backbone or CI environment has to be created and maintained, which can involve a lot of extra effort.

Pure top-down and bottom-up integration can only be applied to systems that have a strict hierarchical structure, which is rare in the real world. In practice, most projects rely on a custom mixture of the strategies detailed above[10].

It is essential to avoid any non-incremental integration (also referred to as the "Big Bang"). This approach involves no real strategy. The team simply waits until all the components are ready and integration means simply throwing them together all at once. At its worst, upstream component testing is skipped too. The drawbacks are obvious:

Avoid the Big Bang!

---

10. For object-oriented, distributed, or real-time systems more specialized integration strategies often make sense.

- The time spent waiting for the "Big Bang" is carelessly wasted testing time. Testing always involves time pressure, so don't waste a single testing day.
- All failures occur at once and it is difficult (or simply impossible) to get the system to run at all. Defect localization and correction is complicated and time-consuming.

3.4.3 System Testing

Terminology

Once integration testing is complete, the next test level is system testing. This level checks that the complete, integrated system actually fulfills its specified requirements. Here too, you might ask yourself why this step is necessary following successful component and integration testing. Reasons are:

Reasons for system testing

- Low-level tests check technical specifications from the software manufacturer's point of view. In contrast, system testing views the system from the customer and end-user viewpoints[11]. System testers check whether the specified requirements have been completely and suitably implemented.
- Many functions and system attributes result from the interaction of the system's components and can therefore only be observed and tested on a system-wide level.

Case Study: VSR-II system testing

For the sales-side stakeholders, the *VSR-II* system's most important task is to make ordering a vehicle as simple as possible. The order process uses nearly all the system's modules: configuration in *DreamCar*; financing and insurance using *EasyFinance* and *NoRisk*; order transmission via *JustInTime*; paperwork saved in *ContractBase*. The system only genuinely fulfills its intended purpose when all of these components work together correctly, and system testing verifies if this is the case.

The test basis

The test basis consists of all documents and other information that describe the test object on a system level. These can be system and software requirements, specifications, risk analyses (if available), user manuals, and so on.

---

11. The customer (who ordered and paid for the system) and the end-user can belong to different groups and organizations that each have their own interests and system requirements.

Once integration testing is finished, you are faced with a complete, ready-to-run system. System testing checks the finished system in an environment that resembles the system's production environment as closely as possible. Instead of stubs and test drivers, all of the hardware, software, drivers, networks, third-party systems, and other components that will be part of its working environment need to be installed in the system test environment.

Test object and test environment

As well as checking user, training and system documentation, system testing also checks configuration settings and should support to system optimization by providing load/performance test results (see section 3.5.2).

To save time and money, system tests are often performed in the production environment itself, rather than in a separate system-testing environment. There are various reasons why this is a bad idea:

System testing requires its own test environment

- System testing is sure to reveal failures! These failures can have a highly negative impact on the customer's production environment. Crashes and data loss at the customer site can be expensive and should be avoided at all costs.
- Testers have limited control over the configuration and the parameters that affect the customer's production environment. If you test while other parts of the customer's system are running, this can subtly alter your results and make the tests you perform extremely difficult to reproduce (see section 3.6.3).

Because of the complex test environment it requires, the effort involved in system testing is often underestimated. [Bourne 97] says experience has shown that usually only half of the required test and QA work has been done by the time system testing begins.

System testing effort is often underestimated

As previously noted, the objective of system testing is to verify whether and how well the finished system fulfills the specified (functional and non-functional) requirements (see sections 3.5.1 and 3.5.2). System testing identifies defects and deficiencies that are due to erroneous, incomplete, or inconsistently implemented requirements. It should also identify undocumented or forgotten requirements.

Test objectives

In systems that rely on databases or other large amounts of data, data quality is an important factor that may need to be considered as part of the system testing process. The data themselves become a "test object" and they need to be appropriately checked for consistency, completeness, and up-to-dateness.

Data quality

> *Side Note:*
> *System testing issues*
>
> In too many projects, the clarification and documentation of the requirements is either patchy or ignored completely. This makes it difficult for testers to know how the system is actually meant to work, and doubly difficult to reliably reveal failures.
>
> *Vague requirements*
>
> Where no requirements exist any system behavior is permissible, or system behavior simply cannot be evaluated. The user (or the internal/external customer) will of course have an idea what to expect from "his" system. Requirements do exist, but only in the minds of some of the people participating in the project. The testers are then given the thankless task of collating all the relevant information regarding the system's planned behavior. One way to deal with a situation like this is using exploratory testing (see section 5.3).
>
> *Missed decisions*
>
> In the process of gathering this information, the testers will find that the various participants have very different ideas and attitudes about what needs to be built. To avoid this situation, the project requirements need to be written down and then agreed upon and approved by all relevant participants.
>
> In other words, as well as gathering requirements, system testing must also enforce clarification and decision-making processes that should have been completed long ago and that are now being done much too late. This kind of information-gathering takes time and is extremely costly, and is guaranteed to delay delivery of the product.
>
> *Some projects fail*
>
> If requirements aren't documented, the developers won't have clear objectives and the probability that the resulting system fulfills the implicit customer requirements is very low indeed. Under such circumstances, nobody expects a usable product to result and system testing can often only "certify" the failure of the project.
>
> *Reduce the risk of early feedback*
>
> Iterative and agile projects require clearly formulated and written requirements too. Again, there is always a risk that some requirements will be incomplete, incorrectly communicated, or simply overlooked. However, in this case each iteration provides the opportunity to check fulfillment of the given requirements, thus reducing the risk of the project failing.
>
> If requirements are not sufficiently met, you can use the next iteration to improve things. You may end up with more iterations than originally planned to ensure that a specific level of functionality is reached. This then equates to a product that is delivered late but works, instead of a project that fails completely.

3.4.4 Acceptance Testing

The types of tests we have looked at so far are all performed by the software manufacturer and/or the development team before the software is delivered to the customer.

Before a system is launched (especially in the case of custom software) it is put through an additional "acceptance test". This type of test takes place from the customer/end-user's viewpoint and is the only test that the customer is directly involved in or is actually responsible for.

3.4 Testing Levels

Typical variants of acceptance tests are:

1. User acceptance testing
2. Acceptance by the system's operator
3. Contractual and regulatory acceptance testing
4. Field tests (i.e., alpha and beta tests)

Acceptance tests can also take place on lower levels and are often distributed over multiple test levels:

- Off-the-shelf software can be tested for acceptance when it is integrated or installed
- The user-friendliness of a component can be acceptance tested as part of the component testing process
- The acceptance of a new function can be checked prior to system testing using a prototype

The scope of acceptance testing is risk-based and is highly variable. In the case of custom software, the risk levels are high, making comprehensive acceptance testing essential. At the other end of the spectrum, if you are installing off-the-shelf software, it can be sufficient to simply install the package and test a couple of typical usage scenarios. If, however, the package accesses interfaces to other systems, the interaction between the separate systems has to be tested too. *How comprehensive do acceptance tests need to be?*

The test basis consists of all documents that describe the test object from the user's point of view—for example, user and system requirements, use cases, business processes, risk analysis, descriptions of the processes that use the system, forms, plus reports and descriptions of system maintenance and admin processes. If the test is based on legal or other formal regulations, it is often referred to as a regulatory acceptance test. *The test basis*

In the case of custom software, the customer will (in cooperation with the manufacturer) perform a contractual acceptance test. Based on the test results and whether or not the guidelines stipulated by the development contract are fulfilled, the customer will then decide whether or not to accept the delivered product. The contract can also be a (less) formal agreement between two company-internal departments that develop the product as joint project. *Contractual acceptance test*

The acceptance criteria detailed in the development contract will serve as test criteria, so these have to be clearly and unambiguously defined. If relevant, any legal stipulations, regulatory standards, or safety regulations are part of the acceptance criteria. *Acceptance test criteria*

In practice, the software manufacturer should usually have checked these acceptance criteria using appropriate test cases during internal system testing. Acceptance testing then can be done by repeating a subset of these system tests which demonstrate to the customer that the contractual requirements have been fulfilled.

Our Tip

- Because it is possible for the manufacturer to misunderstand contractually agreed acceptance criteria, it is essential that customers design their own acceptance test cases (or at least subject the drafted cases to a stringent review).

Acceptance testing at the customer site

In contrast to system testing, which takes place within the software manufacturer's test environment, acceptance tests are performed within the customer's own acceptance-testing environment[12]. The differences between the two environments can cause a fault-free system test case to fail during acceptance testing. Installation and configuration procedures are part of acceptance testing, and are often referred to as operational acceptance testing. The acceptance testing environment has to be as similar as possible to the production environment the system is to be used in. However, acceptance testing within the production environment is to be avoided, as this runs the risk of disrupting critical production processes.

You can use the same methods you used for system testing to derive suitable acceptance tests and test criteria. If you are testing an administrative IT system, you also need to test business cases that occur over a typical period of time and/or billing period (for example, a monthly billing cycle).

User acceptance testing

Another aspect of acceptance testing is user acceptance. This kind of test is especially important if the customer is not actually the end-user.

Case Study: Different user groups and usage situations

In the case of *VSR-II*, the customer is the automobile manufacturer but the end-users are dealership staff and customers who use the *DreamCar* module to configure vehicles at a dealership or online. Staff members at company headquarters also use the system—for example, to update price lists.

---

12. Sometimes, an initial acceptance test run will be performed in the system test environment followed by a second test run in the customer's own environment.

Different user groups will generally have different expectations of a new system. If a user group rejects the system—for example, because they find it "unwieldy", this can mean that the entire implementation is rejected even if the system works according to its functional specifications. It is therefore important to perform acceptance tests tailored to each user group. Such tests are usually organized by the customer, who can select the most appropriate test cases based on established business processes and user scenarios.

Consider all user groups

■ If serious issues crop up at the acceptance testing stage, it is usually too late to change anything except superficial, cosmetic aspects of a system. To avoid such disasters, it is a good idea to let selected end-users evaluate product prototypes as early as possible in the development process.

Our Tip
Show prototypes to end-users as early as possible

Acceptance testing by the system's operator ensures that the system administrators are happy with how the system integrates within the existing IT landscape. These tests include backup and recovery routines, restarts following system shutdown, user administration, and various aspects of data handling and security.

Acceptance testing by the system's operator

If a product is destined to run in multiple, different production environments, it is extremely costly and impractical for the manufacturer to set up system testing environments to mirror each end-user scenario. In this case, the manufacturer will follow system testing with field tests designed to identify (and, if possible, rectify) factors influencing the system from unknown or partially unknown environments. Field tests are especially useful for manufacturers who develop commercial, off-the-shelf software products.

Field tests

In this case, the manufacturer delivers stable, pre-release software to selected customers who represent the market or the environments the product is typically aimed at.

"Typical customer" tests

These customers then perform tests prescribed by the manufacturer or simply test the software under real-world conditions. They then give the manufacturer feedback in the form of comments and defect reports that the manufacturer can use to tweak the product appropriately.

This kind of testing is referred to as "alpha" or "beta" testing. Alpha tests are performed in the developer's test environment by people whose roles lie outside the development organization, while beta tests take place at customer sites.

Alpha and beta testing

A field test must not replace the manufacturer's in-house system test (although some manufacturers think it should). You should only ever release software for field-testing once system testing has proved that it is sufficiently stable.

Acceptance testing in agile projects

All the acceptance test variants mentioned above are relevant to iterative and/or agile development processes.

One of the guiding principles of iterative and agile development is to gather feedback from customers as soon as possible—and that is exactly what acceptance testing is about. You should therefore include some acceptance testing in each iteration, perhaps via a user survey, within a product demo, or in a hands-on test session together with your customer/user. The substance and the focus of acceptance tests may therefore change from iteration to iteration. Rather than conclusive acceptance of a final product version, the feedback is used to steer what can or must be improved in the next release.

The type and scope of the acceptance tests you perform will also depend on the "type" of iteration you are working on. You need to differentiate between iterations that produce an internal release and those that result in a release that is due for external, productive use. For example, the test team doesn't need to perform contractual acceptance testing for a purely internal release.

3.5 Test Types

The previous sections detailed the test levels that you need to cover during software development. The focus and objectives of these tests vary from level to level, so different types of test have to be performed with varying thoroughness. We differentiate between the following basic types:

- Functional and non-functional tests
- Requirements and structure-based tests

3.5.1 Functional Tests

Functional testing includes all test techniques and methods that are used to test the observable input/output behavior of a test object. Functional test cases are built using the "black-box" technique described in section 5.1. The functional requirements are the test basis for the planned system behavior.

Functional requirements[13] specify the behavior expected of a system or system component—in other words, they describe "what" the system (or component) is designed to accomplish, and implementing them is the basic prerequisite for a functioning system. Whether and how well a component fulfills its functional requirements is called its "functional suitability", which is one of the quality characteristics defined in the ISO 25010 standard [ISO 25010] (see section 2.2).

Functional requirements and functional suitability

The following example lists some of the functional requirements for price calculation in the *VSR-II* system (see also section 3.4.1):

R 100: The user can choose a model for configuration from the current catalog

R 101: The deliverable extras will be displayed for the selected model. The customer can select any of these to add to the configuration.

R 102: The price for the current configuration (model plus extras) will be calculated according to the current price list and displayed in real time

R 103: For the currently selected vehicle, only extras that are part of a deliverable configuration will be displayed. Non-deliverable extras for the current configuration will be grayed out.

Case Study: Functional requirements of the VSR-II DreamCar module

Tests that check functional attributes require at least one test case for each functional requirement. Suitable tests for verifying R102 "calculate total price" (see above) might look like this:

Functional test cases

T 102.1: A vehicle model is selected; the price according to the sales manual is displayed

T 102.2: An extra is selected; the vehicle price is increased by the price of this extra

T 102.3: An extra is deselected; the vehicle price is reduced by the price of this extra

T 102.4: Three extras are selected; these are discounted according to the specifications

Case Study: Requirement-based functional test cases

---

13. Specific customer requirements or the assumed requirements of a particular target market

Usually, more than one test case is required to test a functional requirement. In our example, Requirement 102 includes a whole series of price calculation variants that need to be covered by appropriate test cases (102.1—102.4). These cases can be fine-tuned and augmented using other black-box techniques such as equivalence partitioning (see section 5.1.1).

The important thing is that, once the predefined test cases (or a subset thereof as defined in the test specifications) have been run without revealing any faults, the functionality is taken to be correctly implemented.

Functional testing takes place on every test level. For component and integration testing, the test basis comprises the components' technical specifications, the specification of each component's interfaces (its API), or white-box information (see section 3.5.3). For system and acceptance testing, the test basis is made up of functional system requirements (as illustrated in the example above).

Use-case and business-process-based testing

If a software system is designed to automate or support a specific business process (as in the example above), use-case or business-process-based testing techniques are also suitable (see section 5.1.6).

Case Study: Testing a business process

VSR-II supports dealers during the sales process, which might take place as follows:

- The customer selects an available model that is of interest
- The customer looks at equipment and pricing options and configures a vehicle accordingly
- The salesperson suggests various financing options
- The customer makes a decision and places an order

Business process analysis

Business process analysis is usually conducted as part of requirements analysis and shows which business processes are relevant, how often they occur and in which context, which people, companies and external systems are involved, and so on. This information forms the test basis, which is then used to create testing scenarios that emulate typical business events. These test scenarios are prioritized according to the typical frequency and relevance of these events, and also according to the risk factor attached to the corresponding processes.

While requirements-based testing is focused on individual system functions (for example, transmitting an order), business process-based testing checks sequential procedures (such as a sale made up of vehicle configuration, agreeing a purchase, and transmitting the order) using sequences of tests.

As well as the basic select, configure, purchase functionality of our sample *VSR-II* system, user acceptance is also based on how user-friendly a system is. User-friendliness (or usability) is judged by how easy the system is to use, how quickly it "answers", and how clear the output is that it delivers. In other words, alongside functional criteria, we also have to test and validate non-functional system attributes.

3.5.2 Non-Functional Tests

Non-functional requirements describe attributes of a system's functional behavior—i.e., how "well" a system or component should fulfill its function. Its implementation strongly influences customer/user satisfaction and therefore also how well liked the system is. According to [ISO 25010], such characteristics include user satisfaction and efficiency (see section 2.2). From the manufacturer's viewpoint, flexibility and portability are important aspects of a product's maintainability, as these help to reduce maintenance costs.

The following non-functional system characteristics[14] should be covered and checked by corresponding tests (usually in the course of system testing):

- **Load**
  Measurement of system behavior under increasing load (for example, number of parallel users, number of transactions)
- **Performance**
  Measurement of processing speed and response times for specific use cases, usually in conjunction with increasing load
- **Data volume**
  Observation of system behavior dependent on data volumes (for example, when processing very large files)
- **Stress**
  Observation of system behavior in overload situations
- **(Data) Security**
  Combating unauthorized system and/or data access

---

14. According to [Myers 12]

- **Stability/Reliability**
  Under constant use (for example, by measuring the number of system malfunctions per hour for specific user profiles)
- **Robustness**
  When subjected to user errors, programming errors, hardware failure, and similar. Testing exception handling and restart/recovery behavior.
- **Compatibility/Data conversion**
  Testing compatibility with existing systems, especially during data import/export
- **Different configurations**
  For example, using different OS versions, languages, or hardware platforms
- **Usability**
  Testing ease of learning and simplicity of use, including comprehensibility of output for various user groups (see also *Acceptance Testing*, section 3.4.4)
- **Compliance of system documentation with system behavior**
  For example, user manual vs. GUI, or configuration description vs. actual behavior
- **Maintainability**
  Comprehensibility and up-to-dateness of development documentation, modular structure, and so on

Non-functional requirements are often incompletely or vaguely worded. Attributes such as: "The system needs to be easy to use" or "fast response" cannot be tested in their current form.

Our Tip

- Testers should participate in reviews of the requirements documentation and make sure that all the listed (non-)functional requirements are worded in a way that makes them measurable and therefore testable.

Furthermore, many non-functional requirements are ostensibly so obvious that nobody thinks of mentioning or specifying them. Such "assumed requirements"[15] are often highly relevant, and the system must possess the corresponding implicit attributes.

---

15. This is unfortunately also true of functional requirements. Unvoiced requirements ("It was obvious that our system must be able to do that!") are a constant source of difficulties when developing and testing software.

Case Study: Assumed vs. specified requirements

The original *VSR* system was designed to run on an operating system provided by a well-known market leader, and has a look and feel that largely matches the OS styles and conventions.

The new, contemporary user interface in *VSR-II* is browser-based. The marketing department has worked with a web design agency to create a comprehensive style guide that dictates how *VSR-II*'s interfaces should look on a system-wide basis.

Usability tests use checklists (see section 5.3, Checklist-Based Testing) to ensure that the user interface of each module adheres to the specifications stipulated in the style guide. These tests reveal that some of the specified display and interface elements are difficult to read on mobile devices. Although no explicit "easy-to-read" requirement has been formulated, the decision is made to modify the corresponding parts of the style guide so that the assumed requirement of good legibility is fulfilled for all elements of the interface.

Side Note: Testing non-functional attributes using functional tests

It is often expedient to use existing functional tests to verify non-functional attributes. Non-functional tests are usually black-box tests, and can be seen as a kind of "backpack" strapped on to functional tests. An elegant general approach to these kinds of tests is as follows:

The scenarios selected from the functional tests represent a cross-section of the functionality offered by the entire system. The non-functional dimension must be visible in the corresponding test scenario, and is measured during the test run. If the measured value is below a predefined threshold, the test is classified as passed. Practically speaking, the functional test scenario serves as the measurement procedure for determining the non-functional system characteristic you want to test.

3.5.3 Requirements-Based and Structure-Based Testing

Requirements-based testing is a black-box technique in which test cases are designed based on requirements. It is also called specifications-based testing, because it uses the specifications of the externally observable behavior of the software as its test basis. This kind of specification can take various forms—for example, use cases or user stories. The corresponding testing techniques are described in section 5.1. The specifications and the test cases derived from them can relate to functional or non-functional characteristics of the software element in question.

Requirements-based tests mostly take place during system and acceptance testing. If component or integration tests are derived from technical specifications or requirements, these too can be classed as requirements-based testing.

Structure-based testing (structural testing, white-box technique) uses the internal structure/architecture of the software as its test basis. It analyzes things like the control flows within a component or the call hierarchy of procedures or menu structures. The structures within an abstract model of the software can serve as a starting point too. The objective is to cover as many elements of the observed structure as possible during testing. This requires the design of a sufficiently large number of test cases, which again can be based on functional or non-functional attributes of the software element you are investigating.

Structural tests take place mostly during component and integration testing, and sometimes as additional tests on higher test levels (for example, to provide coverage for menu structures). These techniques are discussed in detail in section 5.2.

3.6 Testing New Product Versions

So far, we have simply assumed that a software development project ends when its acceptance tests have been passed and the product has been delivered. However, things look very different in reality. Initial delivery marks only the beginning of a software product's lifecycle. Many software products are used for years, or even decades, and are usually modified, extended, or repaired multiple times during their lifetimes. See our case study section below for an example:

Case Study: Evaluating the VSR-II hotline tickets

VSR-II has replaced the original *VSR* system and has been running for a while. To find potential weaknesses in the new system, the end-user support team analyzes the queries it received in the first few months since the system went live. Here are some examples:

1. A few dealerships have been running the system on a non-approved platform with a legacy operating system. The system's browser cannot display some elements of the user interface and the system sometimes crashes when it accesses the host system.

2. Some customers said that they found selecting extras in the old *VSR* system complicated, especially when comparing the prices of the various equipment packages. As a result, *VSR-II* enables the customer to save various configurations and call them up once changes have been made. However, some customers want even more convenience and would like to be able to compare different vehicle models plus equipment packages.

3. Because the corresponding calculation rule was overlooked when programming the insurance module, some rarely requested insurance tariffs cannot be calculated. A similar problem was already known in *VSR*.

4. In rare cases the order confirmation still hasn't reached the factory computer after waiting for 15 minutes. However, in order to avoid wasting network capacity, *VSR-II* cuts the connection at the latest after 15 minutes. This means the dealer has to repeat the order and send the confirmation to the customer separately later on. This causes customer dissatisfaction due to the unnecessary wait for order confirmation.

Issue #1 is essentially the dealer's problem. However, the manufacturer may modify the system to prevent the dealer having to make costly hardware updates.

Issue #2 will always crop up, regardless of how comprehensive the original system requirements were. A new system delivers a new user experience, and the customer preferences this generates will only be revealed once the system has been running for a while.

Issue #3 could have been found during system testing, although testing is a spot check that doesn't guarantee freedom from defects, but only a certain probability of finding existing failures. A good test manager would check which tests would have been necessary to reveal this oversight and would modify the test schedule accordingly.

Issue #4 was found and remedied using a patch. *VSR-II* no longer loses the order data, but instead automatically repeats the order process multiple times. However, this still doesn"t prevent the customer having to wait if the order confirmation takes a while. A genuine solution would involve modifying the batch processing system on the company's host machine—a solution that lies outside the *VSR-II* remit and thus cannot be remedied in the short term.

These four examples represent typical issues that occur with time, even in the most mature systems:

- The system is used under new, unforeseen, unplanned conditions
- Customers make new, unforeseen requests
- Functionality is required that covers rare (and therefore overlooked) special cases
- Issues evolve and only occur sporadically or once the system has been running for an extended period. These kinds of issues are often caused by external factors.

3.6.1 Testing Following Software Maintenance

Every software system needs to be modified and tweaked during its lifetime. This process is usually referred to as "software maintenance".

Software does not wear out. In contrast to the maintenance of hardware and unlike physical industrial products, the purpose of software maintenance is not to maintain the ability to operate or to repair damages caused by use. The purpose of software maintenance are:

- To correct faults that were unintentionally built into the product
- To improve the quality characteristics of the product
- To adapt the product to changed operating conditions (for example, when a new operating system, a new database, or a new communications protocol is implemented)

The corresponding test processes are called maintenance testing.

Changes in a software product can be triggered by bug fixes, or by planned modification/extension of its functionality that is part of "normal" maintenance and continuing development.

Testing new releases

In both cases, the result is a new product release. New releases are largely identical to earlier releases, but with some modifications to existing functionality and some completely new features.

How does the testing process react to these changes? Do all tests on every test level have to be repeated for each release? Or is it sufficient to test only the elements that are directly affected by the changes that have been made? The following sections discuss these questions.

Maintenance testing

In the case of software maintenance (see above), the basic testing strategy (also called confirmation testing) involves repeating all test cases that revealed failures in the previous version. Such test cases have to be passed in order to classify the corresponding faults as corrected.

If faults have been fixed which were not revealed by previous test cases (for example, because originating from a hotline ticket), you need to draft new test cases to verify that the newly discovered faults really have been corrected.

Correcting previously undiscovered faults often changes the (correct) behavior of nearby program elements. This can be deliberate or accidental, making additional test cases necessary. Theses are either modified or new test cases that verify whether the changes achieve their intended effects. You also need to repeat the existing test cases that verify that "the rest" of the modified element remains unchanged and still functions properly.

Hotfixes

Some software failures cause immediate threats to system integrity and therefore require prompt attention. In such cases, an emergency "hotfix" is more expedient than a well-thought-out long-term solution. Concentrating on the most important confirmation tests helps to deliver a speedy hotfix, but you will nevertheless need to perform comprehensive testing (as described above) as soon as possible.

Maintenance testing is always simpler and more successful if the project manager plans maintenance releases in advance and includes them in the overall test schedule. When dealing with legacy systems, you will often only have access to outdated specifications (or no specifications at all), which makes maintenance and maintenance testing much more difficult. Appropriate planning makes this aspect of testing much easier.

Maintenance mustn't be used as an excuse to skip tests. If you skip testing because "a future release will correct defects anyway", you haven't properly understood the costs and risks that software defects can cause.

Impact analysis

Confirmation testing per se, or new tests in the vicinity of a modification are not really sufficient. Apparently simple local changes can cause unexpected and sometimes disastrous consequences and side effects in other (often distant) parts of the system. How many and which types of test cases are necessary to reduce this risk has to be determined by a highly specific "impact analysis" of the potential effects of the changes you make.

Maintenance testing following modification

When software is modified to suit changed operating conditions, you need to run tests to ensure that the system operator accepts the modified system. This is because various aspects of the non-functional system attributes[16] (such as performance, resource requirements, or installation preconditions) could (following modification) behave differently in the customer's environment.

If modifications involve data conversion or migration, you also need to test data completeness and integrity. Apart from these factors, the overall strategy for testing a modified system is the same as when you are testing a system following maintenance (see above).

---

16. The functional behavior remains unchanged—otherwise, this wouldn't count as an adaptation to a new environment. It is in the nature of such modifications that they don't always work flawlessly.

3.6.2 Testing Following Release Development

Alongside the maintenance required by fault correction, project management will also plan extensions and other changes to the system in order to keep it competitive and expand the customer base. Most systems are subject to continuous development—for example, to build improved releases of the product. Such releases are usually coordinated with scheduled maintenance work. For example, these may be quarterly maintenance releases and "real" functional updates on an annual basis.

Case Study: VSR-II development planning

The *VSR-II* development plan for Release 2 includes the following changes:

1. The *ConnectedCar* communications software is to be extended to ensure compatibility with the new generation of IoT sensors built into the latest model range.
2. Various functional extensions that were not ready in time for Release 1 will be delivered with Release 2.
3. The installed base is to be extended to include the company's dealers worldwide. This requires localization work for additional countries and includes translation of the system menus and manuals.

Change #1 results from a planned change in external resources and systems. Change #2 is a function that was planned from the beginning but hasn't yet been implemented due to time restrictions. Change #3 is part of a set of extensions that are required for preplanned market expansion.

None of these changes are due to fault correction or unforeseen customer requests, but rather part of *VSR-II*'s normal iterative/incremental product development process.

Testing following such release development follows two main objectives:

1. Checking that every new or extended function works as intended
2. Checking that pre-existing functionality is not (unintentionally) impaired

In order to achieve objective #1 you need to develop and perform new test cases. Objective #2 requires appropriate regression testing (see section 3.6.3 below).

Testing before decommissioning

An interesting case occurs when a system is due to be permanently retired. Here, you need to check before decommissioning whether the system data can or must be archived or transferred to the successor system.

3.6.3 Regression Testing

The process of repeating tests following changes to a program is referred to as "regression testing".

Regression testing utilizes existing test cases to check that the changes made have produced no new faults and have had no unintentional side effects. In other words, the objective is to ensure that the parts of a revised system that haven't been changed still work as they used to before the changes took place.

The simplest way to do this is to perform existing tests on the new version of the program.

In order for existing test cases to be useful for regression testing they have to be repeatable. This means that manual test cases have to be sufficiently well documented. Test cases that are used in regression testing will be used regularly and often, and are therefore predestined for test automation. Automation of regression test cases is extremely useful (see section 7.2) as it ensures precise repeatability and simultaneously reduces the cost of each test repetition.

Regression testing and test automation

Which of the existing tests should be used to ensure successful regression testing?

The extent of regression testing

Because we are checking that existing functionality has not been (unintentionally) impaired, we basically need to re-run all the tests that cover this pre-existing functionality[17].

If very few (or no) tests are automated, and you therefore have to perform regression testing manually, you will have to select the smallest possible subset of the manual tests. To select the appropriate test cases you have to carefully analyze the test specifications to see which test cases relate to which pre-existing functionality and which to the new, modified functionality.

If you have automated test cases, the simplest strategy is to simply re-execute all of them for the new product version:

- Test cases that return a "passed" result indicate an unchanged component/feature. This can be either because the required change hasn't been made or because the "old" test cases weren't sufficiently precisely formulated to cover the modified functionality. In both cases, the cor-

---

17. If the existing test cases are patchy, regression testing will be patchy too. Specialized tools that measure code coverage during individual test runs can help to judge whether this is the case.

responding test cases need to be modified to ensure that they react to the new functionality.

- Test Cases that return a "failed" result indicate modified functionality:
  - If this includes features that weren't flagged for change, a fail is warranted as it indicates that—contrary to planning—the corresponding feature has been changed. Because such unintentional modifications are revealed by the "old" test cases, no further changes are required.
  - For features that need to be changed, the test cases need to be adapted too so that they cover the new functionality.

The result of all this is a suite of regression tests that verify the planned alterations to functionality. Test cases that cover completely new functions are not yet part of this suite and have to be developed separately.

Complete vs. partial regression testing

In practice, complete regression testing that runs all existing tests is usually too costly and takes too much time, especially when (as mentioned above) manual tests are involved.

We are therefore looking for criteria that help us to decide which legacy test cases can be ignored without losing too much information. As ever in a testing context, this requires compromise between minimizing costs and accepting business risks. The following are common strategies for selecting test cases:

- Repeat only the tests that were given high priority in the test schedule.
- Leave out special cases for functional tests.
- Limit testing to certain specific configurations (for example, test only the English-language version, test only for a specific operating system, and similar).
- Limit testing to specific components or test levels.

The rules listed here apply primarily to system testing. On lower test levels, regression-testing criteria can be based on design documentation (such as the class hierarchy) or on white-box information.

3.7 Summary

- Software development lifecycle models structure the software development process in sections, phases, or iterations. The two basic model types are "sequential" and "iterative/incremental".
- Sequential development models are characterized by development activities that are conducted in a linear (i.e., sequential) fashion.
- Iterative/incremental models produce regular extended and/or improved product releases that enable timely feedback from the customer and the system's users. This approach reduces time to market and also reduces the risk of developing a product that doesn't fulfill the customer's expectations. All agile development methods are classed as iterative/incremental.
- The V-model is an important sequential development model that defines component, integration, system, and acceptance test levels. It differentiates between verification and validation und provides principles for good testing practice that can be applied to any development model:
  - Each phase of development has a corresponding test level
  - Tests are divided into categories or test types according to their objectives, which are pursued with differing priorities on different test levels:
    - Functional testing
    - Non-functional testing
    - Structure-based testing
    - Change-based testing
  - Test planning and design need to take place as early as possible in the corresponding development phase
  - Testers should be involved in reviews from the very beginning of the project
  - The number and scope of test levels needs to be adapted to suit the constraints and conditions specific to the project at hand
- The sooner a defect is discovered, the less it will cost to rectify it. The V-model therefore requires verification procedures (such as reviews) at the end of every development phase. This helps to prevent the spread of subsequent defects.

- Component testing examines single software components. Integration testing examines the collaboration of these components. Functional and non-functional system testing examine the entire system from the user's viewpoint. In acceptance testing, the customer checks the product for acceptance with respect to the contract, and acceptance by users and operational personnel. If the system is to be installed in multiple environments, field tests provide an additional opportunity to get experience with the system by running pre-release versions of the product.

- Maintenance and incremental development continuously create new software product versions throughout the product's lifecycle. Each new version has to be tested in its own right, and the scope of such regression testing depends on the results of corresponding risk analysis.

4 Static Testing

Static testing and analysis of work products (documentation and code) contributes measurably to increased product quality. This chapter describes static testing in general as well as the specific process involved, with its activities and the roles that have to be filled. We describe four proven techniques and their specific advantages, as well as the factors that ensure success when applying them. We conclude by comparing static and dynamic testing techniques.

Static testing (or "static analysis") can be performed in a tool-based environment or manually, and is a testing technique that is often neglected. While the test object for a dynamic test (see Chapter 5) is an executable program that is run using test data, static testing can be performed on any kind of work product that is relevant to the development of a product. Static testing can take the form of close examination by one or more persons (see section 4.3) or can be performed using appropriate analysis tools (see section 7.1.3).

An underestimated technique

The underlying concept of static testing is prevention. Errors[1] and other deviations from plan are identified before they can have a negative effect during further development. All relevant work products are quality assured before anyone does any further work on them. This prevents faulty interim work products from entering the development flow and causing costly faults later on.

It's all about prevention

Static tests can be performed in a variety of situations (see below), and are often an integral part of the development process (i.e., testing resources are made available at the planning stage). For example, in safety-critical industries such as aviation and medicine, static analysis is an extremely important factor in ensuring the required product quality.

---

1. Errors in the code or other work products.

4.1 What Can We Analyze and Test?

A versatile technique

As well as the code itself, software development produces a lot of other work products too. Most documents play some kind of role in the further development of a product, making the quality of each individual document an important factor in the overall quality of the results.

Work products that can be checked using static analysis (especially reviews, see below) include specifications, business requirements, functional and non-functional requirements, and security requirements. Specification errors need to be found before they are converted into code. In agile projects, epics [URL: Epic] and user stories are subject to static testing. The kinds of defects that static analysis reveals include inconsistencies, ambiguities, contradictions, gaps, inaccuracies, and redundancies.

During the software design process, architecture and design specifications (such as class diagrams) are created that can be tested statically just like program code. The code that makes up a website can be tested this way too (for example, automatic verification of links and their corresponding target sites). Code can be checked for consistency with the project's programming guidelines[2].

Generally speaking, static testing verifies that any predefined standards have been adhered to in the documents being analyzed.

It is also advisable to examine and verify all documents, definitions, and tools that are created during testing (such as the test plan, test cases, test procedure and scripts, acceptance criteria). Other documents and work products that can be verified by static testing include contracts, project plans, schedules, budgets, and user manuals.

Furthermore, the results of static testing can also be used to improve the overall development process. If certain kinds of defects occur repeatedly during specific development steps, this is a sign that this step requires investigation and, if necessary, optimization. This kind of process is usually accompanied by additional staff training.

---

2. Preferably using appropriate tools.

4.2 Static Test Techniques

Human mental and analytical skills can be used to analyze and evaluate complex situations through close investigation of the documents in question. It is essential to the success of such analysis that the people involved understand the documents they are reading and comprehend the statements and definitions they contain. Static tests are often the only effective way to check the semantics of documentation and other work products.

Human mental and analytical skills

They are various static testing techniques that differ in their thoroughness, the resources they require (i.e., people and time), and the objectives they pursue. Some common static testing techniques are detailed below. The terminology used is based on the ISTQB® syllabus and the ISO 20246 [ISO 20246] standard[3].

The commonest and most important static testing technique is the review[4]. In this context, the term "review" has multiple meanings. It is used to describe the static analysis of work products but is also used a general term for all static analysis techniques performed by humans. The term "inspection" is also used to describe a similar process, although it is often used to mean the formal execution of a static test (and the collection of metrics and data) according to predefined rules.

"Review" has multiple meanings

Reviews can be conducted informally or formally. Informal reviews don't adhere to a predefined process and there is no clear definition of the intended results or what is logged. In contrast, the formal review process (see section 4.3.1) is predefined and the participants (see section 4.3.3) document a planned set of results.

Different review processes

The type of review process you choose will depend on the following factors:

- The development lifecycle model: Which model are you using? Which places in the model and interim results are suitable for conducting a review?
- The maturity of the development process: How mature is the process and how high is the quality of the documents that are to be checked?
- The complexity of the documents to be tested: Which output shows a high degree of complexity and is therefore suitable for a (formal) review?

---

3. For more detail on review procedures, see [Gilb 93], [Wiegers 02].
4. *www.meriam-webster.com* defines "review" as "A critical evaluation (as of a book or play)".

- Legal or regulatory requirements and/or the necessity for a traceable audit trail: Which regulations have to be adhered to and which proofs of quality assurance (and therefore reviews) are required?

Different objectives

The desired objectives of a review also determine which type of review process you choose (see section 4.4). Are you focusing on defect detection or on the general comprehensibility of the tested work products? Do new team members have to become familiar with a specific document by reviewing it? Does the review help the team reach a consensus decision? The type of review you conduct will depend on your answers to these questions.

4.3 The Review Process

Review activities

The process of reviewing work products comprises planning, commencement, preparation by the participants (specialists, reviewers, inspectors), communicating and analyzing the results, fault correction, and reporting (see figure 4-1).

Fig. 4-1
Review process activities

4.3.1 Review Process Activities

The following sections go into detail on the individual activities mentioned above.

Planning

At the planning stage, management—or, more accurately, project management—has to decide which documents (or parts of documents) are to be subject to which type of review (see section 4.4). This decision affects the roles that have to be filled (see section 4.3.3), the necessary activities and, if required, the use of checklists. You also need to decide which quality characteristics to evaluate. The estimated effort and timespan for each review have to be planned too. The project manager selects a team of appropriately skilled participants and assigns them their roles. The project manager also has to check with the author(s) of the review object(s) that they are in a reviewable state—i.e., they have reached at least a partial conclusion and are as complete as possible.

Define your objectives and choose a type of review

Formal reviews require predefined entry and exit criteria. If the plan includes entry criteria, you need to check that these have been fulfilled before proceeding with the review.

Checking a document from different viewpoints or having individuals check on specific aspects of a document increases the effectiveness of the review process. These viewpoints and/or aspects have to be defined at the planning stage.

Different viewpoints increase effectiveness

You don't have to review a document in its entirety. It often makes sense to select the parts that contain high-risk defects, or sample parts that enable you to draw conclusions about the quality of the document as a whole.

If you want to hold a pre-review meeting, you need to decide when and where it takes place.

Initiating a Review

The start (or "kick-off") of the review process is the point at which the participants are provided with all the necessary physical and electronic materials. This can be a simple written invitation, or a pre-review meeting at which the importance, the purpose, and the objectives of the review are discussed. If participants are not already familiar with the review object's setting, the kick-off can also be used to briefly describe how the review object fits into its field of application.

Baseline documents

Alongside the work products that are to be reviewed, review participants require other materials. These include any documents that help to decide whether what they are looking at is a deviation, a fault/defect, or a correct statement. These are the basis against which the review object is checked (for example, use cases, design documents, guidelines, and standards). These documents are often referred to as the "baseline". Additional test criteria (perhaps in the form of checklists) help to structure the procedure. If you are using forms to log your findings, these need to be distributed at the start of the process.

If you are conducting a formal review, you need to check that the entry criteria have been fulfilled. If they are not, the review should be canceled. This saves time that would otherwise be wasted reviewing "immature" work products.

Individual Review Preparation

Studying the review object

A review can only be successful if all participants are well prepared, so each member of the review team has to prepare individually for the review.

The reviewers (or "inspectors") subject the review object to intense scrutiny using the provided documentation as their baseline. Any potential defects, recommendations, questions, or comments are noted.

Individual preparation can take a number of forms. For more detail on these, see section 4.3.2.

Issue Communication and Analysis

Collating your findings

Following individual preparation, the findings are collated and discussed. This can take place at a review meeting or, for example, in a company-internal online forum. The potential deviations and defects found by the team members are discussed and analyzed. You also have to define who is responsible for correction of the identified faults, how to monitor correction progress (see section 6.4.4), and determine whether a follow-up review of the fixed document is required or necessary.

The quality characteristics under investigation are defined during planning. Each characteristic is evaluated and the results of the analysis documented.

The review team then has to provide a recommendation regarding acceptance of the review object:

- Accepted without changes or with slight changes
- Revision necessary due to extensive changes
- Not accepted

If a review meeting takes place, try to observe the following recommendations:

- Limit the duration of the meeting to two hours. If further discussion is necessary, hold a follow-up meeting at the earliest on the following day.
- The moderator (see below) has the right to cancel or suspend a meeting if one or more reviewers are absent or are present but insufficiently prepared
- The object of the discussion is the work product, not its author:
  - Reviewers need to mind their phrasing.
  - The author mustn't be required to defend himself or his work. However, justification of his decisions can be useful.
- The moderator cannot be a reviewer too
- General questions of style that are not covered by the review criteria are not to be discussed
- The development and discussion of potential solutions is not the review team's job (see below for exceptions to this rule)
- Every reviewer must be given sufficient opportunity to present her findings
- The reviewers should try to reach and record a consensus
- Findings should not be formulated as fault correction instructions for the author. Suggestions for correction or improvement of the review object can, however, help to improve product quality.
- Individual findings are to be classed[5] as:
  - Critical (the review object is not suitable for its intended purpose, defect has to be corrected prior to release)
  - Major defect (usability of the object is limited, fault has to be corrected prior to release)
  - Minor defect (slight deviation from plan—for example, grammatical error in print, doesn't affect usage)
  - Good (free of defects, don't alter during revision)

Side Note: Recommendations for review meetings

Fixing and Reporting

The final activities in the review process are reporting your findings and correcting any defects or inconsistencies the review has revealed. The minutes of a review meeting often contain all the required information, so that individual reports aren't necessary for defects that require the review object to be modified. As a rule, the author will rectify any defects revealed by the review.

Correcting defects

---

5. See section 6.4.3 Class 2 and 3 defects are major, whereas class 4 and 5 defects are minor.

As well as writing reports, any defects you find can also be communicated directly to the responsible person or team. However, this involves good interpersonal skills, as nobody really likes to talk about their own mistakes (see section 2.4).

Formal reviews involve more work

In a formal review, you need to record the current status of a defect or its report (see section 6.4.4). Changing the status of a defect is only possible with the agreement of the responsible reviewer. You also need to check that the specified exit criteria have been fulfilled.

Evaluating the results of a formal review meeting will help you to improve the review process, and to keep the corresponding guidelines and checklists up to date. This requires the gathering and evaluation of appropriate metrics.

The results of a review vary considerably depending on the type of review and the degree of formality involved (see section 4.4). The following sections detail different ways to approach the review process, and go on to discuss the roles and responsibilities involved in a formal review.

4.3.2 Different Individual Review Techniques

Collating your findings

The basic review process usually requires each participant to prepare for the team review. There are various individual review techniques[6] that help to reveal defects. These techniques can be applied to all types of review (see section 4.4), although their effectiveness can vary depending on the type of review you are conducting. The following sections describe various individual review techniques.

Ad hoc

No rules

As the name suggests, this technique involves no predefined rules regarding individual preparation. The reviewer usually reads the work products sequentially and notes any issues, findings, or defects that are found. The type of documentation is also arbitrary. Because they require very little (or no) preparation, ad hoc reviews take place quite frequently and, because there are no rules involved, the results depend heavily on the skills of the individual reviewer. If a review object is reviewed by more than one person, some issues are sure to be flagged multiple times.

---

6. These techniques can also be seen as an independent review if no other, overarching review process is planned.

Checklist-Based

Using checklists is a great way to structure your reading and thus increase the effectiveness of an individual review. You can define which checklists are used by which reviewers. A review checklist contains a list of questions based on potential defects that have been discovered in the course of earlier projects. The questions can also be based on formal guidelines or standards that need to be observed, as illustrated by the following example.

Using checklists

Checklist for reviewing a requirements document:

- Is the document's structure standardized?
- Is there an explanation of how the document is to be used (i.e., an explanatory introduction)?
- Is a project summary included in the requirements document?
- Is a glossary available to aid consistent comprehension?
- …

Case Study: Using checklists

Our example shows a checklist for reviewing a requirements document, but checklists can be formulated to aid reviewing any type of work product (for example, a code review). Checklists have to be updated regularly to include questions on newly recognized issues and to remove questions related to outdated or resolved issues. Checklists should generally be kept short and should only include key questions.

The main benefit of the checklist-based technique is that it systematically covers all typical types of defects. One potential downside of this technique is that it tends to "focus" the review on specific questions, thus reducing the likelihood of discovering defects that are not related to the listed questions. Always try to keep an open mind when using this technique.

Using Scenarios and Dry Runs[7]

A scenario-based review is based on predefined, structured guidelines that dictate how to run through the review object. The availability of specific use cases simplifies this type of review, as all you have to do is perform "dry runs" of all the use cases. For example, in our *VSR-II* case study, we

Use case run-throughs

---

7. This is very similar to the "walkthrough" technique, which takes place in a team rather than individually.

can check whether all the "configure vehicle" and "select special edition" cases are correctly implemented (see also section 5.1.6).

In the case of a code review, such scenarios can also be based on classes of defects. For example, one reviewer can concentrate on error handling in the code, while another concentrates on checking that boundaries are adhered to. Scenarios help a reviewer to find specific types of defects and are often more effective than simply working through lists of questions.

However, exclusive use of scenarios makes it more difficult to identify other types of defects (such as missing attributes), and should be avoided if possible.

Role- and Viewpoint-Based

Different roles and perspectives

During a role-based review, the reviewer is tasked with checking the review object from a specialist's point of view. To do this, the reviewer has to either already work in the specialist role, or at least empathize strongly with it. The basic idea of a role-based review is to utilize the skills each role provides. Of course, the person playing a role has to have the appropriate skills. For example, it is always useful to have testers review requirements, as they can check early on in the development process whether the requirements are sufficiently precisely defined to effectively derive test conditions and test cases from them.

Utilizing specialist skills

Other typical review roles are those of stakeholders such as end-users or the operator of the system within the customer's organization. If end-users or the system's operator cannot take part in review sessions (which is usually the case), these roles have to be played by others. The "end-user" role can be further refined depending on whether the person is "experienced" or "inexperienced". If the system is to be used within an organization, a reviewer can play the role of system or user administrator.

Case Study: A role-based review

A requirements document is due for role-based review. During the review, Joe Smith is assigned the role of designer. Ideally, Joe will know about software system design and will fulfill this role within the real-world project. Joe analyzes the requirements to see what changes are necessary to the system's architecture in order for the requirements to be adequately implemented. Jane Brown is a tester and adopts this role for the review. During the review, she will check whether it is possible to unambiguously decide (following implementation and testing) that each requirement has been fulfilled. Jane flags the requirement "The system will enable rapid operation' as insufficiently quantified. There are no numbers that can be measured, and there are no preconditions or constraints that determine specific situations in which timing can be considered adequate. Other roles need to be filled, too, in order to further scrutinize the requirements.

Different viewpoints

All the available roles point to different defects, inconsistencies, and gaps. Role-based reviewers take on the viewpoints of various stakeholders, thus examining different aspects of the system. The (often subjective) viewpoints of the stakeholders themselves need to be included in the review. The following example illustrates the differing interests that exist in a scheduling review for the next iteration in our case study project.

Case Study: A perspective-based review

The sales department view says that a particular requirement requires high priority in the requirements document, as this feature has been requested by an important customer and needs to be implemented as soon as possible. From the tester's viewpoint, this feature is very similar to other features that have already been implemented, so there shouldn't be any serious issues involved in implementing and testing it. She therefore recommends timely implementation of the new feature.

However, another new feature is more critical from a testing point of view, as it is the first in this project to implement artificial intelligence (AI). So far, the team has no experience in this field. The tester therefore assumes that this feature will require a lot of implementation and testing effort, so more resources need to be assigned to it.

The basic principle that underlies a perspective-based review is that each reviewer looks at the review object from a different viewpoint and runs through different scenarios as a result. The findings can then be used not only to evaluate the document in question but also to estimate the urgency and scope of any required changes. To do this, each reviewer runs through a different scenario[8] and uses the results to evaluate the document under investigation. Utilizing different stakeholder perspectives increases the depth of each individual review, and the distribution of roles reduces duplicate naming of defects and other issues. Using checklists is also a great way to increase the effectiveness of this kind of review.

Empirical studies (see [Sauer 00] and [Shull 00]) view perspective-based reviews as the most effective way to check requirements and technical descriptions. One of the keys to its success is the inclusion of many stakeholder viewpoints when analyzing and evaluating risk.

---

8. There are obvious links between this and the scenario-based technique described above.

4.3.3 Roles and Responsibilities within the Review Process

The roles and responsibilities[9] involved in the review process have already been roughly described in the course of discussing the general principles of reviewing. The following sections go into more detail on roles and their responsibilities within a typical formal review.

Not every role has to be filled by one person, and there are overlaps between roles that justify having one person fill multiple roles (for example, moderator and review leader). However, which roles can be combined depends on the nature of the project and the quality criteria you need to achieve. The individual activities associated with individual roles also vary according to the type of review you are conducting (see section 4.4).

Management[10]

Management Management selects which work products and supporting materials are to be included in the review and which type of review is to take place. Management is also responsible for planning reviews and allocating the required resources (people, time, money), and needs to keep an eye on cost-effectiveness. If the results of a review aren't conclusive, management needs to step in and take controlling decisions.

Side Note A member of the management team who is also the review object's author's boss shouldn't take part in review meetings, as this involves an implicit evaluation of the author rather than his work, and can limit the freedom of the review discourse. It may also be the case that management doesn't have appropriate IT skills to take part effectively in technical review meetings. This is, of course, not true for project planning meetings and other management-led tasks, where project and general management skills are of the essence.

Review leader

Review leader The review leader holds the overall responsibility and is therefore needs to make sure planning, preparation, execution, revision, and any follow-up work all contribute to achieving the review objectives. The review leader decides who participates in a review, as well as when and where it takes place.

---

9. The ISO 20246 standard [ISO 20246] details further roles.
10. In this case project management.

Facilitator/Moderator

The job of a facilitator (also often referred to as a moderator) is to ensure the smooth running of review meetings. The success of a review meeting often depends on the moderator's chairing and diplomatic skills. He or she has to be good at bringing together opposing viewpoints and keeping discussions brief without hurting anyone's feelings. Also required is a good degree of assertiveness and the ability to detect undertones within the conversation. A facilitator mustn't have preconceived ideas or a personal opinion of the review object, is responsible for collecting any resulting metrics, and ensures that a report of the meeting is written.

Facilitator

Author

The author in this case is the author of the review object. If there are multiple authors, one of them takes on the role of sole author for the duration of the review meeting. The author ensures that the entry criteria are fulfilled—in other words, that the review object is in a "reviewable" state. Usually, the author is responsible for rectifying any defects found during the review and therefore also for the fulfillment of the exit criteria. The author must never take criticism of the work personally. The review process serves solely to improve the quality of the review object.

Author

Reviewer

Reviewers (sometime also referred to as "inspectors") are a group of up to five experts who take part in a review following appropriate preparation. Reviewers are usually part of the project team whose work is being reviewed, but can also be other stakeholders who have an interest in the results or people with specialist and/or technical skills.

Reviewer

A reviewer's task is to identify and describe problematic places in the review object. Having reviewers with different perspectives (testers, developers, end-users, system operators, business analysts, usability experts, and so on) aids the effectiveness of a review, although you heed to make sure that only specialists take part whose views are relevant to the review object.

Having individual reviewers concentrate on specific aspects of the review increases the efficiency of the review process. For example, one reviewer can concentrate on adherence to a particular standard while another checks the program syntax. This distribution of roles takes place at the review planning stage.

Reviewers must differentiate clearly between parts of the review object that pass the review and those that require improvement. Defects must be clearly documented so that they are easy to identify and resolve.

Scribe

Scribe The scribe (or "recorder") documents the unresolved issues, open questions, and any other related tasks generated by the review. The documentation has to be brief and precise, and has to include undistorted summaries of all the discussions that took place.

As dedicated tools become more common, the job of review scribe is slowly becoming obsolete. If such tools are in use, every reviewer can record defects, open questions, and decisions directly in the tool interface without the need for separate documentation.

Side Note: Author and scribe For practical reasons, the author is often also the scribe. The author usually knows exactly what needs documenting in order to perform the changes requested by the reviewers.

4.4 Types of Review

Side Note: Management reviews Two types of review can be identified when looking at review objects:

- Reviews of documents that are created as work products during the development process
- Reviews that analyze the project or the development process itself

Reviews in the second group are referred to as "management", "project", or "process" reviews. Their aims include investigating whether regulations and plans are adhered to, analyzing the implementation of the required tasks, and the effectiveness of changes made to the process.

- The review object is the entire project and the main review objectives are to establish its current technical and economic state, as well as checking whether it is on schedule and how project management is doing
- Management reviews are often conducted when the project reaches a particular planning milestone, a development phase is completed, or as a "post mortem" analysis that supports the learning process for future projects
- In agile projects, such reviews often take the form of "retrospective" meetings. These are usually held following every sprint, and enable the team to compare notes and collect ideas on how to improve things in the next sprint.

4.4 Types of Review

The following sections go into detail on the first type of review, whose main objective is to identify defects by investigating documents. The type of review you perform will depend on the nature of the project, the available resources, the type of review object, potential risks, the business area, company culture, and other criteria.

The main objective is always to identify defects

The review can be an informal review, a walkthrough, a technical review, or an inspection. All of these can be conducted as a "peer review"—in other words, with the participation of colleagues on the same an identical or similar level within the company hierarchy.

A single review object can be reviewed using more than one type of review. For example, an informal review can be conducted to verify that the review object is in a fit state for a subsequent technical review and that the effort involved is justified.

Informal Review

An informal review is a kind of "soft" review that nevertheless follows the standard review process (see section 4.3) but without a strict, formal structure. The main aim of an informal review is to identify defects and provide the author of the review object with short-term feedback. It can also be used to develop new ideas and suggest solutions to existing issues. Minor issues can also be resolved during an informal review.

No strict guidelines

An informal review is usually initiated by the author. The planning stage involves selecting the participants and setting a date for delivering the results. The success of an informal review is highly dependent on the skills and motivation of the reviewer. Checklists can be used, but an informal review usually does without a separate session for discussing the results. In this case, an informal review is really just a simple author/reader feedback cycle.

Author/reader feedback cycle

An informal review is therefore a simple double-check of the review object by one or more colleagues—a "buddy check". The learning effect and interaction between team members are welcome side effects. A list of the issues found or a corrected/commented copy of the review object usually suffices as far as results are concerned. Techniques such as "pair programming", "buddy testing", and "code swapping" can also be seen as kinds of informal review. Because they are easy to organize and involve relatively little effort, informal reviews are widely used in all kinds of projects, and not only in an agile context.

Walkthrough

Running through the review object

As well as identifying defects, a walkthrough can be used to check for conformity with required standards and project specifications. This is also a forum for discussing alternative implementations, and an exchange of ideas about procedures or variations in style can also result and contribute to the participants' learning curve. The results of a walkthrough should be a consensus opinion.

The focus of a walkthrough is a meeting that is usually led by the author. The results need to be recorded, but there is no real need to prepare a formal transcript or summary report. Use of checklists is also optional. There is little individual preparation involved compared with a technical review or an inspection, and a walkthrough can be conducted with no preparation at all.

During the meeting, typical usage scenarios are named and walked through in a process-oriented fashion. Simulations or test runs of program parts (so called "dry runs") are also possible, and individual test cases can also be simulated. The reviewers use the comments and questions raised by the participants as a basis for identifying potential defects.

The author is responsible for making any changes that are required, and there is usually no further supervision involved.

Side Note

> This technique is suitable for small teams of up to five people, and little or no preparation and follow-up are required. It is great for checking non-critical objects. In practice, walkthroughs range from extremely informal to quite formal.
>
> Because the author usually leads a walkthrough, you have to take care that the review object is nonetheless critically and impartially scrutinized. Otherwise, the author's potential bias may lead to insufficient discussion of critical issues, thus distorting the results.

Technical Review

Alternative suggestions welcome

Alongside identifying defects, the main focus of a technical review[11] is forming a consensus. Other objectives include evaluating product quality and building confidence in the review object.

New ideas and suggestions for alternative implementations are welcome in a technical review, and technical issues can be solved by special-

---

11. "Specialist review" is perhaps a more precise term, as a technical review involves specialists who discuss specialized issues that are not exclusively technical.

ists. To make the most of this kind of discussion, colleagues of the author who work in the same or closely- related technical domain should participate as reviewers. Additionally, involving experts from other fields can help prevent the team from becoming blind to their own habits.

Individual preparation is critical in technical reviews. Checklists can be used too. If possible, the review meeting should be led by a trained review moderator, but not by the author. Discussion amongst the reviewers mustn't get out of control and should stick to finding a consensus about what the author can do to improve his work in the future. A meeting isn't mandatory, and the discussion can take place in other forums—for example, on the company intranet.

The results of the review need to be recorded, but not by the author. Usually, a list of descriptions of potential defects and a summary review report are prepared.

Technical reviews, too, can take many forms, from completely informal to strictly organized with predefined entry and exit criteria for each step of the process, and mandatory use of reporting templates.

> It helps to focus the review session on the most important points if the reviewers submit the findings from their individual reviews to the session moderator in advance. The moderator can then prioritize this input and use the meeting to discuss the most important points and the most obviously divergent opinions.
>
> The results of a technical review are the responsibility of all participants. If you cannot reach a consensus during the meeting, you can hold votes to settle discussions and log the results in the review report.
>
> It is not the responsibility of participants in a technical review to consider the consequences of the suggestions they make. This is down to management.

Side Note

Inspection

An inspection is the most formal type of review and follows a strict predefined flow[12]. All participants are project specialists or specialists in other aspects of the review object, and each adopts a specified role during the review. The review process is governed by rules that define check criteria for each aspect of the process. Each testing step has its own entry and exit criteria.

The objectives of an inspection are identifying defects and inconsistencies, determining the quality of the inspection object, and the building

Formal predefined flow

---

12. This is the most comprehensive of the types of review discussed here.

of confidence in the work products. Here too, reaching a consensus is an important part of the process. The findings of an inspection should help the author to avoid similar mistakes in the future and—like a technical review—help to improve the quality of future work.

An additional objective is the improvement of the software development process (see below). The objectives of an inspection are defined at the planning stage and the number of issues that the reviewers need to address is limited from the start.

The inspection object is formally checked for "reviewability" and the fulfillment of the entry criteria is verified before the inspection begins. The reviewers' individual preparation takes place according to predefined rules or standards using checklists.

A sample inspection meeting

A sample inspection meeting could take place as follows: The meeting is led by a trained moderator (not the author) who introduces the participants and their roles, and also provides a brief summary of the subject matter due for inspection. The moderator asks all the reviewers if they are sufficiently well prepared (for instance, by making sure that all the checklist questions have been answered). The moderator may also ask how much time the reviewers spent and how many defects they have identified.

General inconsistencies that affect the entire object are discussed and logged first.

A reviewer then makes a concise and logical presentation of the contents of the inspection object. If necessary, parts of the material can be read out (but not by the author). This is where other reviewers can ask questions and where the selected aspects of the object can be discussed in detail. The author (who mustn't be the review leader, the moderator, or the scribe) answers any direct questions. If the reviewer and the author cannot agree on how to deal with an issue, this is put to a vote at the end of the session.

If the discussion wanders off the point it is up to the moderator to intervene. The moderator also has to make sure that all selected aspects of the inspection object (and the object in general) are covered, and that all defects and inconsistencies are clearly recorded.

At the end of the session, all defects are presented and checked for completeness by all participants. Any unresolved issues are briefly discussed, but no suggestions for possible solutions are discussed. If there is no consensus as to whether an open issue represents a defect, this discrepancy is recorded in the report. The final report summarizes all results of the inspection and provides a list of descriptions of all potential defects.

To conclude, the inspection is evaluated and a decision is made as to whether the inspection object needs more work. During an inspection, any changes that are made and follow-up work that is done are formally regulated.

Some of the data collected during an inspection can also be used to identify the causes of weaknesses in the development process and thus to improve its quality. The data can also be used to improve the inspection process itself. Any improvement in the quality of both processes can be verified by comparing data collected before and after any changes are made.

Additional evaluation of the development and review processes

> This type of review is often referred to as a design, code, or software inspection. The name is based on the type of documents that are being inspected. However, if formal review criteria exist, all types of documents can be inspected.

Side Note

> **Selection Criteria**
>
> When and what type of review you use depends on the objectives you are pursuing, the required quality, and the effort this will cost. The project environment is critical to these decisions too, and it is impossible to make specific recommendations. You have to decide from project to project which type of review is best suited to the situation at hand. The following questions will help you decide which type of review to conduct:
>
> - The form of the review's results can be a factor. Do you need a comprehensive report, or is an undocumented implementation of the results sufficient?
> - Is scheduling easy or difficult? Finding a date when five, six, or seven specialists all have time can be hard work.
> - Does the review require experts from multiple disciplines?
> - How much specific knowledge of the review object do the reviewers need?
> - How motivated are the reviewers to spend time and effort concentrating on the planned review?
> - Is the planning effort commensurate with the expected results?
> - How formal is the review object? Can tool-based analysis take place in advance of the review?
> - How much management support do you have? Are reviews likely to be limited or even axed if time is running out?

Selecting the type of review

4.5 Critical Factors, Benefits, and Limits

Improving quality and lowering costs

Reviews are an efficient tool for assuring the quality of the work products under investigation. Ideally, reviews will take place immediately a work product is finalized. This way, any inconsistencies or defects are identified in a timely manner and the author receives feedback as soon as possible. Resolving any issues leads to improved quality in the documents in question and thus has a beneficial effect on the development process, which is then pursued with fewer defects in tow. Furthermore, static tests often reveal defects that are difficult (or impossible) to find using dynamic tests (see section 4.6).

Early identification and correction of defects through reviews is usually cheaper than resolving defects later when the application has reached an executable stage of development. This is especially true when earlier versions of an application have been delivered or are already in use.

Static tests are generally cheaper than dynamic tests (see Chapter 5) because defects can be corrected directly in the document and further checks are no longer necessary[13]. Correcting failures that appear during dynamic testing generally requires additional confirmation or regression testing. Reviews often save significant amounts of development time.

However, it is not always accurate to say that a review will reduce costs. For example, if a static test finds a memory leak, remedying the issue can be extremely time-consuming. Here, you need to differentiate between the cost of conducting a review and the cost of correcting the defect(s) the review identifies. The cost of correcting text in a document is negligible. In other words, the effort involved in making a correction depends on the nature of the issue that requires attention.

Dynamic testing can involve less effort if a code review has already removed faults in the test object (i.e., the code) and the risk of discovering further faults has been reduced thanks to the review.

A reduced number of defects and inconsistencies in the reviewed and corrected document will also reduce costs during the system's lifetime. For example, reviews can reveal inaccuracies in customer requirements that can be resolved in advance of implementation. Reviews also lead to a reduction in the number of failures that occur when the system is running. Additionally, productivity during development increases, as the team will be working with improved designs and code that is much easier to maintain (i.e., to understand and alter).

---

13. In the case of major defects or significant corrections, a repeat review can be scheduled.

As well as increasing quality and reducing costs, reviews have positive effects on the collaboration within the development team too:

Improved team communication

- Because reviews always take place in a group environment, they encourage the exchange of know-how among the participants. This leads to improvements in the working methods of individuals and thus to a general improvement in quality of the work they produce.
- The group environment makes it essential to present material in a way that is clear and comprehensible for all involved. This need for clarity often generates insights that the author wouldn't otherwise have had.
- The entire team feels responsible for the quality of the review object, and the result is a document that everyone understands.

In order to increase review quality, or to have a successful review in the first place, various organizational and people-related factors need to be considered. The following sections list the most important of these.

Organizational Success Factors

- Project management supports the review process by providing adequate resources for reviews throughout the development process.
- Formal reviews are planned well in advance and are organized with clear, verifiable objectives.
- Participants are given sufficient time to prepare for a review.
- In principle, all types of review (for example, checklist-based or role-based) are suitable for identifying defects in the review object. The most appropriate type can be selected based on the agreed objectives, the type and level of the investigated object, and the skills of the participants.
- Checklists cover the most important risks and are always up to date.
- Large-scale documents are reviewed in parts rather than as a whole so that defect feedback can be provided as quickly as possible to the authors.

Organizational factors

People-Related Success Factors

- You need to select the "right" participants to reach your planned review objectives. It is most productive to select people whose skills and viewpoints mean that they need to understand the review object anyway in

People-related factors

order to continue their work. Because the review object will usually be used as the basis for designing test cases, it makes sense to have testers take part in a review. The testers are then familiar with the project documents from the start of the development process and can begin specifying test cases right away. Such a test-based viewpoint also aids other aspects of quality assurance, such as verifying an object's testability.

- Reviews serve to assure the quality of the investigated object(s), so the identification of defects, inaccuracies, and deviations from plan is intended and should be encouraged. However, the reviewers must communicate their findings in an objective, unbiased manner. Reviews must be held in a trusting, confidential atmosphere, and participants should avoid using gestures that indicate boredom, frustration, or hostility to other participants. The author has to be sure that the results of a review don't influence his standing in the company. The author should see a review as a positive experience and all participants should end up feeling that taking part in the review was time well spent.

- Participants take the time to concentrate on details. Reviews are held so that participants don't lose their concentration. Don't attempt to review large documents in one sitting, and limit the length of the review session in advance.

- If necessary, offer participants additional training in advance of the review, especially for a formal review such as an inspection.

- Try to encourage a learning atmosphere so that everyone benefits from each review. This also improves the quality of the review process and individual review techniques.

Side Note:
Why reviews sometimes fail

- If a review fails because of insufficient preparation, this is usually due to poor scheduling
- If the reviewers don't understand the significance of the review or the effectiveness of the review process in quality improvement, you can use figures from the current project (or from earlier projects) to underscore the importance of the review process
- Reviews can fail due to insufficient or incomplete documentation. Alongside the review object, you have to make sure that all supporting documentation is available with the necessary depth of detail. A review should only go ahead if this is the case.

4.6 The Differences Between Static and Dynamic Testing

Static and dynamic tests can be used to achieve the same objectives (see section 2.1.2), but complement each other by identifying different types of defects. Static tests identify faults directly in documents and other work products, whereas dynamic tests usually identify failures in the source code rather than other types of documents (with the exception of executable models). Any failures you discover have to be traced back to the faults that cause them if they are to be successfully resolved. Failures often remain undiscovered for a long time—for example, if the corresponding code is only rarely executed. It therefore requires a lot of effort to design appropriate test cases. These kinds of faults in the source code are usually easier to identify using static tests.

Identifying different types of defects

Dynamic testing verifies the visible, external behavior of the test object, whereas static tests focus on improving the internal quality of the object under investigation.

Checking "inner" quality

The following sections detail typical defects and inaccuracies that can be identified quickly and cheaply, and therefore quickly resolved, using reviews:

Typical defects found by reviews

- **Requirements defects**
  Typical defects found in requirements documents are: inconsistencies, ambiguities, contradictions, gaps, inaccuracies, or redundancies.

- **Software design defects**
  Where defects are identified in the architecture documents that specify the system's internal interfaces. When the degree of dependency (or "coupling") between individual components or modules is high, it can be difficult to fully understand and test them, not least because the effort involved in creating a corresponding test environment is disproportionately to the importance of the results. The cohesion between components/modules can also be analyzed. A strongly coherent component is responsible for a single, clearly defined task.

  A component that performs a loose selection of tasks indicates low cohesion, which is just as disadvantageous as a high degree of coupling. Algorithms and database structures that have been inefficiently designed can be identified too.

- **Coding defects**
  If you have sufficient time and appropriately skilled personnel, all programming faults can be identified using code reviews. This enables you to detect variables with no value or redundant variables that are never called. You can also use a review to detect unreachable or duplicate code. These types of defects can also be detected by a compiler or by using automated static analysis tools, which is often quicker and cheaper than a human-based technique.

- **Deviations from standards**
  Standards and guidelines help to achieve high quality products, while insufficient adherence to programming guidelines leads to the opposite, namely: poor quality. If it is clear that adherence to certain guidelines will be checked, the motivation to stick to them from the start is much greater.

- **Faulty interface specifications**
  The names of the interfaces between components and their parameters (number, data type, and sequence) must be checked individually, as not all discrepancies will be found during integration.

Example: Incorrect interface definitions

The NASA Mars probe *Mars Climate Orbiter* is a famous and well-documented example of incorrectly specified interfaces [URL: Mars Climate Orbiter]. The system programmers used multiple measuring systems (metric and imperial), and this oversight led to the loss of the probe. A formal code review would probably have identified this inconsistency in the measurement system's specifications.

- **Security vulnerabilities**[14]
  Alongside dynamic security tests, static tests can also help uncover these kinds of vulnerability. For example, when buffer overflows occur because constraints weren't explicitly checked, or when input data or SQL queries are deliberately manipulated.

- **Gaps or inaccuracies in test basis traceability or coverage**
  We discussed the importance of traceability and degree of coverage in section 2.3.8. Gaps in traceability make traceability itself useless, as you can no longer make a connection between the requirements and the corresponding test cases. Inaccuracies in the exit criteria and the required degree of coverage make these aspects unusable too, and can

---

14. Tool-based analysis probably delivers more reliable results in this type of situation (see Chapter 7).

lead to incorrect estimates or distorted results. A review report can, for example, point out missing tests for fulfilled exit criteria.

Software systems often have surprisingly long lifecycles, making maintainability an important aspect of any system. Most shortcomings in maintainability can be identified using static tests. These include incorrect modularization (see coupling and cohesion above), bad reusability of individual components, and complex code that is difficult to modify (i.e., not "clean code" as defined in [Martin 08]) and therefore increases the risk of creating new faults when changes are made.

Maintainability

4.7 Summary

- Every work product (i.e., every document) can be reviewed, provided that all participants in the review are aware of how to read and understand the document in question.
- Reviews are static tests that—unlike dynamic tests—don't require code to be executed. This means that reviews can be applied at any time to all forms of work products that are used in or created by the software development process.
- Multiple pairs of eyes see more than a single pair, and the same applies to software development. Reviews used to monitor and increase quality are based on this principle. Documents are inspected by more than one person, and the results are discussed and recorded in a dedicated meeting.
- The activities involved in the review process are planning, initiation, individual preparation (i.e., individual review), discussion of the findings (issue communication and analysis, usually in a dedicated meeting), fixing and reporting.
- In order to better identify defects at the individual review stage, there are various different review techniques you can use:
  - **Ad hoc**
    No rules
  - **Checklist-based**
    Pre-formulated questions support the review process
  - **Scenarios and dry runs**
    Scenarios are run through

- **Role-based**
  Participants adopt specific roles for the review
- **Perspective-based**
  Different views on the review object

- The roles that need to be assigned for a review are manager, review leader, facilitator (moderator), author, reviewer (expert), and scribe.

- There are many types of review and, because the related standards don't use a unified terminology, the names used to describe them can vary. In this chapter we have discussed the following four review types:
  - An *informal review* doesn't follow any formal rules, and the form of the resulting documents is not regulated. Because it involves relatively little effort, the informal review process has become a widely accepted and well-used technique.
  - A *walkthrough* is an informal technique that sees the author presenting a document to reviewers in a meeting. Here too, preparation is minimal. Walkthroughs are ideal for small development teams who need to discuss alternatives and distribute know-how within the team.
  - A *technical review* follows a more strictly regulated flow in which individual reviewer preparation is essential. Reviewers should be professional colleagues of the author so that alternative realizations can be discussed.
  - An *inspection* is the most formal of these types of review. Preparation is based on checklists, and each review steps has its own entry and exit criteria. The review session is led by a trained facilitator. Alongside checking the quality of the work product, the objective of an inspection is to improve the development and review processes.

- To make them as effective as possible, reviews are generally tailored to the specific requirements of the company. One of the most important factors is establishing a cooperative atmosphere among all participants in the software development process.

- If you keep appropriate organizational and people-related success factors in mind, and as long as you take care to avoid known pitfalls, a review can be a seriously effective tool for increasing quality in software development projects.

- Reviews typically identify different defects than dynamic testing.

5 Dynamic Testing

This chapter describes the process of testing software by running it on a computer. It uses examples to illustrate various ways to specify test cases and exit criteria. Dynamic testing is based on black-box, white-box, and experience-based techniques. We explain what each category means and how to choose the appropriate one for your situation.

When we talk about software testing, most people imagine that it involves running a program on a computer. The term "dynamic testing" helps to clarify the situation. The test object has to be executable and is fed with input data before it is run. Because low-level test objects (component and integration tests) are not usually executable, dynamic testing requires use of a unit test framework (see figure 5-1).

Running the test object on a computer

The test object will usually use predefined interfaces to call other components, which are simulated by placeholders called stubs or mocks if the components themselves are not yet ready. Stubs simulate the input/output behavior of the components they represent.

A unit test framework is required

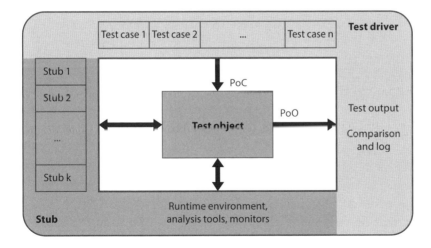

Fig. 5-1
Test framework

The test framework also provides the test object with input data, which usually requires simulation of the component that calls the test object. This task is performed by a test driver. The test driver and the stubs make up the test framework that, together with the test object, forms an executable program.

The test framework is usually developed by testers, either from scratch or by adapting the interfaces in a generic test framework to work with the current project. Once an executable test object is available, dynamic testing can begin.

Systematic development of test cases

The test objective is to verify that the specified requirements are fulfilled by the implemented component, and to identify any failures or deviations from the requirements. The objective is to use as little effort as possible to test as many requirements and identify as many failures as possible. To achieve this objective, you need to develop your test cases systematically. Poorly structured "gut reaction" testing won"t guarantee that all real-world situations faced by the test object will be tested.

Necessary steps

Dynamic testing involves the following steps:

- Define the test conditions and preconditions, and the objectives you wish to achieve
- Specify individual test cases
- Define the test execution schedule (usually made up of a sequence of multiple test cases)

These steps can be executed in an informal, undocumented fashion or, as described here, formally. The degree of formality of the process depends among other factors on the planned system usage (for example, safety-critical), the maturity of the development and test processes, time constraints, and the skills of the team members (see section 5.4).

Conditions, preconditions, and objectives

Starting at the test basis (i.e., the general test conditions), you need to analyze which aspects of the system require dynamic testing (for example, correct execution of a transaction). The objectives for verifying fulfillment of system requirements through test cases are then defined, with particular attention paid to the risks involved if the system should fail. Any necessary preconditions and constraints for dynamic testing have to be identified too—for example, the availability of appropriate data in a database.

Traceability

Traceability between individual requirements and their corresponding test cases enables us to analyze the impact of changes to requirements on the testing process (for example, designing new test cases, discarding redundant test cases, or modifying existing test cases). It also enables you to define a degree of coverage as an exit criterion for dynamic testing.

In practice, the number of test cases required can lie in the hundreds or even thousands, and traceability makes it possible to identify which of these are affected by changes to the requirements (see sections 2.3.8 and 7.1.1).

In order to design a test case, you need the input values for the test object, which can be derived using the techniques described later in this chapter. A test case also needs to fulfill any preconditions, and must include the expected results and postconditions in order to decide whether it has detected a failure. The expected results (output, changes in internal states, and so on) must be defined and documented before the test is executed. If you don't adhere to these rules, an incorrect test result might be interpreted as fault-free, thus allowing a system failure to go unnoticed.

Test case specifications

Defined expected system behavior and results

It usually makes sense to execute multiple tests in sequence (often referred to as a test suite or scenario). Which tests are performed and their sequence is defined in the test execution schedule, which usually lists test cases thematically according to their objectives. Test priorities and technical/logical dependencies between tests and regression test cases should also be included in the plan. Assignment of test cases to individual testers and test scheduling are also part of the test execution schedule (see section 6.3.1).

Test sequences are usually automated using scripts written in a chosen programming language or similar notation. A test script can also include preconditions and a comparison between the expected and actual results. As an example, JUnit is a test framework that facilitates the coding of simple Java test scripts (see [URL. xUnit]).

Execute test cases

There are many techniques available for systematically deriving and designing test cases. These are generally divided into black-box and white-box[1] categories. Experience-based testing techniques can also be used to derive test cases.

Black-box and white-box techniques

Black-box techniques can be applied to functional and non-functional tests. As the name suggests, the point of observation for a black-box test is outside the test object and you need no knowledge of its code or inner

Black-box testing

---

1. Also referred to as glass-box or open-box techniques. Although you can't actually look into a "white box", this has established itself as the term of choice.

structure. Apart from choosing input data or setting appropriate preconditions, you have no influence over the test itself. Black-box techniques concentrate solely on the test object's input and output behavior.

The design of test cases and test conditions, and the choice of test data will depend on the specifications/requirements and on use cases and user stories. Software and system components are often designed using formal and informal models, and both can be used to systematically derive appropriate test cases.

Identifying gaps in the requirements

Test cases can also be used to identify discrepancies or deviations between requirements and their implementation. However, these benefits can only usually be realized if you systematically derive test cases using black-box techniques.

You can stop testing once you have achieved the degree of coverage of the tested items in the test basis (see *exit criteria* in section 6.3). A minimal exit criterion might be defined as performing at least one test case for each requirement.

White-box techniques

Unlike black-box techniques, white-box testing techniques focus on the structures and behavior within the test object. This is why white-box techniques are also known as structural or structure-based testing techniques.

Here too, test cases, test conditions and test data are derived from the test basis. As well as requirements (for example, to define the expected result), the test basis also includes information about the code base, the system architecture, design details, and other aspects of the structure of the component(s) you are testing.

Running a test analyzes the inner state of the test object (i.e., the point of observation, or PoO) lies within the test object). In exceptional cases, you can intervene in the object's operation—for example, if you can't provoke the desired operating error using the component's own interface, you will have to perform a "hard" set of the operation. In other words the point of control (PoC) is within the test object. Test cases can be derived from the structure of the application's code or specifications (see figure 5-2). The objective of white-box techniques is to verify a specified degree of structural coverage (for example, 80% of the statements in the test object need to be covered by test cases). You can then increase the degree of coverage by systematically deriving further tests.

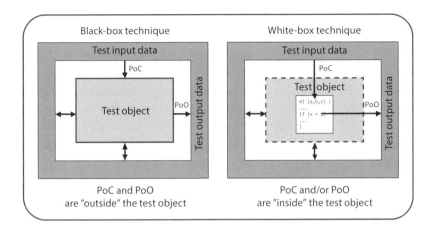

Fig. 5-2
PoC and PoO for black-box and white-box techniques

White-box test techniques can be applied on the lower component and integration test levels. A system test that is based on code makes little sense. Black-box techniques can be used on all test levels. All techniques that define test cases before coding (such as test-first/test-driven development) are by definition black-box techniques.

Systematic derivation of test cases

Most test techniques belong clearly to one or other of these types. Techniques that include elements of both are often referred to as "grey-box" techniques.

Experience-based test techniques leverage the know-how and experience of testers, developers, users, and other stakeholders to design test cases, test conditions, and test data. This approach also uses knowledge of the software's planned usage, its environment, and the probable type and location of faults in the test object. A specific degree of coverage is difficult to ascertain and therefore cannot be effectively used as an exit criterion. Experience-based test techniques are often used in conjunction with white-box and black-box techniques.

Experience-based test case design

The following sections go into more detail on black-box, white-box, and experience-based testing.

5.1 Black-Box Test Techniques

Because a black-box test has no knowledge of the inner workings of the test object, test cases are derived from (or, ideally, are already part of) the specifications. Because they are derived from specifications (i.e., requirements or system behavior), these techniques are also referred to as specification-based, or behavior-based. A complete test sequence that covers all possible permutations of input data values is impossible to perform (see section 2.1.4). You have to select an appropriate set of test cases using the techniques outlined below.

5.1.1 Equivalence Partitioning

Here, the absolute number of possible concrete input values for the input data (a single parameter of the test object) is divided into partitions (also called "classes"). An equivalence partition contains all data values that the tester expects the test object to process in the same way. In other words, it is assumed that testing only one member of an equivalence partition is sufficient.

The input value range is divided into equivalence partitions

Alongside partitions for valid input, you also need to create partitions that contain invalid input values.

Case Study: Equivalence partitioning

This example also uses the discount calculation example we looked at in section 2.3.4. We recall: the software enables the manufacturer to give its dealers various discounts. The corresponding requirement reads thus:

> For prices below $15,000 there is no discount. For prices up to $20,000, a discount of 5% is appropriate. If the price is below $25,000, a 7% discount is possible. If the price is above $25,000, a discount of 8.5% is to be applied.

Four equivalence partitions containing valid input values (vEP) can easily be derived for calculating the discount:

Table 5-1 Valid equivalence partitions and representatives

Parameter	Equivalence partitions	Representative
Price	$vEP_1: 0 \leq x < 15000$ $vEP_2: 15000 \leq x \leq 20000$ $vEP_3: 20000 < x < 25000$ $vEP_4: x \geq 25000$	14500 16500 24750 31800

In section 2.3.4, we used the representatives 14500, 16500, 24750, and 31800 (see table 2-3). Each of these values represents one of the four equivalence partitions. It is assumed that a test run using the values 13400, 17000, 22300, and 28900 would reveal no further failures and therefore doesn't need to be performed. Tests using boundary values (such as 15000) are discussed in section 5.1.2.

You need to create equivalence partitions with invalid input values and test these too.

Equivalence partitions with invalid values

For our example, we use the following invalid equivalence partitions[2] (iEP):

Case Study

Parameter	Equivalence partitions	Representative
Price	iEP$_1$: x < 0 (negative price)	-4000
	iEP$_2$: x > 1000000 (unrealistically high price[3])	1500800

Table 5-2
Invalid equivalence partitions and representatives

To systematically derive test cases, you first have to define a range for each input variable (for example, function or method parameters for a component test, or form fields for a system test). This range constitutes the equivalence partition for all valid input values, and the test object has to process them all according to the specifications. Values outside of the range belong to the equivalence partition of invalid input values, and you also need to check the test object's behavior using these.

The next step involves fine-tuning the equivalence partitions you have established. Any elements of an equivalence partition that, according to the specifications, are processed differently are assigned to a new equivalence sub-partition. You then need to keep splitting the equivalence partitions until each requirement has its own corresponding partition, from which a representative is selected for testing.

Sub-dividing equivalence partitions

As well as a representative, each test case includes the expected result and, if necessary, any preconditions required for the test to run.

This principle of breaking things down can be applied just as well to output values. However, deriving test cases is more difficult because you

Equivalence partitions for output and other values

---
2. In other words, an equivalence partition for invalid values.
3. This is a random value. The manufacturer has to specify which price range is actually considered "unrealistic".

also need to determine the corresponding input value that results in each representative output value. Additional equivalence partitions for invalid output values need to be established too.

You can build equivalence partitions for any coherent data element used by the test object (i.e., not just input and output values). These can be internal values, time-related values (for instance, before and after an event), or interface parameter values that are checked during integration testing.

Make sure that every input/output value belongs to only one equivalence partition. You need to take care when dividing values into equivalence partitions and selecting representatives, as this strongly influences which test cases are performed and therefore the likelihood of successfully identifying failures. Deriving equivalence partitions from specifications and other documents is definitely a non-trivial task.

Equivalence partition boundaries

High-quality test cases test the boundaries of an equivalence partition, where ambiguities and inaccuracies in the requirements are often found. It is difficult to formulate precise mathematical situations using written language, and this makes it tricky to decide which boundary values belong to which equivalence partition. The written requirement "… less than \$15,000 …" can be represented by the precise value 15000 within the equivalence partition (EP: $x \leq 15000$) or outside it (EP: $x < 15000$). An additional test case using $x = 15000$ could reveal a possible misinterpretation and a hitherto undiscovered failure. Section 5.1.2 goes into detail on boundary value analysis.

Case Study: Equivalence partitions with integer input values

The following example illustrates the principle of forming an equivalence partition using integer input values. The integer parameter `extras` for the `calculate_price()` method gives us the following equivalence partitions:

Table 5-3 Equivalence class with integer input values

Parameter	Equivalence partitions
extras	vEP_1: [MIN_INT, … , MAX_INT] [4] iEP_1: NaN

Note that, unlike in the world of mathematics, the value range in a computer is limited by given maxima and minima. Using values outside of this range usually causes failures, as they cannot be processed properly by the system.

---

4. MIN_INT and MAX_INT represent the smallest and largest integers that can be represented by the computer. These can vary from machine to machine depending on the hardware in use.

5.1 Black-Box Test Techniques

The equivalence partition of invalid values is made up of all values that are non-numerical[5] or larger or smaller than the range boundary values. If we assume that the method always reacts the same way to invalid input values (for example, an exception handler that returns the error code NOT_ VALID), it is sufficient to assign all invalid input values to a single equivalence partition called NaN ("Not a Number"). Floating-point numbers are included in this partition, as it is assumed that an input value such as 3.5 will also return an error message. In this case, we don't need to form any equivalence sub-partitions, as all incorrect input produces the same result. However, an experienced tester will include a test case for a floating-point number to check that the system doesn't round non-integer input values up or down and use the result for subsequent calculations. This is a great example of an experience-based test case (see section 5.3).

In most cases positive and negative values need to be handled differently, so it makes sense to further divide the equivalence partition for valid values (vEC$_1$). Zero is an input value that often causes failures.

Parameter	Equivalence partition	Representative
extras	vEP$_1$: [MIN_INT,...,0[[6] vEP$_2$: [0,...,MAX_INT] iEP$_1$: NaN	-123 654 "f"

Table 5-4
Equivalence partitions and representatives for integer input values

For each equivalence partition we chose a random representative and added the boundary values MIN_INT, -1, 0, and MAX_INT (see section 5.1.2). Strictly speaking, there are no boundary values for the equivalence partition for invalid values.

In the end, equivalence partitioning (including boundary values) gives us a total of seven values for the integer parameter extras:

{"f", MIN_INT, -123, -1, 0, 654, MAX_INT}.

We now have to define the expected result or test object reaction for each, so that we can effectively decide whether the test reveals a failure or not.

The integer input values we used in our example make it simple to build equivalence partitions and select representatives. As well as elemental data types, the value range can be made up of composite data structures or object sets. Here too, we have to select appropriate representatives.

Equivalence partitions for atypical input data types

---

5. Which values the computer interprets as invalid depends on the programming language and the compiler you use—for example, when the test driver attempts to call the method. Our example assumes that the compiler doesn't recognize invalid values, and therefore that invalid input values have to be checked during dynamic testing.
6. "[" indicates an open range that doesn't include its own boundary value. Because we are talking about integers, the range [MIN_INT, …, -1] defines the same number of values.

Case Study: Selecting input values from a set

The following example helps to illustrate the principle. If the test object reacts differently to different types of customer (e.g., employee, student, trainee, senior), each different type needs to be covered by its own individual test case. If the test object's expected reaction is the same regardless of the customer type, one test case based on one of the types should be sufficient.

The *EasyFinance* module is sure to deliver different results for each customer type (employee, student, trainee, senior) and thus requires four separate test cases. Precise details of what to test can be derived from the requirements. Each resulting calculation needs to be tested for potential failures.

For the *DreamCar* online configuration module it is probably sufficient to test just one of the four customer types. It is likely that the software doesn't care who is configuring a vehicle, so the representative here can be a student or a senior (although once again, we need to look to the requirements for precise details). However, the tester needs to be aware that if the test is performed using the "employee" input value, this provides no evidence that the chosen configuration works properly for the other customer types.

Our Tip
Building equivalence partitions

Here are some guidelines for building equivalence partitions:

■ Establish the specified limits and conditions for input and output values.

■ Build equivalence partitions for each limit and/or condition:
  - If a contiguous value range is specified, you need to build one "valid" and two "invalid" equivalence partitions.
  - If the specifications state that a specific number of characters has to be entered (for example, a name consisting of at least five and a maximum of seven letters), you need to build a "valid" equivalence partition that includes all possible valid values, and two "invalid" equivalence partitions that cover "less than 5" and "more than 7".
  - If a set of values is specified that requires different handling, you need to build an equivalence partition for each individual value in the set, and one "invalid" equivalence partition.
  - If a limit or condition describes a situation whose fulfillment is obligatory, you need to build two equivalence partitions—one for "valid" and one for "invalid".

■ If you have any doubts about whether values within an equivalence partition are to be handled the same way, you need to further divide the partition to avoid ambiguities.

Test Cases

A test object will usually have more than one input parameter. Equivalence partitioning provides at least two equivalence partitions for each parameter (for valid and invalid values), and thus at least two representative test input values.

Rules for designing test cases

When specifying a test case, you have to assign an input value to each parameter, so you have to decide which of the available representatives can be combined to form an input data set. In order to provoke all necessary test object reactions (according to the decomposition of the equivalence partitions), you need to observe the following rules when combining representatives:

- For the "valid" equivalence partitions, your test cases have to cover all possible combinations of representatives. Each of these combinations forms a "valid test case".

Combining representatives

- A representative from an "invalid" equivalence partition should only be combined with representatives from other, valid equivalence partitions. In other words, every "invalid" equivalence partition requires an additional "negative" test case (see below).

Test invalid values separately

The total number of "valid" test cases is therefore the product of the number of valid equivalence partitions per parameter. This type of multiplicative combination can quickly produce hundreds of valid test cases for just a few parameters. It is rarely possible to deal with so many test cases, so we need to apply rules that help to reduce their number:

Limiting the set of test cases

- Combine representatives from all test cases and sort them according to the frequency of typical usage profiles, then prioritize them according to this sequence. This ensures that you only use the test cases that are most relevant to real-world usage scenarios.

- Preference is given to test cases that cover boundary values or combinations of boundary values (see section 5.1.2).

- Make sure that every representative in an equivalence partition is combined with every representative in the other equivalence partitions used in a test case (i.e., pair-wise combination instead of exhaustive combination—see section 5.1.5).

- Your minimum requirement should be that every representative occurs in at least one test case.

- Don't combine representatives from equivalence partitions with invalid values.

Test invalid values separately

Representatives from invalid equivalence partitions are not combined multiplicatively. An invalid value should only be combined with valid ones. This is because an invalid parameter value triggers an exception regardless of the other parameter values. Combining multiple invalid values in a single test case quickly leads to mutual fault masking, with only one of the possible exceptions being triggered. Furthermore, when an exception does occur, it is not clear which of the invalid values caused it and unnecessary further analysis ensues[7].

Case Study: Testing DreamCar price calculations

Once again, the following example uses the *VSR-II DreamCar* module's calculate_price() method as its test object (see section 3.4.1). The test serves to check whether the method calculates a correct total price for all input values according to the system's specifications. The functional specifications and its interface are known, but its inner workings remain a black box:

```
double calculate_price (
    double baseprice,      // Vehicle base price
    double specialprice,   // Special edition markup double
    double extraprice,     // Price of optional extras
    int extras,            // Number of optional extras
    double discount        // Dealer discount
```

Step 1 Identify the range

We use equivalence partitions to design the input parameter test cases. The first step is to establish the range for each input parameter, which provides us with equivalence partitions containing valid and invalid values (see table 5-5).

Table 5-5 Valid and invalid equivalence partitions for our method's parameters

Parameter	Equivalence partition	
baseprice	vEP_{11}:	[MIN_DOUBLE, ... , MAX_DOUBLE]
	iEP_{11}:	NaN
specialprice	vEP_{21}:	[MIN_DOUBLE, ... , MAX_DOUBLE]
	iEP_{21}:	NaN
extraprice	vEP_{31}:	[MIN_DOUBLE, ... , MAX_DOUBLE]
	iEP_{31}:	NaN
extras	vEP_{41}:	[MIN_INT, ... , MAX_INT]
	iEP_{41}:	NaN
discount	vEP_{51}:	[MIN_DOUBLE, ... , MAX_DOUBLE]
	iEP_{51}:	NaN

---

7. To provoke additional failures, it sometimes makes sense to design additional test cases by combining representatives from invalid equivalence partitions with each other.

The specifications alone provide us with a valid and an invalid equivalence partition for each parameter (see also test data generators in section 7.1.2).

In order to divide these equivalence partitions, we require further information about the functionality of the method, which we glean from the method's specifications (see section 3.4.1). These deliver the following statements that are relevant to our test:

- Parameters 1-3 are (vehicle) prices. Prices are never negative. No price limits are specified.
- The discount given for optional extras (10% for extras ≥ 3, 15% for extras ≥ 5) depends on the extras value. extras represents the selected number of optional extras and is thus not negative[8]. No upper limit to the number of extras is specified.
- The discount parameter is given as a percentage between 0 and 100. Because the discount brackets for extras are specified as percentages, the tester can assume that the dealer discount is given as a percentage too. However, it would be prudent to check this with the customer.

Step 2
Fine-tuning equivalence partitions based on the specifications

These considerations are based on the functional specifications, which reveal a number of gaps. The tester "fills" these gaps by making plausible assumptions based on common sense and testing experience, or on information gained by talking to other testers and developers. In case of doubt, it is always best to talk directly to the customer about what is really required. This analysis enables us to further decompose the equivalence partitions we have built. The more precise the partitioning, the more accurate the resulting test will be. The partition process is complete when all the specified conditions and all the tester's experience-based assumptions are covered.

Gaps in the requirements

---

8. Floating-point numbers belong to the NaN ("Not a Number") equivalence partition (see case study: *equivalence partitions with integer input values* above).

Table 5-6
Partitioning the equivalence partitions for the `calculate_price()` *method's parameters*

Parameter	Equivalence partition		Representatives
baseprice	vEP11:	[0,..., MAX_DOUBLE]	20000.00
	iEP11:	[MIN_DOUBLE,...,0[	-1.00
	iEP12:	NaN	"abc"
specialprice	vEP21:	[0,..., MAX_DOUBLE]	3450.00
	iEP21:	[MIN_DOUBLE,...,0[	-1.00
	iEP22:	NaN	"abc"
extraprice	vEP31:	[0,..., MAX_DOUBLE]	6000.00
	iEP31:	[MIN_DOUBLE,...,0[	-1.00
	iEP32:	NaN	"abc"
extras	vEP41:	[0,...,2]	1
	vEP42:	[3,4]	3
	vEP43:	[5,..., MAX_INT]	20
	iEP41:	[MIN_INT,...,0[	-1
	iEP42:	NaN	"abc"
discount	vEP51:	[0,...,100]	10.00
	iEP51:	[MIN_DOUBLE,...,0[	-1.00
	iEP52:	]100,...,MAX_DOUBLE]	101.00
	iEP53:	NaN	"abc"

This results in a total of 7 equivalence partitions for valid parameters and 11 for invalid parameters.

Step 3
Selecting representatives

To derive test input values, we have to select a representative for each equivalence partition. Equivalence partition theory tells us that this can be any value within the range covered by the equivalence partition. However, in practice, the decomposition of an equivalence partition seldom works perfectly. Partitioning usually stops at a particular level, due either to a lack of detailed information, a lack of time, or simply because it is too much effort. You may find that some equivalence partitions overlap[9]. When selecting representatives, note that a single equivalence partition can contain values that cause varying reactions in the test object, so values that occur more often when the system is in everyday use.

The valid representatives selected in the case study example (see table 5-6 above) are plausible values that we assume will occur regularly when the system is in use.

Step 4
Combining test cases

The next step involves combining representatives to build test cases. The rules listed above give us 1×1×1×3×1 = 3 "valid" test cases (through multiplicative combination) and 2+2+2+2+3 = 11 "invalid" test cases (through separate tests for each

---

9. Ideally, the partitions you build will be free from overlaps (like disjointed mathematical equivalence classes). The informal partitioning process described here doesn't guarantee this.

invariant representative). This gives us a total of 14 test cases for 18 equivalence partitions (see table 5-7).

Table 5-7
Test cases for the calculate_price() method

Test case	Parameter					result
	baseprice	special-price	extra-price	extras	discount	
1	20000.00	3450.00	6000.00	1	10.00	27450.00
2	20000.00	3450.00	6000.00	3	10.00	26850.00
3	20000.00	3450.00	6000.00	20	10.00	26550.00
4	-1.00	3450.00	6000.00	1	10.00	NOT_VALID
5	"abc"	3450.00	6000.00	1	10.00	NOT_VALID
6	20000.00	-1.00	6000.00	1	10.00	NOT_VALID
7	20000.00	"abc"	6000.00	1	10.00	NOT_VALID
8	20000.00	3450.00	-1.00	1	10.00	NOT_VALID
9	20000.00	3450.00	"abc"	1	10.00	NOT_VALID
10	20000.00	3450.00	6000.00	-1	10.00	NOT_VALID
11	20000.00	3450.00	6000.00	"abc"	10.00	NOT_VALID
12	20000.00	3450.00	6000.00	1	-1.00	NOT_VALID
13	20000.00	3450.00	6000.00	1	101.00	NOT_VALID
14	20000.00	3450.00	6000.00	1	"abc"	NOT_VALID

For the valid partitions that are combined with an invalid partition, we used the same representatives for our test cases to ensure that changing only the invalid parameter provokes the expected reaction in the test object.

Because four of the five parameters have only one valid equivalence partition, there are only a few "valid" test cases. In other words, there is no reason to further reduce the number of test cases.

Once the test cases have been set up, the expected result has to be determined. In the case of the "invalid" test cases in the table above, all we have to do is enter the error message generated by the test object. The expected results for the "valid" tests have to be calculated separately, perhaps using a spreadsheet.

■ Table 5-7 lists all the test cases for the calculate_price() method, including ones like #10 that tests a negative number of optional extras. In practice, a negative value like this won't be handed over to the calculate_price() method, but instead checked and intercepted in advance (see *Design by Contract* [Meyer 13]).

Our Tip

Defining Exit Criteria

An exit criterion can be defined by the relationship between the number of tested values and the total number of equivalence partitions:

EP coverage = (Number of tested EPs / total number of EPs) ×100%

In our example, 18 input value equivalence partitions are derived from the specifications, of which 15[10] are used to build test cases, which equates to equivalence partition coverage of 83%:

EP coverage = (15/18) ×100% = 83.33%

Case Study: Equivalence partition coverage

The 14 test cases (see table 5-7) include representatives from all 18 equivalence partitions. In other words, executing all 14 test cases results in 100% equivalence partition coverage. If the final three tests are left out due to time constraints, all three invalid equivalence partitions for the discount parameter remain untested and coverage is reduced to 15/18 = 83.33%.

The degree of coverage defines testing thoroughness

The greater the degree of coverage you aim for, the more thoroughly the test object will be tested. The coverage figure defines the desired depth of testing and is used as a reference criterion to check that the required testing objective have been achieved.

Returning to our example above, if the test plan defines equivalence partition coverage of 80%, this figure is achieved and equivalence partition testing is complete when 15 out of the 18 possible test cases has been executed.

Our example shows how important the decomposition of input data into equivalence partitions can be. If not all the possible equivalence partitions and their representatives are identified, you can achieve a high degree of coverage that is, unfortunately, based on an incorrect number of equivalence partitions. In other words, an apparently good result doesn't accurately mirror the actual thoroughness of the test. The test cases you build using equivalence partitions are only as good as the amount of care you take identifying the appropriate equivalence partitions.

---

10. It doesn't matter which 15 equivalence partitions these are.

Benefits and Limitations

The formation of equivalence partitions ensures that specified conditions and limits aren't overlooked during testing and that no unnecessary tests are performed. Unnecessary test are those that use input data from an equivalence partition that has already been covered and thus produces the same behavior in the test object.

As well as input and output data for methods and functions, equivalence partitions can be used to test internal values and states, time-based values (for example, before and after an event), and interface parameters. They can thus be used for system, integration, and component testing.

However, equivalence partitions can only be used to test individual input or output conditions. Testing dependencies or interactions between these conditions is much more difficult and involves complex decomposition of the equivalence partitions and combination of the resulting values.

However, when used in conjunction with boundary value analysis it can be an extremely effective testing technique.

5.1.2 Boundary Value Analysis

Boundary value analysis provides a useful addition to test cases determined using equivalence partitioning. This is because faults often occur at the boundaries of equivalence partitions where error-prone special cases occur. Tests with boundary values often reveal previously undiscovered defects. Boundary value analysis can only be applied if the data set in an equivalence partition is numerically ordered or can be (at least partially) defined using some kind of order. The boundaries themselves have to be clearly identifiable. The test cases include the precise boundary value and the two neighboring values (inside and outside the partition). Where floating-point numbers are involved, you have to select a suitable degree of computational accuracy that equates to the smallest available increment in each direction.

A useful addition

Each boundary therefore yields three test cases. If the upper boundary of one partition coincides with the lower boundary of the next, the corresponding test cases coincide (see figure 5-3).

Fig. 5-3
Coincidental boundaries in neighboring equivalence partitions

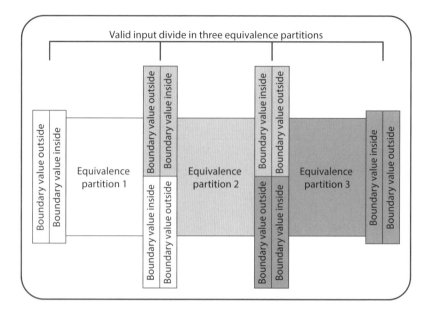

In many cases, there is no "real" boundary value, as the boundary value actually lies within one of the neighboring equivalence partitions. In such cases, it is usually sufficient to test the boundary using two values that lie just outside the equivalence partition (but within the neighboring partition) on either side of the boundary.

Case Study: Boundary values for calculating discounts

Four valid equivalence partitions were determined and corresponding representatives selected for the discount calculation (see table 5-1). Equivalence partitions 3 and 4 are specified with vEP_3: $20000 < x < 25000$ and vEP_4: $x \geq 25000$. To test the boundary between the two partitions (25000), we use the values 24999 and 25000 (using whole dollar values for simplicity). The value 24999 lies within vEP_3 and is the highest possible value in this partition. The value 25000 lies within vEP_4 and is the lowest possible value. The values 24998 and 25001 lie "deeper" within their respective equivalence partitions and therefore provide no useful additional results.

Side Note:
Two tests or three?

When are the two test cases 24999 and 25000 sufficient and when do we need to add a third case (25001) to test the boundary value 25000?

A closer look at the way the query is formulated helps to answer the question. In our example, we assume that the corresponding place in the program includes the query *if (x < 25000)*[11]. Which boundary values can we use to check whether this condition has been correctly implemented? Using the test values 24999, 25000, and 25001 returns the logical values true, false, and false, and the corresponding program paths are executed. Testing the value 25001 appears to provide no additional benefit as 25000 already returns false, and therefore facilitates the switch to the neighboring equivalence partition. Running the flawed query *if (x ≤ 25000)* returns the logical values true, true, and false. Here too, we can do without testing 25001, as 25000 already returns the wrong result and reveals the fault. If we run the completely erroneous query *if (x <> 25000)*, we receive the results true, false and true, so in this case we have to test 25001 as well to reveal the faulty query. The values 24999 and 25000 deliver the expected results (i.e., the same as when the query is correctly formulated).

Note: *if (x > 25000)* returns false, false, true; *if (x ≥ 25000)* returns false, true, true; and *if (x == 25000)* returns false, true, false. These queries return two or three deviations from the required logical results, so again we only need to execute two test cases (using 24999 and 25000) to reveal the fault(s).

Table 5-8 illustrates the situation with a list of all the queries and the corresponding logical values returned by the boundary values.

Table 5-8
Three boundary values used to test the query

Implemented query	24999	25000	25001	Notes
x < 25000 (correct version)	true	false	false	Expected results
x ≤ 25000	true	**true**	false	25000 reveals the fault
x <> 25000	true	false	**true**	25001 reveals the fault
x > 25000	**false**	false	**true**	24999 and 25001 reveal the fault
x ≥ 25000	**false**	**true**	**true**	All three values reveal the fault
x == 25000	**false**	**true**	false	24999 and 25000 reveal the fault

---

11. If the programmer implements the query if ($x \leq 24999$) there is no semantic difference between the two queries, but the boundary values derived from the requirements (24999, 25000, and 25001) still don't completely verify the query if ($x \leq 24999$). The possibly faulty implementation ($x == 24999$) returns the same results (true, false, false) for all three boundary values. A code review would here reveal the difference between the requirement (i.e., the selected boundary values) and the implementation.

You always have to decide when two values are sufficient and when you need three to test a boundary value. The defective code *if (x <> 25000)* can be revealed by a code review, as the query tests non-equality instead of a boundary value *(if (x < 25000))*. *However*, this fault is still easy to overlook. Only a boundary value test with three values at every boundary is certain to reveal every defective implementation of the query.

Case Study:
Integer input

The integer input example described in section 5.1.1 yields five additional test cases, giving us a total of 12 test cases with the following input values:

```
{"f",
MIN_INT-1, MIN_INT, MIN_INT+1,
-123,
-1, 0, 1,
654,
MAX_INT-1, MAX_INT, MAX_INT+1}
```

The test case with the value -1 tests the maximum value in the equivalence partition EP_1: [MIN_INT, ... , 0[and also the minimum under-run of the lower boundary (0) in the equivalence partition EP_2: [0, ... , MAX_INT]. From the point of view of the latter equivalence partition, the value -1 lies outside the partition. Note that for technical reasons, values above the upper boundary or below the lower boundary can sometimes not be used as concrete input values.

Our example only lists the input variables. However, each test case must also include the expected behavior of the test object (i.e., its output) according to the test oracle, and the corresponding pre- and postconditions.

Is the testing effort justified?

Here too, you need to decide whether the effort involved in testing every boundary and its neighboring values is justified. You could leave out the test cases with the representatives of equivalence partitions that don't test boundaries. In our example, these are the test cases with the input values -123 and 654. Because the maximum and minimum values in the equivalence partition already have their own test cases, it is assumed that test cases with input values taken from the middle of the partition won't provide any additional insights. In our example, these are the values MIN_INT+1,1 and MAX_INT-1.

No boundary values
in the set

If we use the input value "potential buyer" in the example above, we cannot determine boundaries for the input value range. Mathematically speaking, the input value has to be selected from one of the four elements of the set (employee, student, trainee, senior). There are no identifiable boundaries and it makes no sense to order the member of the set according to their age. Students can be of any age, so it is more likely that a person's job status is more conclusive.

Boundary value analysis can of course be applied to equivalence partitions populated with output values.

Test Cases

The same way that test cases can be derived from equivalence partitions, the valid boundaries within an equivalence partition can be combined to build test cases. Invalid boundaries have to be tested separately and cannot be combined with other invalid boundaries.

In the example described above, values from the middle of an equivalence partition do not need to be tested if both boundary values within the partition have already been earmarked for use in test cases.

If we apply boundary value analysis to the valid equivalence partitions for testing the calculate_price() method, we end up with the boundary-based test data shown in table 5-9:

Case Study:
Boundary value tests for
calculate_price()

Parameter	Lower boundary [Equivalence partition] Upper boundary
baseprice	0-δ^{12}, [0, 0+δ, ..., MAX_DOUBLE-δ, MAX_DOUBLE], MAX_DOUBLE+δ
specialprice	The same values as baseprice
extraprice	The same values as baseprice
extras	-1, [0, 1, 2], 3 2, [3, 4], 5 4, [5, 6, ..., MAX_INT-1, MAX_INT], MAX_INT+1
discount	0-δ, [0, 0+δ, ..., 100-δ, 100], 100+δ

Table 5-9
Boundary values for the
calculate_price()
method's parameters

Considering only the boundary values that lie within the equivalence partition, we have 4+4+4+9+4 = 25 boundary-based representatives. Two of these (extras: 1, 3) are already covered (Test cases 1 and 2 in table 5-7). This leaves us with the following 23 boundary values for input in further test cases:

```
baseprice:     0.00, 0.01¹³, MAX_DOUBLE-0.01, MAX_DOUBLE
specialprice:  0.00, 0.01, MAX_DOUBLE-0.01, MAX_DOUBLE
extraprice:    0.00, 0.01, MAX_DOUBLE-0.01, MAX_DOUBLE
extras:        0, 2, 4, 5, 6, MAX_INT-1, MAX_INT
discount:      0.00, 0.01, 99.99, 100.00
```

---

12. The required degree of accuracy δ depends on the nature of the task and the way the computer displays numbers.
13. 0.01 is the assumed degree of accuracy tolerance.

Because these are all valid boundary values, they can all be combined to form test cases (see table 5-10).

Table 5-10
Additional test cases for the calculate_price() method

Parameter						
Test Case	baseprice	specialprice	extraprice	extras	discount	result
15	0.00	0.00	0.00	0	0.00	0.00
16	0.01	0.01	0.01	2	0.01	0.03
17	MAX_DOUBLE-0.01	MAX_DOUBLE-0.01	MAX_DOUBLE-0.01	4	99.99	>MAX_DOUBLE
18	MAX_DOUBLE-0.01	3450.00	6000.00	1	10.00	>MAX_DOUBLE
19	20000.00	MAX_DOUBLE-0.01	6000.00	1	10.00	>MAX_DOUBLE
20	20000.00	3450.00	MAX_DOUBLE-0.01	1	10.00	>MAX_DOUBLE
...						

The expected results of a boundary value test are not always clearly defined in the test object's specifications. An experienced tester therefore has to define appropriate target behavior using the available test cases:

- Test case 15 checks all the valid lower boundaries for the calculate_price() method's parameters. The test case appears to have no direct reference to reality[14]. This is due to the imprecise specification of the method that doesn't specify lower and upper boundaries for the parameter values (see below)[15].

- Test case 16 is analogous to test case 15 but tests computational accuracy[16].

- In test case 17 the expected result of a 99.99% discount is highly speculative. The specifications of the calculate_price() method state that prices are added, so it makes sense to test the maxima individually (see test cases 18-20). The values for the other parameters were taken from test case 1 in table 5-7. Further useful test cases result if we set the other parameter values to 0.00 to test whether the maxima are correctly processed without further addition (no overflow?).

- Similarly to test cases 17-20, test cases for the value MAX_DOUBLE need to be executed too.

- Additional test cases need to be set up for the boundary values that haven't yet been tested (extras = 5, 6, MAX_INT-1, MAX_INT and discount = 100.00).

The boundary values outside the valid equivalence partitions are not included here.

---

14. Note: Testing baseprice using 0.00 makes sense but only at a system testing level, as the calculate_ price() method is not necessarily responsible for handling this input value.
15. The dependency between the number of optional extras and their price (if no extras are selected, no price should be stated) cannot be tested using equivalence partitions or boundary value analysis. In this case, we need to use decision tables (see section 5.1.4).
16. Values such as 0.005 are required to precisely test the rounding accuracy.

This example shows clearly the effects that imprecise specifications can have on testing[17]. If a tester gets information about the parameter range directly from the customer before setting up any test cases, the overall testing effort will be reduced.

It is never too early to think about testing. Start with the specifications!

The following example illustrates the principle.

The customer provides the following information:

- The base price lies between 10000 and 150000
- The special edition premium is between 800 and 3500
- There are up to 25 optional extras with prices between 50 und 750
- The maximum dealer discount is 25%

Forming equivalence partitions for these numbers results in the following valid parameter values for boundary testing:

```
baseprice:     10000.00, 10000.01, 149999.99, 150000.00
specialprice:  800.00, 800.01, 3499.99, 3500.00
extraprice:    50.00, 50.01, 18749.99, 18750.00[18]
extras:        0, 1, 2, 3, 4, 5, 6, 24, 25
discount:      0.00, 0.01, 24.99, 25.00
```

All of these values can be freely combined to form test cases. A single test case is required for each value that lies outside of an equivalence partition:

```
baseprice:     9999.99, 150000.01
specialprice:  799.99, 3500.01
extraprice:    49.99, 18750.01
extras:        -1, 26
discount:      -0.01, 25.01
```

It is obvious that precise specifications provide clear expected results and require fewer test cases.

Precise specifications reduce the number of test cases

Adding a test case for the "machine boundary values" (MAX_DOUBLE, MIN_DOUBLE and so on) is recommended. This ensures that any potential failures caused by hardware limitations are successfully identified.

---

17. And of course on coding too.
18. The maximum price for the extras cannot be precisely determined, as the dependency between the number of extras and the total price cannot be included. The assumed maximum is 25×750 = 18750. An additional boundary value of 0 for the extras was not included, as the dependency between the number of extras and the total price cannot be tested using equivalence partitions or boundary value analysis.

Here too, you have to decide whether a boundary needs to be tested with two or three input values. The following tips assume that code reviews have already detected any faulty queries and that two input values are therefore sufficient.

Our Tip
on setting up test cases using boundary value analysis

- For every input value range, you need to include the boundary values and the neighboring values outside the range. For example, for the range [-1.0; +1.0], the test data are -1.0 and +1.0, -1.001 and +1.001[19].

- If a file contains a number of records specified between 1 and 100, boundary value analysis results in the following options: the file contains no records, the file contains one record, the file contains 100 records, the file contains 101 records.

- If test cases are based on an output range, you could proceed as follows: If the expected output is a whole number between 500 and 1000, you need to test the results 500 and 1000, as well as 499 and 1001. Determining the corresponding input values might involve significant effort and you may find that it is impossible to provoke defective output. Nevertheless, considering how to do this will help you to identify additional faults.

- If the number of output values is critical, you need to proceed the same way as for input values—i.e., for 1-4 output values, you need to set up test cases that check for 1, 4, 0, and 5 output values.

- For ordered data sets, the first and last elements in the set are the most important when it comes to testing.

- If the input or output values are complex data structures, you can include a zero matrix or an empty list as a test boundary value.

- For numerical calculations, your test cases need to include closely neighboring values and ones that lie far apart.

- Boundary value analysis only makes sense for invalid equivalence partitions if you expect the boundary values to produce differing behaviors in the test object.

- Always perform additional test with very large data structures, lists, tables or similar objects to check the test object's behavior when buffer, file, and memory limits are exceeded. When testing lists and tables, the first and last elements (and empty lists) are the most useful cases to watch out for, as these are often subject to coding errors (so-called *off-by-one* issues).

---

19. The required degree of accuracy depends on the specified problem.

Defining Exit Criteria

As with equivalence partitions, a measurable degree of boundary value (BV) coverage can be defined as an exit criterion:

BV coverage = (number of tested BV / total number of BV)×100%

Note that this calculation includes the boundary values and their direct neighbors on either side of the boundary, but that only unique values are used. Because they are covered by only one test case, coincident values from neighboring equivalence partitions count as one value.

Benefits and Limitations

Boundary value analysis is most useful when used in combination with equivalence partitions, as errors at the boundaries of equivalence partitions are more common than ones based on values from the middle of a class. Both techniques offer a good degree of freedom in the selection of concrete test data.

In combination with equivalence partitions

Boundary value analysis may appear simple, but determining the relevant boundaries is a complex task. Selecting appropriate boundary test data requires a high degree of creativity, especially when analysis isn't based on purely numerical data ranges.

5.1.3 State Transition Testing

Alongside input data, preceding steps in the program flow also influence output and general system behavior. In other words, you also need to pay attention to the history of the system you test. State models and state diagrams are used to help design state transition tests.

The present system state depends on the past

Based on its initial state, a system or test object can adopt various new states. Changes in state or transitions between states can be initiated by events such as function calls or system input. If an event leads to two or more potential transitions from a single state, you have to differentiate clearly between them using "guard conditions" that clearly define which transition (and therefore which successor state) follows the event.

Guard conditions

Changes in state may trigger actions, and a completed event is said to be in its "end state". State transitions are modeled using state transition diagrams and/or state transition tables.

Side Note:
About state machines

This side note goes into some detail on state machines and assumes that you are already familiar with the basic concept.

A state machine changes its state according to its current state and the next input, which can also be an event. The machine has a finite number of states. The machine can perform an action (such as producing output) in every state or during every transition from one state to the next. It is assumed that:

- Actions are related to transitions, not states
- A state machine is deterministic—i.e., from a given initial state and following a given sequence of inputs (events), the machine will be in an unambiguously defined successor state
- The state machine is finite—i.e., there is a transition for every input in every state. This is not always the case in state transition models. However, this situation can be remedied by extending the machine so that for previously unknown inputs a transition either
  - leads to the same state without preforming an action, or
  - causes a fault

Case Study:
Finite state machine for a vehicle software update

Here is an example of a (highly simplified) state transition test:

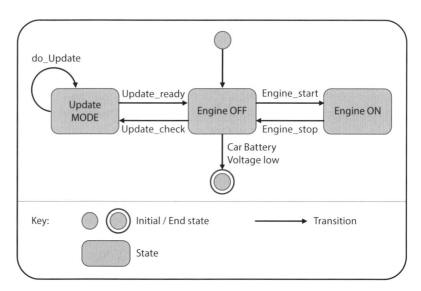

Fig. 5-4
State machine for a vehicle software update

The vehicle software can be updated "over the air" (OTA), but only when the vehicle is not being driven (the "Engine OFF" state in the diagram).

The situation is modeled in a state transition diagram (see figure 5-4). There are three states (Update MODE, Engine OFF, Engine ON), and transitions between the states are indicated by the arrows. The machine has initial and end states.

Under the precondition that the battery supplies sufficient current, the machine transitions from its (pseudo-) initial state to the "Engine OFF" state. From here, there are three possible successor states. If the engine is started, the vehicle is in the "Engine ON" state. This can only change if the "Engine_stop" event takes place and the vehicle switches back to the "Engine OFF" state. If the driver checks whether an update is available by activating the button in the vehicle's display (the "Update_check" event), the vehicle transitions to the "Update MODE" state. The vehicle remains in this state until the update is completed (the "Update_ready" event) and the vehicle transitions back to the "Engine OFF" state. If the battery is then depleted, the machine switches to its (pseudo-) end state.

The specifications have to define which event (Engine_start, Engine_stop, Update_check, do_Update, Update_ready) can occur in which states and is allowed to trigger an event.

The state transition table (see table 5-11) for this finite state machine (without its initial and end states) looks like this:

Current state event	Engine OFF	Engine ON	Update MODE
Engine_start	Engine ON	–	–
Engine_stop	–	Engine OFF	–
Update_check	Update MODE	–	–
do_Update	–	–	Update MODE
Update_ready	–	–	Engine OFF

Table 5-11
State transition table for a vehicle software update

The state machine is equivalent to the table, which shows the successor state for every state, depending on the input/events that occur. While the table illustrates all the possible permutations, the diagram doesn't show transitions that the specifications don't allow (indicated by a "-" in the table). These non-specified (i.e., invalid) transitions are nonetheless relevant for testing, as they enable us to identify potential system failures.

Here is a sample test case with its pre- and postconditions:

    Precondition: The engine is off ("Engine OFF" state)
    Event: Engine_start
    Expected reaction: State transition to "Engine ON" state
    Postcondition: State is "Engine ON"

A Sample concrete test case

A state transition test object can be a complete system with various states or, in an object-oriented system, a class with various states. A state transition test is required every time the historical system flow leads to differing behaviors.

More sample test cases

There are various possible levels of testing thoroughness. The minimum requirement should be that the test object reaches all its possible states. In our example, these are Engine OFF, Engine ON, and Update MODE. The following test case evokes all three ([State], Event[20]):

Test case 1
[Engine OFF], Engine_start [Engine ON], Engine_Stop [Engine OFF], update_check [Update MODE]

However, this test case doesn't cover all the possible events. If the minimum requirement also states that all events have to be triggered, the test case above needs to be extended to include "do_Update" (no transition), "Update_ready" (transition to "Engine OFF"), and "Car battery voltage low" (transition to the end state).

Test criteria

A useful test criterion to aim for is triggering every possible event for each state at least once. This way, you can be sure to verify that the state model matches the specified system behavior.

Test invalid transitions too

In critical systems, the transitions included in the table but not specified for the state diagram need to be tested too. For example, you could test whether the "Update_check" event can be triggered in the "Engine ON" state, thus triggering a non-specified change of state.

Side Note

Simply testing states and/or transitions separately doesn't really do justice to the complexity of a finite state machine. A finite state machine describes cycles of virtually any desired depth. In our example, constant switching between the "Engine OFF" and "Engine ON" states is possible and mirrors daily, real-world usage. But how "deep" should testing really go? How can we handle cycles to "pry them open"?

The issue of endless cycles

The following sections introduce test case creation using a transition tree, and testing transition sequences of differing lengths (N-switch coverage).

Transition trees

Test cases created using a transition tree concentrate on testing separate sequences of transitions that always begin with the initial state.

A transition tree illustrates all the state transition diagram's possible event and input sequences while simultaneously eliminating repeat cycles. If the current sequence leads us to a previously reached state (a simple cycle), the tree is not expanded any further.

→

---

20. These test cases are simplified to help you retain an overview of what's going on.

The state machine diagram is traversed and the process generates a transition tree as follows:

1. The initial state represents the tree root
2. Each possible transition is represented by a new branch, which in turn ends in a node that represents the successor state. Each pair of nodes is connected by the event that triggers the transition. This "branch creation" step is repeated until:
   - previously visited state is reached (thus preventing repeat cycles), or
   - state offers no outgoing transitions (i.e., the path/branch has reached its end state)

The transition tree shown in figure 5-5 represents all the possible paths[21] that lead from the initial state to an end state (or a state that is already part of the path you are on). Each path from the root to a leaf represents a test case (i.e., a unique sequence of inputs and/or events). Each such sequence contains no repeat cycles.

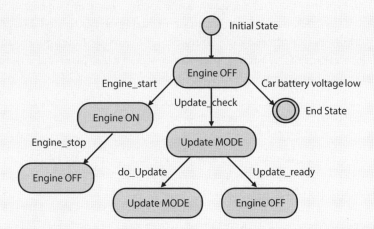

Fig. 5-5

The transition tree for our example

This transition tree describes four test cases that all begin with the same initial state. You can create an extended transition tree by including events that the current state is not designed to react to. If they can be triggered at all, testing such invalid transitions should lead to the event being rejected or ignored, or to an error message.

Triggering every event and visiting each state at least once is a relatively simple exit criterion for a state transition test. However, depending on the requirements, this base criterion won't always be sufficient. A comprehensive test suite includes paths of varying lengths. For example, if individual transitions (or sequences of transitions) are to be tested from the initial state *Za* to the end state *Zz*, a sequence of events has to be executed that leads to the initial state (*Za*) of the transition sequence you wish to test. You then need to execute the inputs and/or events that trigger the actual sequence of transitions (from *Za* to *Zz*) that is due for testing.

---

21. In this case, a "path" is a sequence of states and transitions.

n-switch coverage

> The length of the transition sequences can vary according to the thoroughness of the test. The process of testing sequences of varying length is called *n-switch coverage*, where *N* is the number of states between the initial and the end state of the sequence being tested. The term *0-switch coverage* is used if only one transition is required to go from the initial state to the end state. Correspondingly, if there are two transitions (i.e., one additional state), the aim is 1-switch coverage, while a transition with two successor states requires 2-switch coverage, and so on. Note that successive states can be the same if the previous input doesn't trigger a change of state. This technique enables you to test for cycles in state machines and limit the number of potential cycles.

Transition state testing is a useful technique for system testing graphic user interfaces (GUIs). A GUI usually consists of a whole raft of masks and dialogs that the user navigates using menu commands and keyboard input, or by clicking buttons. If a mask or dialog box is treated as a state and inputs as transitions, you can model all the navigation options using a finite state machine. You can then derive suitable test cases and coverage criteria using the techniques described above.

Case Study: Testing the DreamCar GUI

The previous *VSR* version of the window-based *DreamCar* GUI was tested as follows:

The test begins in the main mask of the *DreamCar* module (State 1). The action[22] *Settings>Vehicles* triggers the switch to the *Edit Vehicle* dialog (State 2). The *Cancel* action closes the dialog and transitions the system back to State 1. "Local" tests (in this case to test the functionality of the mask) can take place within a state. This technique can be used to navigate through sequences of menus/dialogs that can be as complex as you like. The transition state model of the GUI helps to ensure that all the available dialogs are included in the test.

---

22. This two-level menu selection is counted here as a single action.

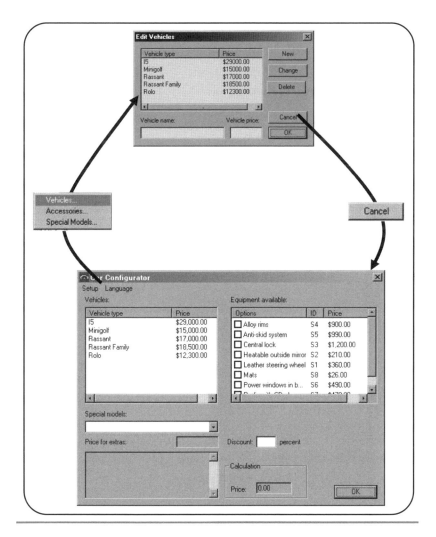

Fig. 5-6
The transition tree for our example

Test Cases

The complete definition of a transition state test case must include the following information:

- The initial state of the test object (precondition)
- Input data for the test object
- The expected result/behavior
- The expected state of the test object following the test case (postcondition)

Additionally, the following aspects of each transition also have to be defined:

- The state prior to the transition
- The event that triggers the transition
- The expected reaction to the transition
- The expected successor state

It is not always easy to determine the state(s) of a test object. The current state is often the result of changes in the values of multiple variables, making it tricky to verify and evaluate individual test cases.

Our Tip
- Assess the state transition diagram for its testability at the specification stage. If there are too many states and/or transitions, point out the additional testing effort that this would entail and request simplification of the specifications where possible.
- Insist at the specification stage that the various states are as simple as possible to determine, with as few variables and combinations of variables as possible.
- State variables should be simple to query. Additional functions that enable you to read, set, and reset states are a boon to testing.

Defining Exit Criteria

Coverage and exit criteria can also be defined for state transition tests:

- Each state has to be reached at least once
- Every transition is executed at least once
- All transitions that contravene the specifications have to be checked

As with the other testing techniques we have looked at, percentage exit criteria can be defined using the ratio of the available requirements to the requirements that are actually covered by test cases.

Further checks   Highly critical applications can be subjected to further-reaching state transition tests, such as:

- All possible combinations of transitions
- All transitions in every possible sequence using all the available states (if necessary, multiple consecutive times)

However, this depth of testing with its huge number of test cases makes it difficult to achieve an appropriate degree of coverage. It usually makes sense to restrict the number of combinations and/or transition sequences (see the side note on n-switch coverage above).

Benefits and Limitations

State transition tests are useful for any situation in which states influence the behavior of a system or where functionality is affected by the state of the test object. The other testing techniques we have discussed can't do this because they don't account for the effects of the system flow in time or the current state that past activities produce.

■ Objects that are part of an object-oriented system can take on varying states, so the method used to manipulate an object therefore has to react to these differing states. State transition testing is therefore a widely used technique for testing object-oriented systems.

Our Tip
Especially suitable for testing object-oriented systems

5.1.4 Decision Table Testing

The techniques discussed so far view multiple input parameters separately from one another, and test cases are designed on the basis of individual values. Dependencies between the various input parameters and their effects on the test object's output are not an explicit part of the test case specifications.

[Myers 12] describes *Cause-Effect Graphing*—a technique that takes this kind of dependency into account when designing test cases. Part 4 of the ISO 29119 standard [ISO 29119] also describes this approach to testing. The logical relationships between cause and effect and the impact they have on a component or system are illustrated using a cause-effect graph. The precondition for this kind of analysis is that causes and their effects can be derived from the specifications. Each cause is described as an input condition comprised of input values or a combination of input values. Inputs are combined using logical operators (such as AND, OR, and NOT). The input condition—and therefore the cause—either holds true or it doesn't. In other words, it can be true or false. The corresponding effects are handled analogously and recorded graphically (see figure 5-7).

→

Side Note:
Cause-Effect Graphing

Withdrawing cash from an ATM serves to illustrate the principle. In order to do this, the following conditions have to be met[23]:

- The customer's card is valid
- The correct PIN is entered
- A maximum of three PIN input attempts is allowed
- Money is available (in the account and in the ATM)

The possible (re)actions of the ATM are as follows:

- The card is rejected
- The user is asked to re-enter the PIN
- The card is confiscated
- The user is asked to enter a different sum of money
- Money is paid out

Figure 5-7 shows this example in the form of a cause-effect graph.

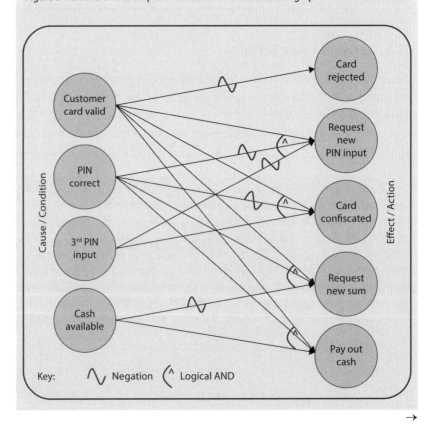

Fig. 5-7
Cause-effect graph for an ATM

---

23. Note that this is a symbolic rather than an exhaustive description of the process.

The graph makes it clear which combinations of conditions need to be met to cause a specific effect/action.

To derive test cases, the diagram has to be converted into a decision table (see table 5-15 below). The steps involved in the conversion are as follows:

1. Select an effect
2. Check the graph for combinations of causes that provoke the desired effect (or not)
3. Create a decision table with one column for all the cause combinations you have found and one for the states caused by the other effects
4. Check for duplicate entries in the decision table and remove if necessary

Decision tables are often created without the help of cause-effect graph. They are often used during project specification (i.e., before testing) to help clarify certain situations.

Decision table testing

Tests based on decision tables serve to identify "interesting" combinations of input values that are likely to cause system failures.

Decision tables are ideal for recording complex business rules (i.e., conditions) that the system must implement correctly. Different combinations of conditions usually cause varying results, and these can be systematically tested using a decision table.

In its simplest form, every combination of conditions yields a test case. However, conditions can influence or preclude each other, making some combinations redundant.

The upper portion of a decision table contains the causes and the lower portion the effects. The columns on the right define the individual test situations—i.e., the combinations of conditions and their expected effects.

Decision table structure

A decision table is divided into four sections:

- **Upper left**
  This is where the causes (conditions) are recorded in such a way that they can be answered with "yes" or "no"
- **Upper right**
  This is where all possible combinations of causes are recorded (n causes result in 2^n combinations)
- **Lower left**
  Contains all the effects (actions)
- **Lower right**
  Contains records of which effect (action) should be provoked by which combination of causes

Creating a decision table

A decision table is created as follows:

1. All conditions that affect the issue at hand have to be determined. Each condition has to be formulated so that it can be answered with "yes" or "no". Each condition is recorded in a single row at the upper left of the table.
2. All relevant actions have to be determined and are recorded in individual rows at lower left.
3. All possible combinations of conditions are recorded at upper right with no regard for potential dependencies.
4. All combinations of conditions (i.e., all columns on the right-hand side) have to be analyzed in order to decide which action should result from each. A cross (X) indicates an action that is to be executed. Multiple crosses are possible if multiple actions are required.

Every condition should correspond to at least one "yes" and at least one "no" in the table.

Optimize and consolidate

The decision table is complete when every possible combination of conditions is included. The table thus has as many columns as combinations. Columns that contain impossible combinations or possible but non-executable combinations can be deleted. The table can be further consolidated if different combinations of conditions lead to the same result. Once you have weeded out the unwanted cases, every column represents a test case, and no combinations and/or actions (i.e., test cases) are duplicated. Decision tables can also be checked for completeness, freedom from redundancy, and consistency.

Case Study: Decision table example

This example illustrates the basic principle.

A special offer for a limited period is aimed at increasing vehicle sales. All standard models receive an 8% discount and all special editions (for which no optional extras are available) a 10% discount. If more than three extras are selected for a standard model, these receive an additional 15% discount. All other models receive no additional base discount and no extra discount for additional extras.

The upper part of the corresponding decision table (with all the possible combinations) looks like this (see table 5-12):

Table 5-12
The upper part of the decision table showing all combinations of conditions

Decision table		TC1	TC2	TC3	TC4	TC5	TC6	TC7	TC8
Conditions	Special edition?	Yes	Yes	Yes	Yes	No	No	No	No
	Standard model?	Yes	Yes	No	No	Yes	Yes	No	No
	Extras > 3	Yes	No	Yes	No	Yes	No	Yes	No

Because some of the conditions preclude each other, the table can be correspondingly edited ("–" is interpreted as "don't care", see table 5-13):

Decision table		TC1	TC2	TC3	TC4	TC5	TC6	TC7	TC8
Conditions	Special edition?	Yes	Yes	Yes	Yes	No	No	No	No
	Standard model?	–	–	–	–	Yes	Yes	No	No
	Extras > 3	–	–	–	–	Yes	No	–	–
Actions	10% discount	X	X	X	X				
	8% discount					X	X		
	15% discount for extras					X			
	No discount							X	X

Table 5-13
Decision table including "don't care" cases

The table can now be consolidated. Test cases 1–4 are identical and can be treated as one, as can test cases 7 and 8. The result is the following decision stable with a total of four test cases, each of which leads to a different action or sequence of actions (see table 5-14).

Decision table		TC1	TC5	TC6	TC7
Conditions	Special edition?	Yes	No	No	No
	Standard model?	–	Yes	Yes	No
	Extras > 3	–	Yes	No	–
Actions	10% discount	X			
	8% discount			X	X
	15% discount for extras		X		
	No discount				X

Table 5-14
Consolidated decision table

This simple example shows that relatively few conditions and/or dependencies can quickly produce large, complex decision tables.

Side Note:
Cause-Effect Graphing
continued

To round out the ATM example cited above, here is the consolidated decision table created using cause-effect graphing:

Decision table		TC1	TC2	TC3	TC4	TC5
Conditions	Customer Card valid?	No	Yes	Yes	Yes	Yes
	PIN correct?	–	No	No	Yes	Yes
	3rd PIN input?	–	No	Yes	–	–
	Cash available?	–	–	–	No	Yes
Actions	Card rejected	X				
	Request new PIN input		X			
	Card confiscated			X		
	Request new sum				X	
	Pay out cash					X

Table 5-15
Consolidated ATM decision table

Test Cases

This technique enables you to read the input conditions and dependencies, and the corresponding expected actions for each test case directly from the columns of the decision table. The table defines concrete test cases that, if necessary, can be augmented with preconditions, postconditions, and constraints before testing begins.

Defining Exit Criteria

Simple exit criteria

As with all the other techniques we have looked at, it is relatively simple to define exit criteria for decision table-based tests. The minimum requirement should be that every column in the table is covered by at least one test case. This ensures that every meaningful combination of conditions and reactions is tested.

Benefits and Limitations

This systematic and highly formal technique often reveals combinations of conditions that other test case creation techniques overlook. This technique helps to reveal gaps in the requirements, but you have to be careful not to unintentionally reject relevant test cases when consolidating the table.

As we have already seen, a decision table can quickly become very large and unwieldy with increasing numbers of conditions and corresponding actions. This makes the process difficult to handle without the support of dedicated tools.

Decision table tests can be applied on all test levels in any situation in which the system or component's behavior depends on combinations of conditions.

5.1.5 Pair-Wise Testing[24]

The testing techniques we have looked at so far are all based on system specifications and their associated considerations. If there are no direct dependencies between individual inputs (i.e., all inputs can be feely combined), mathematics can help us select appropriate combinations and design the corresponding test cases.

Side Note:
n-wise combinatorial testing

Here is a simple example to get you started. If we have three Boolean input parameters that can be freely combined, we have eight possible combinations, as shown in table 5-16.

Combination	Parameter A	Parameter B	Parameter C
1	True	True	True
2	True	True	False
3	True	False	True
4	True	False	False
5	False	True	True
6	False	True	False
7	False	False	True
8	False	False	False

Table 5-16
All combinations of three Boolean parameters

How do things change if we only look at the following four combinations?

Combination	Parameter A	Parameter B	Parameter C
1	True	True	True
4	True	False	False
6	False	True	False
7	False	False	True

Table 5-17
Selection of four combinations

---

24. Part 4 of the ISO 29119 standard [ISO 29119] also describes this technique (Combinatorial Test Design Techniques, Pair-wise Testing). This section is largely quoted from the German-language OpenBook *Lean Testing for C++-Programmers*.

These four combinations give us the following situation: If we look at only two parameters, we see that for the parameter pairings A/B, B/C, and A/C, all four combinations of results are covered (true/true, true/false, false/true, and false/false). In other words, all four combinations result whichever combination of two columns we choose.

The core concept of combinatorial pair-wise testing

This illustrates the core concept of pair-wise testing. Instead of testing all possible combinations of all parameters, you only need to test all combinations of two, three or more parameters, although these combinations do then have to be tested completely.

Case Study: A sports club offers various types of sports

To clarify the process, here is a more complex example. A sports club offers its members table tennis, gymnastics, volleyball, basketball, handball, and fitness training. For organizational reasons, each sport is assigned to a department, with volleyball, basketball, and handball combined under "ball sports". This also reflects the differing costs of the various sports. The result is four basic types of sports (table tennis, gymnastics, ball sports, fitness) that club members can choose from. These options give members a total of 16 different combinations of sports. However, we can cover all the possible pair-wise combinations (table tennis/gymnastics, table tennis/ball sports, table tennis/fitness, gymnastics/ball sports, gymnastics/fitness, and ball sports/fitness), each with its own four combinations, using just six test cases. These are shown in table 5-18.

Table 5-18 Types of sports (all four combinations for gymnastics and ball sports are highlighted)

Test case	Table tennis	Gymnastics	Ball sports	Fitness
1	Yes	No	No	No
2	No	Yes	Yes	Yes
3	Yes	Yes	No	Yes
4	No	No	Yes	No
5	Yes	Yes	Yes	No
6	No	No	No	Yes

This example shows that some combinations occur more often than others. For example, for table tennis/gymnastics, the Yes/Yes and No/No pairings both occur twice, while all other combinations occur only once.

It is also clear that more "interesting" combinations, such as no sports (No/No/No/No) or all sports (Yes/Yes/Yes/Yes), don't occur at all.

Test case	Table tennis	Gymnastics	Ball sports	Fitness
1	No	No	No	No
2	No	Yes	Yes	Yes
3	Yes	No	Yes	Yes
4	Yes	Yes	No	Yes
5	Yes	Yes	Yes	No

Table 5-19
A selection of five combinations

There is more than one way to select test cases that cover all four pairs of parameters. Table 5-19 fulfills this condition using just five combinations.

Orthogonal and Covering Arrays

The example shown in table 5-16, with its three Boolean parameters, is very simple. In practice, you will have to combine multiple parameters with more than two possible values, and the selections you make have to follow a strictly defined process. This process is based on a so-called orthogonal array, which is a two-dimensional array in which every combination of two columns contains all possible combinations of the values in both columns.

Orthogonal arrays guarantee even distribution of combinations and are often used in the process of statistical experiment design, whereby the factors being investigated must not be mixed with each other and should be equally distributed. In an orthogonal array, every combination occurs the same number of times, whichever pair of columns you select.

Tables 5-16 and 5-17 are orthogonal arrays. Each true/false combination occurs exactly twice in every combination of two columns in table 5-16 (for example, see parameters B and C, rows 1/5, 2/6, 3/7, and 4/8). In table 5-17, every combination occurs exactly once for any combination of two columns.

Covering Arrays are similar to orthogonal arrays but differ in that every combination occurs at least once. They are therefore not able to fulfill the "even distribution of values" requirement. This is not a major drawback when testing and offers the benefit of smaller arrays compared with the orthogonal technique. Covering arrays are sometimes referred to as "minimal" or "optimum" arrays if coverage of possible combinations is reduced to its absolute minimum. Our sports club example requires an orthogonal array with eight rows (from a possible 16) if any two columns are to contain all possible true/false combinations. In this case, each would appear twice.

If we do without the limitation of each combination occurring the same number of times, we end up with the covering array shown in table 5-18 (with six combinations). Table 5-19 (with its five combinations) reduces the level of complication again to produce the corresponding minimal covering array.

Orthogonal and covering arrays represent a mathematical model for selecting a smaller but nevertheless complete set of input combinations. The covering array that

A little bit of math

Covering Arrays

→

Pair-wise Testing

table 5-19 is based on contains all possible sports pairings without having to list all 16 possible combinations.

n-wise Testing

Pair-wise testing is limited to all discrete combinations of pairs of parameters values—i.e., the n in the section heading = 2. Both of the examples above illustrate paired combinations. However, pair-wise testing doesn't guarantee even distribution, and only ensures that each pair occurs at least once. The objective of pair-wise testing is to identify failures that occur due to the interaction of pairs of parameters. Including three or more interwoven parameters in the combinations increases the reliability of the test process.

The corresponding technique is called "n-wise testing", which determines all possible discrete combinations of n-parameter values.

Case Study: A sports club offers various types of sports (continued)

Table 5-20 extends our previous example to illustrate the principle of n-wise testing for combinations of three parameters. The eight possible combinations of table tennis, gymnastics, and fitness training are highlighted (in this respect, test case 6 is redundant due to test case 5). The table is based on a covering array in which the individual combinations occur different numbers of times (i.e., it is not an orthogonal array).

Table 5-20 A covering array for all 3s combinations of sports

Test case	Table tennis	Gymnastics	Ball sports	Fitness
1	No	No	No	Yes
2	No	No	Yes	No
3	No	Yes	No	No
4	No	Yes	Yes	Yes
5	Yes	No	No	No
6	Yes	No	Yes	No
7	Yes	Yes	No	Yes
8	Yes	Yes	Yes	No
9	Yes	No	Yes	Yes

As you can see, this technique involves more combinations. For four parameters (i.e., $n = 4$), a table offering complete coverage would contain $2^4 = 16$ possible permutations. The variable n is therefore referred to as the "strength" of a covering array. For the purposes of this book, we will steer clear of too much math and stick to the practical applications of the technique.

5.1 Black-Box Test Techniques

So far, we have only considered parameters that can take on the values `true` or `false`. However, some parameters can be represented by a range of values, as in the example below. In such cases, orthogonal arrays are not always practical, while covering arrays usually fit the bill.

n-wise testing can be used to drastically reduce the number of required test cases. To illustrate the principle, let's take a look at the example we used in section 2.1.4. We recall that the product owner wanted to calculate the number of possible equipment variants for each vehicle and came up with the following results:

Case Study:
Testing effort and vehicle variants
(section 2.1.4 continued)

10 models, each with 5 different types of engine; 10 types of wheel rims, each with summer or winter tires; 10 colors, each in matt, gloss, or pearl effect; and 5 different entertainment systems. These options give us 10×5×10×2×10×3×5 = 150,000 different combinations[25]. If testing each combination takes 1 second, testing all the possible variants would take 1.7 days of testing time.

So how do we use combinatorial test design techniques to reduce this huge number of potential test cases?

Consider the following: Each possible value for each of the seven parameters (10 vehicle types, 5 engines, 10 wheel rim types, 2 tire types, 10 colors, 3 paint effects, and 5 entertainment systems) should occur in at least one test case. We begin by selecting the parameter(s) with the highest number of values (in this case, vehicle type, wheel rim type, and color, each with 10 different values). This gives us a maximum of 10 test cases required to cover each value in at least one test case (see table 5-21). However, this is not a particularly good solution, as the resulting 10 test cases cover only a small selection of the available combinations.

1s combinations

Table 5-21
Every possible parameter value occurs in at least one test case (1s combinations)

Test case	Vehicle type	Engine	Wheel rims	Tires	Color	Paint effect	Entertainment
1	Model1	Engine1	Rim10	Summer	White	Gloss	Ent1
2	Model2	Engine2	Rim9	Winter	Yellow	Pearl	Ent2
3	Model3	Engine3	Rim8	Summer	Red	Matt	Ent3
4	Model4	Engine4	Rim7	Winter	Blue	Gloss	Ent4
5	Model5	Engine5	Rim6	Summer	Gray	Pearl	Ent5
6	Model6	Engine5	Rim5	Winter	Orange	Matt	Ent1
7	Model7	Engine4	Rim4	Summer	Pink	Gloss	Ent2
8	Model8	Engine3	Rim3	Winter	Green	Pearl	Ent3
9	Model9	Engine2	Rim2	Summer	Light blue	Matt	Ent4
10	Model10	Engine1	Rim1	Winter	Black	Gloss	Ent5

---

25. We have left the other 50 optional extras out of this example.

2s combinations

So how do things look if we want to test every possible combination of two out of seven parameters? A quick scan of the table shows that we require a total of at least 100 test cases just to check all combinations of colors and wheel rims[26]. Can we perhaps "handle" the other pair-wise combinations of the other parameters using these tests? Yes, we can.

Test case	Vehicle type	Engine	Wheel rims	Tires	Color	Paint effect	Entertainment
0	Model1	Engine2	Rim1	Summer	White	Gloss	Ent2
10	Model2	Engine5	Rim1	Winter	Yellow	Gloss	Ent1
20	Model3	Engine1	Rim1	Winter	Red	Matt	Ent5
30	Model4	Engine3	Rim1	Winter	Blue	Pearl	Ent5
40	Model5	Engine5	Rim1	Winter	Gray	Gloss	Ent3
50	Model6	Engine5	Rim1	Winter	Orange	Pearl	Ent2
60	Model7	Engine5	Rim1	Winter	Pink	Pearl	Ent1
70	Model8	Engine5	Rim1	Winter	Green	Pearl	Ent5
80	Model9	Engine5	Rim1	Winter	Light blue	Pearl	Ent5
90	Model10	Engine5	Rim1	Winter	Black	Pearl	Ent5

Table 5-22
Test cases with 2s combinations (excerpt)

Table 5-22 shows a portion of the table containing all 100 test cases (available for download at the book website [URL: Softwaretest Knowledge])[27]. The test case numbers are taken from the online table. The 10 test cases in the table here combine Rim1 with each available color, but also cover other pairs. For example, test case 0 also tests Model1 & Engine2, Model1 & Rim1, Model1 & Summer, Model1 & White, Model1 & Gloss, Model1 & Ent2. It also tests Engine2 & Rim1, Engine2 & Summer, Engine2 & White, Engine2 & Gloss, Engine 2 & Ent2, and also Rim1 & Summer and so on.

With these 100 test cases, each vehicle type is combined with each value for all the other parameters at least once, and the same is true for all the other parameters too. If each of these test cases takes 1 second, all 100 would require 1,66 minutes of testing time.

3s combinations

What about *3s* combinations? Table 5-23 shows some (but not all) of the combinations for the parameters with fewer possible values (5x engine, 2x tires, and 3x paint effect). The table doesn't include the 18 test cases that are derived from the 6 combinations for Engine3, Engine4, and Engine5.

---

26. This example uses all possible combinations to explain the principle of pair-wise testing. In practice, combinations of parameters that have nothing to do with each other are not included.
27. The tables were created with the open source ACTS tool [URL: ACTS].

5.1 Black-Box Test Techniques

Test case	Vehicle type	Engine	Wheel rims	Tires	Color	Paint effect	Entertainment
0	Model1	Engine1	Rim1	Winter	Black	Matt	Ent1
19	Model1	Engine1	Rim2	Winter	Light blue	Gloss	Ent5
11	Model1	Engine1	Rim2	Winter	White	Pearl	Ent3
32	Model1	Engine1	Rim4	Summer	Yellow	Matt	Ent5
16	Model1	Engine1	Rim2	Summer	Orange	Gloss	Ent5
5	Model1	Engine1	Rim1	Summer	Gray	Pearl	Ent2
15	Model1	Engine2	Rim2	Winter	Gray	Matt	Ent3
51	Model1	Engine2	Rim6	Winter	White	Gloss	Ent5
6	Model1	Engine2	Rim1	Winter	Orange	Pearl	Ent1
10	Model1	Engine2	Rim2	Summer	Black	Matt	Ent5
1	Model1	Engine2	Rim1	Summer	White	Gloss	Ent2
38	Model1	Engine2	Rim4	Summer	Green	Pearl	Ent5

A total of 1,014 test cases are necessary to cover *3s* combinations for all seven parameters—or, more precisely, any three of the seven parameters are completely combined with their possible values. The complete table with its 1,014 test cases is available for download at [URL: Softwaretest Knowledge].

Table 5-23
Test cases for 3s combinations (excerpt)

Using an automated tool (see below), enables the team to determine the required number of test cases for other combinations too. *4s* combinations result in 5,374 test cases, *5s* in 25,000 test cases, *6s* in 75,000 test cases, and *7s* combinations provide complete coverage (i.e., 150,000 test cases).

n-wise testing can significantly reduce the number of test cases

Based on these data, the product owner and the testing/QA leader decide to perform the *3s* combinations with 1,014 test cases. Both consider the 17 minutes (with an execution time of 1 second per test case) required to execute the entire test suite to be justifiable, compared with the 1.7 days required to execute tests for all 150,000 possible combinations. They also assign three experienced testers to perform a maximum of two hours' exploratory testing on the test object.

From 1.7 days to 17 minutes!

The only issue remaining is to determine the expected results for the 1,014 selected test cases. The decision is taken to implement an additional mini-application that calculates the expected prices for all these combinations, independent of the *VSR-II* system's calculate_price() method. The prices it calculates serve as the basis for the pass/fail decisions. To ensure that the new mini-app does not perform incorrect calculations, the most experienced coder is given the job of programming it and a code review is agreed upon.

Expected results?

> **Side Note**
>
> ### Test Cases
>
> The rows in the covering arrays list the combinations of (input) parameters that need to be converted into test cases. To effectively decide whether a test reveals a failure, the parameter values have to be precisely defined, potential preconditions have to be recorded, and the expected result noted.
>
> ### Defining Exit Criteria
>
> There are two techniques for test objects with multiple, freely combinable parameters:
>
> - Each parameter value occurs in at least one test case. The maximum number of test cases is then equal to the number of values that the parameter with the most values has.
>
> - All possible combinations of parameter values are to be combined and assigned to separate test cases. However, the sheer number of test cases this can produce often results in an unjustifiably large testing effort, or is simply beyond the scope of the project.
>
> Both techniques are relatively simple to illustrate and explain. If each value is to be used in a single test case, it is easy to achieve the required coverage—i.e., every parameter value is tested. Based on the example with three Boolean parameters shown in table 5-16, we would only need to use combinations 1 and 8 (or instead 2 and 7, 3 and 6, or 4 and 5) to achieve complete coverage. To cover all possible combinations, we would have to use all eight rows of the table for the test cases. Complete coverage is the exit criterion that determines whether testing is complete and can be terminated.
>
> *n*-wise testing is a great technique for determining a number of test cases that lies between these two extremes. The scope of the test (i.e., whether it is based on 2s, 3s, 4s combinations, and so on) is up to the tester to decide, and usually depends on the importance of the test object. The greater the risks involved in a system failure, the more thoroughly the test object needs to be tested. Furthermore, n-wise test cases are defined so that a specific combination of values is always tested completely, which also provides a definition of the required coverage. For example, if all 3s combinations of sports are to be tested, all nine test cases listed in table 5-20 have to be executed. The required coverage is thus achieved and the exit criterion fulfilled.
>
> The exit criterion for an n-wise test is derived from the selected number of combinations. The greater the value *n* the more combinations there are, and the greater the number of test cases that have to be designed and executed. In order to achieve 100% test coverage, all test cases have to be executed, although impossible combinations can be excluded before testing begins (see below). If the value *n* is very large, achieving 100% coverage involves a lot of effort and is often not a practical solution.
>
> An alternative technique is to increase *n* by 1 once a failure has been discovered and remedied, and to repeat the process until no more failures occur on the next level up. Because it involves a lot more effort than simple pair-wise testing, this particular technique is only really suitable for mission-critical test objects.

Use each parameter value once or combine all parameter values with each other?

n-wise testing is often the best compromise

→

Benefits and Limitations

Combinatorial test design techniques for deriving test cases are convincing and easy to follow. They provide testers with the certainty of testing a systematically derived set of test cases, even if all possible test cases cannot be included in the test suite. This technique also offers tiered testing based on varying combinations (2s, 3s, ...) that cover everything from basic coverage (i.e., each parameter value occurs in at least one test case) to complete coverage of every possible combination of parameters and values.

Reducing the number of test cases reduces testing thoroughness

This creates test cases that don't actually exist in practice, so these have to be filtered out before testing begins. The remaining test cases also have to be adapted to factor in any dependencies between parameters.

This technique is highly practical but not a magical solution to all of a tester's problems. The mathematical approach helps to formulate useful sets of test cases, but additional test cases are usually required too. If we take a closer, test-oriented look at tables 5-19 and 5-20, we discover the following:

- **2s** combinations (table 5-19):
  - There is no test case that includes all four categories of sports
  - Apart from Test Case 1 (no sports selected), all other test cases include some combination of three categories of sports
  - There are no test cases that combine two categories of sports

Drawback: Some combinations are ignored

- **3s** combinations (table 5-20):
  - There are no test cases that include all four categories of sports
  - There are no test cases for which no categories of sports are selected
  - There is only one test case that combines two categories of sports (Test Case 6: Yes/No/Yes/No)

In spite of these apparent drawbacks, n-wise testing is a great way to test multiple parameters. The tester needs to be aware of the pros and cons of the technique and, if necessary, adapt or augment the resulting tests accordingly.

Remember: there is no single testing technique that can reliably identify all the defects in a system. You will always need to apply a selection of testing techniques that are suited to the test object at hand.

Testing Tools

You are sure to be asking yourself which formulae you can use to derive your n-wise test cases. Fortunately, there are plenty of dedicated software tools available that do (most of) the work for you.

Open-source tools

We are not in the business of advertising, but the authors of the German-language OpenBook "Lean Testing for C++-Programmers" recommend the free, open-source *Advanced Combinatorial Testing System* (ACTS) from the National Institute of Standards and Technology [URL: ACTS].

5.1.6 Use-Case Testing

Use cases and business cases are often used to determine and document system requirements. These are generally illustrated using use case diagrams. Such diagrams describe typical use/system interactions and are used to specify requirements on a fairly abstract level. Figure 5-8 shows a use case diagram for part of the *VSR-II* vehicle selection process.

Example

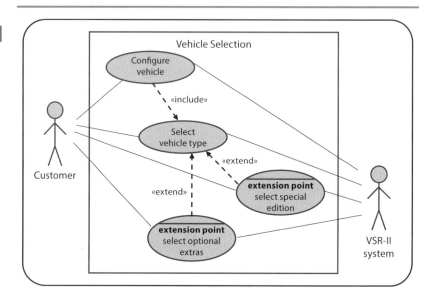

Fig. 5-8
Use-Case diagram for vehicle selection in VSR-II

The individual use cases in this example are "configure vehicle", "select vehicle type", "select special edition", and "select optional extras". Relationships between these are classed using the "extend" and "include" tags. "Include" relationships always occur, whereas "extend" relationships only occur under specific circumstances at "extension points". In other words, there are either alternatives to an "extend" relationship or the relationship simply doesn't come into effect.

The diagram represents the following situation: To configure a vehicle, a customer has to select a vehicle type. Once this has happened, there are three alternative ways to proceed. The customer can select a special edition, optional extras, or neither of these. The *VSR-II* system is involved in all three actions, which require their own detailed use case diagrams.

Use case diagrams usually depict the external view of a system, and serve to clarify the users' view of the system and its relationships to other connected systems. Lines and simple drawings such as the stick figures in the diagram above indicate relationships with external entities, such as people or other systems. Use case diagrams can include a wide range of other symbols and cyphers, but these are not part of this book's remit.

The view from outside

Every use case defines a specific behavior that an object can execute in collaboration with one or more other entities. Use cases are described using interactions and activities that can be augmented with pre- and postconditions. Natural language can also be used to extend these descriptions in the form of comments or additions to individual scenarios and their alternatives. Interactions between external entities and the object can lead to a change in the object's state, and the interactions themselves can be illustrated in detail using workflows, activity diagrams, or business process models.

Every use case is subject to specific pre- and postconditions that need to be met for the use case to be successfully executed. For example, one of the preconditions for a vehicle configuration is that the customer is logged on to the system. Postconditions come into play once the use case has been run—for example, once a vehicle has been successfully selected, the configuration can be ordered online. The sequence of use cases within a diagram (i.e., the "path" taken) also depends on pre- and postconditions.

Pre- and postconditions

Use cases and use case diagrams serve as the test basis when designing use-case-based tests. Because this type of test models an external view of the system, it is highly suitable for system and acceptance testing. If a diagram models the interaction and dependencies between individual system components, it can be used to derive integration test cases too.

Suitable for system and acceptance testing

Use case diagrams illustrate the "usual", or most probable sequence of events and their alternatives, so the tests derived from them are used to check typical system usage scenarios. If a system is to be accepted, it is important that it works error-free under "normal" conditions. This makes use-case-based tests extremely important for the customer, and therefore for developers and testers too.

Testing "normal" system usage

A use case often comprises multiple variants of its basic behavior. In our example, one variant is the selection of a special edition, which in turn makes it impossible for the customer to select any other optional extras. More detailed test cases can also be used to model special cases and error handling as well.

Test Cases

Every use case relates to a specific task and a specific expected result. Events can occur that lead to further activities or alternative actions and postconditions are present following execution. To design a test case, you need to know:

- The initial situation and required preconditions
- Any relevant constraints
- The expected results
- The required postconditions

However, specific input values and results for individual test cases cannot be directly derived from use cases. Each test case has to be fleshed out with appropriate data. All alternative scenarios shown in the use case diagram (i.e., the "extend" relationships) have to be covered by individual test cases too. Test cases designed on the basis of use case scenarios can be combined with other specification-based testing techniques.

Defining Exit Criteria

One possible exit criterion is that each use case (or sequence of use cases) in the diagram is covered by at least one test case. Because the alternative paths and/or extensions are use cases too, this criterion demands that each alternative/extension is executed.

The degree of coverage can be measured by dividing the number of use case variants you actually test by the total number of available use cases. Such a degree of coverage is usually expressed as a percentage.

Benefits and Limitations

Use-case-based tests are ideal for testing typical user/system interactions, making them ideal for acceptance and system testing. "Foreseeable" exceptions and special cases can be illustrated in the use-case diagram and can be covered by additional test cases. However, there is no simple, methodical way to derive further test cases that cover situations that are beyond the scope of the diagram. For situations like this, you need to use other techniques, such as boundary value analysis.

This section hasn't covered all the available black-box testing techniques. This side note offers brief explanations of some other commonly used techniques, and should help you to decide whether they are appropriate for your particular situation.

Side Note: Other techniques

A syntax test derives test cases based on formally specified input syntax. The corresponding syntactical rules are used to derive test cases that test both compliance with and violation of these syntax rules.

Syntax test

Random testing uses randomly selected representatives from the complete set of possible input values. If the values show a statistical distribution (for example, a normal distribution), this should be used to select the representatives. This way, the test cases will be as realistic as possible and will provide meaningful predictions regarding the system's reliability.

Random test

A smoke test is a "quick and dirty" technique that primarily tests the minimum robustness requirements of the test object. Such tests are usually automated and are limited to testing the object's main functionality without looking in detail at the results. The test only checks whether the system crashes or shows any obvious failures. This technique saves resources by doing without a test oracle to derive the expected result. Smoke tests are usually based on a selection of existing (rather than new) test cases. If a smoke test delivers an "everything OK" result, other "proper" tests can then be performed. The term goes back to the times when electrical devices "went up in smoke" when they failed. A smoke test is often performed before all other types of tests to see if the test object is sufficiently mature to warrant further resource-hungry testing. Smoke tests are often used to put software updates through an initial quick functional test.

Smoke test

5.1.7 Evaluation of Black-Box Testing

All black-box testing techniques are based on the requirements and/or specifications of a system or its components and their interactions. If the requirements include erroneous definitions or an erroneous specification was used as the basis for an implementation, black-box testing will not reveal these defects. This is because there will be no deviation between the erroneous requirement and the system's actual behavior—i.e., the test object behaves as specified, even if the specification is erroneous. If a tester uses common sense and views requirements critically, erroneous requirements can be identified when designing test cases. Otherwise, you will need to schedule reviews (see section 4.3) to identify inconsistencies and defects in the specifications.

Faulty specifications or requirements are not revealed

Black-box techniques are also not able to check whether the test object has other functionality that goes beyond the actual specifications (often a reason for security issues). These additional functions are neither specified

Non-required functionality is not recognized

nor are they part of the customer's requirements, and test cases that cause them to be executed are only performed coincidentally, if at all. The coverage criteria that determine when testing is complete are based entirely on the requirements/specifications, not on functions that haven't been described and whose existence is only surmised.

Checking basic functionality

The focus of all black-box testing techniques is the functionality of the test object. It is certainly undisputed that the correct functioning of a software system has the highest priority and thus black box test procedures must always be used.

5.2 White-Box Test Techniques

Structure-based testing

White-box test techniques are based on the test object's internal structure, and are often referred to as structural or structure-based tests. Another term for this technique is code-related testing. This type of test relies on the availability of the source code and the ability to manipulate and adapt it if necessary. White-box test techniques can be used on all test levels, but the techniques described below are aimed squarely at the component testing level.

Other techniques

Alongside the techniques included in the ISTQB® syllabus (statement and decision testing) there are many other techniques that aim to achieve a greater degree of code coverage and therefore increased testing thoroughness (see the side note below for more details). These techniques are usually used to test security- or business-critical systems.

Every part of the code must be executed

The underlying concept of white-box testing is to make sure that all parts of the test object's code are executed at least once. Process-based test cases are designed and executed based on the program's logic. It is clear that the object's specifications also play a role in designing test cases and also in deciding whether defective behavior has been detected when a test is run.

The subject of a white-box test technique can, for example, be the object's statements, and the aim is to achieve a predefined degree of coverage of the statements during testing—i.e., to get as many of the statements in the program to execute as possible.

5.2 White-Box Test Techniques

We can differentiate between the following types of white-box test techniques:

- Statement Testing
- Decision Testing
- Condition Testing
  - Branch Condition Testing
  - Branch Condition Combination Testing
  - Modified Condition Decision Coverage Testing
- Path Testing

The following sections go into detail on each of these techniques.

5.2.1 Statement Testing and Coverage

The test object's individual statements are the focus of this type of test. You need to identify test cases that execute a predefined percentage (or all) of the program's executable statements.

This technique (and decision testing too) can be illustrated and explained using a control flow graph, which can be created based on the source code.

The graph illustrates the possible flows within the test object and enables you to precisely define the required coverage. Statements are represented by nodes, and the control flow by directed edges that connect the nodes. If the program contains a sequence of unconditional statements this is represented by only one node, as executing the initial statement leads to execution of all the subsequent statements too. Selection statements (IF, CASE) and loops (WHILE, FOR) have multiple exit edges.

Once the test cases have been run, you have to verify which individual statements were executed (see section 7.1.4). If the required degree of coverage has been achieved, the test is considered complete. Generally, you will need to execute all (100%) of the statements, as it is impossible to judge whether a statement that hasn't been executed works as intended.

No information on statements that aren't executed

Example This example is based on a simple piece of code that contains just two IF-statements and a single loop (see figure 5-9).

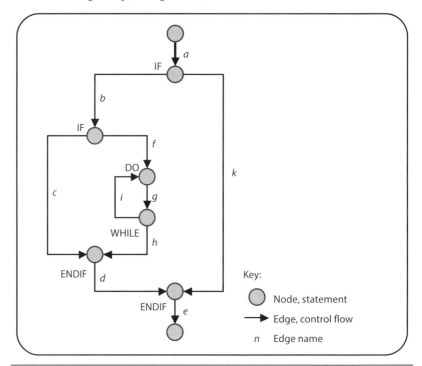

Fig. 5-9
Control flow graph for a system component

Test Cases

Node coverage in the control flow diagram

In our example, all the statements (i.e., all the nodes) can be reached using one single test case. This test case has to traverse all the edges in the following order:

a, b, f, g, h, d, e

A single test case is enough

Once all the edges have been traversed, all the statements (nodes) have been executed once. There are sure to be other sequences that also provide 100% coverage. Remember though, that minimizing overall effort is one of the guiding principles of testing—i.e., you need to fulfill the predefined degree of coverage with as few test cases as possible.

The expected behavior of the program and the expected results have to be defined based on the specifications and, once the test has been executed, you need to compare the expected results with the actual results in order to identify any divergence or failures.

Defining Exit Criteria

The exit criteria for this type of test can be clearly defined using the following formula:

Statement coverage =
(number of executed statements / total number of statements)×100%

This measure for calculating statement coverage is also known as C0 (C-zero) coverage, and provides only a weak exit criterion. Achieving 100% statement coverage can be difficult—for example, if the program includes exceptions that are difficult to produce during testing without expending a lot of extra effort.

C0 coverage

Benefits and Limitations

If 100% coverage is required but some statements cannot be executed by any test cases, this can be a sign of unreachable, or "dead" code.

Identifying dead code

If a condition (IF-statement) only executes statements once it is fulfilled (the THEN part) and there is no ELSE part, the control flow graph has a THEN edge with at least one node starting at the condition, plus a second outgoing ELSE edge without any intermediate nodes (no statements in the ELSE part). The control flow of these two edges is reunited at the terminal (ENDIF) node of the IF-statement. An empty ELSE edge (between IF and ENDIF) is irrelevant when calculating statement coverage, and any missing statements in this part of the program will not be detected by using statement testing.

Empty ELSE edges are ignored

Statement coverage is measured using appropriate tools (see section 7.1.4).

5.2.2 Decision Testing and Coverage

A more advanced criterion for white-box testing is decision testing and coverage, whereby decisions within the source code are the focus of the testing process. In this case, the effect of a decision is assessed and, as a result, a decision is made as to which statement(s) to execute next. This situation has to be considered during testing. Decisions in the code are triggered by IF and CASE statements, loops, and other similar statements. The query implicit in an IF-statement is analyzed and a Boolean "true" or "false" result is returned (i.e., an IF is a decision with two possible outcomes). A CASE (or SWITCH) statement has an outcome for each available option, including the default option.

More test cases required

Decision testing or branch testing?

Decision tests, too, can be illustrated using control flow graphs, but are then referred to as branch testing with corresponding branch coverage. The individual edges in the graph (i.e., the "branches" between nodes) are the focus of the testing procedure.

Side Note: The difference between decision and branch testing

One of the differences between decision and branch testing is the degree of coverage the two techniques achieve. Let's look at an example: In the case of an IF-statement with an empty ELSE part, a decision test will achieve 50% coverage if the condition for "true" is evaluated. An additional test case for "false" increases coverage to 100%. Branch testing is based on the control flow graph and delivers a different result. For example, if the THEN branch consists of two branches and one node and the ELSE branch consists of one branch with no nodes (i.e., no statements), the IF-statement has a total of three branches. If the test case for "true" is run, two of the three branches are covered, giving us 66% coverage (compared with 50% for the decision test). Executing the second ("false") test cases then gives us 100% branch coverage.

Empty ELSE branches are factored in

Unlike in statement testing, it is irrelevant to decision testing whether the THEN and ELSE parts of an IF-statement contain further statements. In a decision test, an empty ELSE branch has to be included. Decision coverage demands that both branches that follow a query and all branches that follow a CASE statement are tested. In a loop, there is one branch to the loop body, one to return to the start of the loop and, if appropriate, one for bypassing the loop body.

Test Cases

Additional test cases required

Let's begin with an example for a branch test. For our example (see figure 5-9), we need additional test cases if we wish to cover all the branches in the control flow graph. The following edge sequence gave us 100% statement coverage:

a, b, f, g, h, d, e

However, the *c*, *i*, and *k* edges are not executed by this test case. The *c* and *k* edges are "false" outcomes from an IF-statement, and the *i* edge is the return jump to the start of the loop. This means we need a total of three test cases to generate 100% branch coverage:

a, b, c, d, e
a, b, f, g, i, g, h, d, e
a, k, e

Expressed in the form of decisions (only the single test case with 100% statement coverage): For the first IF-statement, one outcome of the decision is missing (the *k* edge isn't executed during the test). The same applies to the second IF-statement (the *c* edge isn't tested either). Furthermore, a repeat of the WHILE loop (the *i* edge) hasn't yet been tested.

Decision outcome coverage in the code

Taken together, the three test cases provide complete coverage of all the edges in our control flow graph (i.e., all possible branches of the control flow in the code are covered by at least one test case). Likewise, all decisions—or, more precisely, all decision outcomes—are covered by these three test cases.

Edge coverage in the control flow graph

As in our example, it is often impossible to avoid executing some edges multiple times. Here, because there are no alternative paths, the *a* and *e* edges are executed by all three test cases.

Here too, the pre- and postconditions, the expected results, and the test object's expected behavior have to be defined in advance and compared with the test results. To help identify runtime discrepancies, it is also helpful to record what decision outcomes are delivered and/or which branches are followed during the test. This is especially important when it comes to identifying missing statements in empty branches.

Defining Exit Criteria

Analogously to statement coverage, decision coverage is calculated as follows:

$$\text{Decision coverage}^{28} =$$
(Number of test outcomes during test / total number of possible decision outcomes in the test object) × 100%

Decision coverage is called C1 coverage. The calculation only looks at whether a decision outcome/branch is traversed, not how often. In our example, the *a* and *e* branches (and the corresponding decision outcomes) are traversed three times—once for each test case.

C1 coverage

---

28. The same formula works for branch coverage too, based on the number of branches in the control flow graph (see above).

Side Note: Differing (intermediate) results

> Assuming that the final test case that includes the *k* edge is not executed, the resulting branch coverage is (9/10) × 100% = 90%, whereas decision coverage is (5/6) × 100% = 83.33%. In other words, even if you use the same test cases, there will be differences in the intermediate degree of decision and branch coverage, even if the final result is 100%. This is because, although there are three decisions with six outcomes, the graph has a total of ten branches that need to be covered.
>
> In comparison, 100% statement coverage is achieved using just one test case.

The exit criterion is defined according to the test object's importance and the degree of risk involved if it fails. For example, 85% coverage might be sufficient for one component, whereas 100% is required for another. As our example illustrates, the greater the required degree of coverage, the more testing effort this involves.

Benefits and Limitations

Decision and branch testing always require more test cases than statement testing, although how many more depends on the structure of the test object. Unlike statement tests, decision tests can reveal missing statements in empty IF branches. One hundred percent decision coverage guarantees 100% statement coverage, but the opposite is not true. Decision coverage is a more comprehensive criterion.

The individual decisions in the test object are viewed independently of one another and no specific combinations of program fragments are required.

Our Tip

- You should always aim for 100% decision coverage
- A test can only be classed as satisfactory if all statements, all branches of the control flow, and therefore all possible decision outcomes are covered by corresponding test cases.

Not good enough for object-oriented systems

Statement and decision testing are generally not comprehensive enough for testing object-oriented systems. The control flows within classes and methods are usually quite simple, so the required coverage can be achieved quite easily. However, the complexity of an object-oriented system is usually hidden in the dependencies between classes, and these require the formulation of additional, more complex coverage criteria. Automated tools are often used to determine the required degree of coverage for statement and/or decision coverage, and these can be utilized to identify uncalled methods and program parts too.

5.2.3 Testing Conditions

In a decision test, only the resulting logical values of a decision are evaluated (true or false). These values are then used to decide which outcome branch to follow and/or which statement is executed next. If a decision comprises multiple conditions that are connected using logical operators, the resulting complexity has to be covered by your tests. The following section discusses varying requirements and degrees of testing thoroughness for complex decisions (see also [ISO 29119]).

Side Note

Accounting for compound decisions

Branch Condition Testing[29]

The objective of branch condition testing is to test every condition of a decision (sometimes referred to as "atomic" subconditions) both ways—i.e., for both true and false values.

A condition contains no logical operators such as AND, OR, or NOT, and instead only relative operators such as ">" or "=".

A single decision contained in the test object's code can be made up of multiple conditions.

Defining "atomic" subconditions

Here is an example of a compound decision: x > 3 OR y < 5. In this case, the decision comprises two conditions (x > 3, y < 5) connected using a logical OR. The objective of branch condition testing is to get each (sub)condition to assume both possible logical results. The test data x = 6 and y = 8 return true for the first condition (x > 3) and false for the second (y < 5). The logical result for the entire decision is true (the only possible outcomes are true OR false). The second test data pair (x = 2 and y = 3) returns false for the first condition and true for the second. The decision outcome is once again true. Both conditions have assumed both logical values and the decision outcome (true) is the same both times.

This branch condition test is therefore a weaker criterion than the decision test, as it doesn't demand different logical decision outcomes.

Example
of a compound decision

Altering a condition without having an effect

Weak criterion

---

29. It is also weaker than the statement test, if there are no empty IF statement parts.

5 Dynamic Testing

All combinations of logical values

Branch Condition Combination Testing

Branch condition combination testing demands that the combinations of the logical values assumed by the conditions are tested. If possible, all available combinations should be tested.

Example (continued)

Continuing with our previous example, the same two conditions (x > 3, y < 5) produce four combinations of test cases using the same test data[30]:

x = 6 (T), y = 3 (T), x > 3 OR y < 5 (T)
x = 6 (T), y = 8 (F), x > 3 OR y < 5 (T)
x = 2 (F), y = 3 (T), x > 3 OR y < 5 (T)
x = 2 (F), y = 8 (F), x > 3 OR y < 5 (F)

Branch condition combination testing subsumes statement and decision testing

The decision outcome now covers both possible logical values, thus fulfilling the same criterion as the decision test. This is a comprehensive criterion, as it also takes compound decisions into account. The downside of this technique is that the number of possible combinations increases exponentially with the number of conditions (for n conditions, there are 2^n possible combinations).

One potential drawback is that not all the possible combinations can be realized using test data.

Example for non-realizable combinations of conditions

Here is an example of non-realizable combinations. For the compound decision $3 \leq x$ AND $x < 5$, not all possible combinations can be realized for a single value of x because the two conditions are not independent:

x = 4: $3 \leq x$ (T), x < 5 (T), $3 \leq x$ AND x < 5 (T)
x = 8: $3 \leq x$ (T), x < 5 (F), $3 \leq x$ AND x < 5 (F)
x = 1: $3 \leq x$ (F), x < 5 (T), $3 \leq x$ AND x < 5 (F)
x = ?: $3 \leq x$ (F), x < 5 (F), this combination cannot be realized because x would have to be simultaneously less than 3 and greater than or equal to 5

---

30. (T) = true and (F) = false.

Modified Condition Decision Coverage Testing (MCDC)

Modified condition decision coverage testing confirms the issues outlined above. You don't need to test all possible combinations of logical values of conditions, but only those where changing a single Boolean value of a condition in a decision changes the result of that decision. In other words, you only need to test the conditions for which changing the Boolean value changes the resulting decision.

Limiting the combinations

Let's take another look at our previous example with the two conditions (x > 3, y < 5) and an OR operator. There are 4 (i.e., 2^2) possible combinations:

Example
(continued)

1. x = 6 (T), y = 3 (T), x > 3 OR y < 5 (T)
2. x = 6 (T), y = 8 (F), x > 3 OR y < 5 (T)
3. x = 2 (F), y = 3 (T), x > 3 OR y < 5 (T)
4. x = 2 (F), y = 8 (F), x > 3 OR y < 5 (F)

For the first combination, if the logical value for the first condition (x > 3) is incorrectly calculated (i.e., an incorrect condition is realized), the logical value of the first condition can be changed from true (T) to false (F), although the final result of the decision remains the same (T). The same applies to the second subcondition (y < 5).

For the first combination, this means that faulty evaluation of one of the conditions is masked and the defect will not be visible. Testing the first combination can therefore be omitted.

However, for the second test case, if the logical value of the first condition is incorrectly calculated due to a fault, its value changes from true (T) to false (F). This changes the value of the decision and thus causes a failure. The same applies to the second condition in the third test case. For the fourth test case, an incorrect realization of both conditions leads to a failure (i.e., changes the result of the decision).

For every logical operator in a compound decision, you have to determine which test cases are sensitive to errors and which combinations of conditions can mask failures. The latter can then be left out at the testing stage.

Keeping the number of test cases low

Test Cases

For every test case, you need to know which input values lead to which evaluation of each condition (and thus the decision), and which program part are due to be executed as the result. In order to correctly identify whether a failure is present, you need to define the expected output and/or behavior of the test object in advance of testing.

Our Tip

- Branch Condition Testing is weaker than decision testing, so always perform decision tests if you can.
- Modified Condition Decision Coverage Testing is preferable when testing compound decisions, as the procedure for designing test cases accounts for the complexity of the decision. It also subsumes statement and decision testing, so you don't have to additionally perform either.

However, during modified condition decision coverage testing, it can be hard work finding input values that produce the logical values for all conditions required by the individual test cases.

Defining Exit Criteria

As for all the previous testing techniques, here too the test completion criteria can be derived from the relationship between the achieved and possible logical values for the conditions and decisions. For cases in which the complexity of the decisions in the test object's code are the focus of the test, it is prudent to aim for 100% coverage. If decision complexity is not relevant to the test at hand, decision testing is usually sufficient.

Benefits and Limitations

Compound decision are often buggy

If compound decisions occur in the code, they need to be tested thoroughly to be sure of identifying any failure. Mistakes are often made when combining logical operators, so thorough testing is key. Remember though, that designing effective modified condition decision coverage test cases involves a lot of effort.

Our Tip

- It can help to divide compound decisions into nested simple IF-statements and then decision test the resulting sequence of IF-statements.
- You may be able to forgo thorough testing or subdivision of compound decisions if the corresponding code is put through a conclusive code review (see section 4.3) before dynamic testing begins.

One disadvantage of all kinds of condition testing is that Boolean expressions are only tested within IF-statements.

5.2 White-Box Test Techniques

Example

In this example, the test doesn't recognize that the IF decision contains multiple conditions and therefore requires modified condition decision coverage testing.

```
...
   Flag = (A || (B && C));
   if (Flag)
       ...;
   else ...;
...
```

However, this drawback can be mitigated if all Boolean expressions in the code are used to derive test cases.

Compilers can cause additional issues when evaluating condition coverage. Some compilers curtail the evaluation of Boolean expression as soon as the result of a decision is known. For example, is one condition of an AND operator has already returned FALSE, the result of the entire decision is seen as FALSE, regardless of the result returned by the second condition. To return a complete result as quickly as possible and sidestep evaluating the other conditions, some compliers also alter the evaluation sequence depending on the type of operator. Test cases designed to achieve 100% coverage can be executed, but the curtailed evaluation makes it impossible to accurately assess the actual degree of coverage.

Compiler curtails statement evaluation

Path Testing[31]

So far, statements or branches in the control flow have been the focus of our test case derivation. However, if the test object includes loops or other kinds of repeat steps, the techniques we have looked at so far don't test sufficiently thoroughly. Path testing demands that all possible paths through the test object are tested.

All possible paths through a test object

---

31. Path testing is not part of the ISTQB® *Certified Tester* syllabus and not part of the ISO 29119 standard. We have included this section because it is actually a kind of extension to statement and decision testing, and because the term itself is often incorrectly used.

> **Example**
> *Sample path test*

This example uses the control flow graph shown in figure 5-9 to explain the term "path" in more detail. The program illustrated in the graph contains a DO-WHILE loop that is automatically executed at least once. The WHILE condition at the end of the loop evaluates whether the flow should jump back to the start of the loop and repeat it or continue with the next statement after the loop. The loop is covered by two of the test cases we derived:

- Loop without jump back/repeat:
  a, b, f, g, h, d, e
- Loop with jump back (i) and single repeat:
  a, b, f, g, i, g, h, d, e

Loops are usually repeated more than once. Other possible paths through the graph are:

a, b, f, g, i, g, i, g, h, d, e
a, b, f, g, i, g, i, g, i, g, h, d, e
a, b, f, g, i, g, i, g, i, g, i, g, h, d, e
and so on

As you can see, there are as many paths through the control flow graph as you care to derive. Even if you limit the number of repeats for the loop, the number of possible paths quickly increases beyond control (see also section 2.1.4).

Combining program parts

> A path describes a possible sequence of individual program parts within a program piece. In contrast, decisions (i.e., branches) are viewed independently of one another. Paths take dependencies between branches into account—for example, loops that jump from the end of a branch to the start of a different branch.

Case Study: Statement and decision coverage in VSR-II

In section 5.1.1, we derived test cases from the *VSR_II DreamCar* module's `calculate_price()` method's parameters using valid and invalid equivalence partitions. The following example evaluates test cases according to code coverage—i.e., according to which parts of the method are executed. The aim is to achieve 100% decision coverage in order to ensure that all decision results are tested at least once.

5.2 White-Box Test Techniques

For clarity's sake, here is the method's code once again (see also section 3.4.1):

```
double calculate_price (double baseprice, double specialprice,
                        double extraprice, int extras,
                        double discount)
{
double addon_discount; double result;
if (extras ≥ 3)
   addon_discount = 10;
else
   if (extras ≥ 5)
        addon_discount = 15;
   else  addon_discount = 0;
if (discount > addon_discount)
   addon_discount = discount;
result   = baseprice/100.0 * (100-discount) + specialprice
         + extraprice/100.0 *(100-addon_discount);
return result;
}
```

The calculate_price() method's control flow graph is shown in figure 5-10.

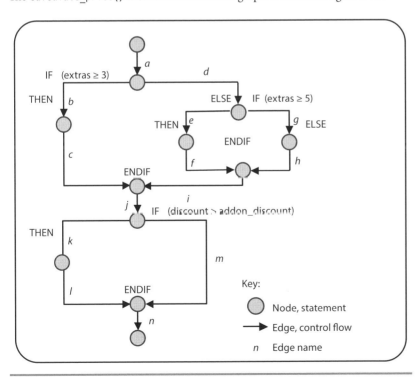

Fig. 5-10
Control flow graph for the method
calculate_price()

Section 3.4.1 detailed the following two test cases:

```
// testcase 01
price = calculate_price(10000.00,2000.00,1000.00,3,0);
test_ok = test_ok && (abs (price-12900.00) < 0.01);
// testcase 02
price = calculate_price(25500.00,3450.00,6000.00,6,0);
test_ok = test_ok && (abs (price-34050.00) < 0.01);
```

These test cases cause the following paths through the graph to be executed:

- Test case 01: *a, b, c, j, m, n*
- Test case 02: *a, b, c, j, m, n*

33% decision coverage

Edges *d, e, f, g, h, i, k,* and *l* haven't been executed. These test cases only execute two out of six possible decision outcomes, thus achieving 33% decision coverage (and 6/14, or 43% branch coverage). Test case 02 achieves no improvement in coverage and is useless as a decision test. However, according to its specifications, test case 02 should execute further statements, as a different discount has to be calculated for five or more optional extras.

To improve coverage, the following test cases are specified:

```
// testcase 03
price = calculate_price(10000.00,2000.00,1000.00,0,10);
test_ok = test_ok && (abs (price-12000.00) < 0.01);
// testcase 04
price = calculate_price(25500.00,3450.00,6000.00,6,15);
test_ok = test_ok && (abs (price-30225.00) < 0.01);
```

These test cases execute the following paths through the graph:

- Test case 03: *a, d, g, h, i, j, k, l, n*
- Test case 04: *a, b, c, j, k, l, n*

83% decision coverage

These test cases also execute the edges *d, g, h, i, k,* and *l*, and thus increase coverage to 5/6 decision outcomes = 83% (and branch coverage of 12/14 = 86%). In this case, edges *e* and *f* are not executed.

Evaluating the conditions

Before we attempt to use new test cases to reach the missing edges, let's take a closer look at the IF-statements. In other words we are going to use the source code as a basis for deriving test cases. In order to reach the edges *e* and *f*, the condition for the IF-statement (extras ≥ 3) has to return FALSE so that the ELSE branch is executed. The THEN part of the IF-statement then has to return TRUE (i.e., extras ≥ 5). In sum, this means we have to find a value for this parameter that fulfills the following condition:

¬(extras ≥ 3) AND (extras ≥ 5)

> Such a value obviously doesn't exist, making the missing edges unreachable. There is clearly a fault in the source code.

We also need to look at the relationships between statement, decision, and path coverage. The test object has a total of three IF-statements, two of which are nested (see figure 5-10).

All statements (nodes) in the graph are reached using the following sequences:

a, b, c, j, k, l, n

a, d, e, f, i, j, k, l, n

a, d, g, h, i, j, k, l, n

These sequences achieve 100% statement coverage, but not all decisions are covered (edge *m* hasn't been traversed). A sample test case that includes the *m* edge looks like this:

a, b, c, j, m, n

If we replace the first sequence of the three listed above with this new one, the resulting test cases provide us with 100% decision coverage and 100% branch coverage.

However, there are other paths through this program that we haven't yet covered, such as:

a, d, e, f, i, j, m, n

a, d, g, h, i, j, m, n

We now have a total of six different paths through the code (i.e., the three paths *to* the *j* edge multiplied by the two possible outcomes *from* the *j* edge). The precondition for this situation is that the statements are independent of one another and the edges therefore freely combinable.

Example
The relationship between different types of coverage

Other paths through the graph

> If a program also includes loops, the possible number of repeats for each loop also counts as a separate path through the program. It is obviously impossible to achieve 100% path coverage during testing for any but the most trivial programs.

Other White-Box Testing Techniques

There are many more white-box testing techniques available than the more common ones described here (see also [ISO 29119]). One of the more interesting of these is data flow testing.

Various techniques use the flow of data through a test object to derive test cases. The basic principle involves observing the use of data within the test. The usage of

Other white-box techniques

Data flow testing

→

each variable is analyzed, whereby the definitions of and read/write access to variables are differentiated form one another. The technique checks whether failures arise if the value of a variable changes when the value is used elsewhere in the program. Furthermore, this technique checks whether the value of a variable is used to calculate the value of other variables or to determine the logical value of a condition. The resulting information can then be used to define various data flow criteria that can be covered by test cases. There is a detailed description of data flow testing in [ISO 29119].

5.2.4 Evaluation of White-Box Testing

Define testing thoroughness

The basis of all the white-box testing techniques described in this chapter is the source code. Suitable testing techniques can be chosen based on the complexity of a program's structure, and testing thoroughness is determined by the source code and type of testing technique you have chosen.

Suitable for lower-level testing

The white-box techniques described here are most suitable for low-level testing such as unit testing. It makes little sense, for example, to demand coverage of individual statements or decisions during system testing.

Use dedicated tools

Code-based white-box techniques require specific program parts to be executed and/or decisions to take on specific logical values. In order to analyze the results, you need to know which parts of the program have already been executed, and which still have to be run. This kind of coverage assessment can be automated using appropriate tools (see section 7.1.3).

Coverage useful at higher levels too

As well as for checking code, the concept of test coverage is useful at higher testing levels too. For example, it can be used during integration testing to evaluate the percentage of modules, components, and (object-oriented) classes that have been executed (module coverage, component coverage, and class coverage). The required percentage value has to be defined in advance and verified once testing is complete.

Missing code cannot be identified

Requirements that are overlooked and therefore not implemented cannot be identified using these techniques. Only requirements that are genuinely put into practice can be tested using white-box techniques. Other techniques have to be used to identify missing code.

5.3 Experience-Based Test Techniques

Alongside methodical test case derivation techniques, testers can use their experience and intuition to derive additional test cases too. Experience-based testing can be used to discover defects that are often overlooked by systematic testing. It is usually prudent to augment systematic testing with experience-based tests. These kinds of techniques can vary in their efficacy at discovering defects, depending on the tester's areas of expertise. Experience-based testing makes it difficult (or simply impossible) to define a degree of coverage that can be used as an exit criterion.

Experience and intuition

Coverage only partially or not at all measurable

A well as testing experience, testers can use their experience developing similar applications, or knowledge of the technologies being used to derive appropriate test cases. For example, a tester with experience of a particular programming language can use defects whose causes lie in the use of the language as the basis for deriving test cases for the current project.

Intuitive Test Case Derivation

Intuitive test case design is based on the intuitive ability to use expected errors, faults, and failures to select suitable test cases. In this case, there is no methodical technique, and the tester has to rely on the ability to recognize situations in which defects occurred in the past (and in other applications), or on knowledge of how earlier versions of the test object worked, or on awareness of what types of errors developers are likely to make. This commonly used test case derivation technique is called "error guessing".

Error guessing

One methodical way to support this technique is to keep lists of errors, faults, and failures that you have discovered in the course of past projects, or that you have compiled from your own knowledge of reasons software fails, and use them to help derive new test cases. Always try to keep such lists current, and update them with new experiences as soon as they occur. You can determine a kind of coverage figure by calculating the percentage of list entries that you use to write test cases.

Record your experiences in checklists

Checklist-Based Testing

As the name suggests, this technique uses checklists as the basis for deriving test cases. A checklist contains aspects of a program (i.e., test conditions) that need to be tested—these include things like exception handling and reliability. Entries in a checklist should remind the tester to include

Have you thought of everything?

these aspects in the resulting test cases. Other aspects include regulations, special cases, or data conditions that require checking. The level of detail in checklists varies enormously from project to project.

Keep your checklists current

Checklists are based largely on an individual tester's experience. They are usually compiled over long periods of time and are updated regularly. However, this doesn't mean you shouldn't use a standardized, unedited checklist.

You can use different checklists for different types of test—for example, one list could contain conditions for functional testing, while another contains the conditions for non-functional testing.

Using checklists can help you retain a degree of consistency when testing. However, because the conditions they contain are worded generally, the test cases derived using them will vary depending on which tester ends up testing which conditions. This variation increases coverage of the individual aspects in the list but reduces the overall level of test repeatability.

Coverage

Here too, you can measure coverage by calculating the percentage of list entries that are covered by test cases. If all the aspects on the list are tested, you have achieved 100% coverage and can stop testing.

Case Study: Checklist-based testing for GUI-Style guide compliance

To ensure that the user interface of the *VSR-II* looks uniform across all modules and their dialogs, a style guide was created in cooperation with a web design agency. This style guide defines the look and feel of the elements in the *VSR-II* user interface (see section 3.5.2).

In order to efficiently test compliance with the style guide, the team transferred the most important style guide requirements into a checklist-based test. To verify a dialog mask, the tester creates a copy of the checklist, which then serves as the test instruction and the test protocol. For example, the test log shown in the following figure documents that three style guide criteria are not met. The test is therefore automatically documented as "failed". If required, more detailed defect reports can be created and assigned, checkpoint by checkpoint.

5.3 Experience-Based Test Techniques

Fig. 5-11 *Results of a checklist-based test session verifying the VSR-II GUI*

Exploratory Testing

If the documents required for deriving test cases are outdated, of low quality, or are simply not available, you can approach the situation using exploratory testing. In extreme cases you may be faced with just the executable code and no other supporting information, or with significant time restrictions. This technique is quicker to implement and perform than other testing techniques and is based largely on the tester's intuition and experience.

Informal testing techniques

This technique sees the various testing activities (see section 2.3) performed almost simultaneously. The testing procedure doesn't follow a predefined structure and no advance planning is involved. The potential elements of the test object and their tasks and functions are "explored" before deciding which elements to test. A few tests follow, and the result are analyzed. Running such tests helps to clarify the test object's as yet "unknown" behavior, and any conspicuous anomalies or other data this yields are then used to write new test cases. This step-by-step technique enables the tester to accumulate knowledge about the test object's purpose and functionality, as well as any quality issues and expectations the program can fulfill. Exploratory testing usually results in conclusions about which other testing techniques to apply (black-box, white-box, or experience-based), provided of course that there is time to conduct further tests.

Session-based testing

Exploratory testing can be structured by defining testing objectives and/or by limiting the time you take to do the exploring (using a "time-box"). Exploratory testing conducted within a limited time-box (not usually exceeding two hours) is usually referred to as "session-based". The tests conducted and the results you achieve are recorded in "session sheets".

Test charter

It makes sense to limit exploratory testing to specific program elements, tasks, or functions. Each selected element is then subdivided into smaller sub-elements, which are then noted in a "test charter". A test charter usually contains just one test objective to guide the testing.

The following questions should be addressed:

- Why is testing being carried out (with what objective)?
- What is to be tested?
- How is it to be tested (using which technique)?
- What problems are to be identified?

The basic principles of exploratory testing are:

Characteristics of exploratory testing

- The results of one test case influence the design and execution of subsequent test cases
- During testing, a virtual model of the program is constructed that details what it does, how it works, and how it behaves (or should behave)
- Tests are performed to verify the model, while simultaneously identifying other aspects of the test object's behavior that are not yet part of the model or are only present in a different form

In order to get feedback about new features implemented in the current development iteration, an exploratory test session will be held.

The test manager invites some team members and some external stakeholders to participate in the test session. He has defined the objective of the session in advance in a "Test Mission" statement and has fleshed out the details in several "Test Charters". For example, the charter "Be a rich customer" where the aim is to configure as many vehicle extras as possible.

Because the Exploratory Test Session is conducted online using *TestBench CS*, all participants can see immediately during test execution what findings, suggestions or praise their colleagues have already recorded or are currently recording. This information not only helps to avoid unnecessary duplication of work, but can also be a source of inspiration for additional test ideas or further test variants.

All participants' notes are discussed and evaluated together after the session. Where necessary, notes can be transformed into formal defect messages or can be marked as test cases which can then be reused in later (non-exploratory) tests.

Case Study: Exploratory testing of VSR-II

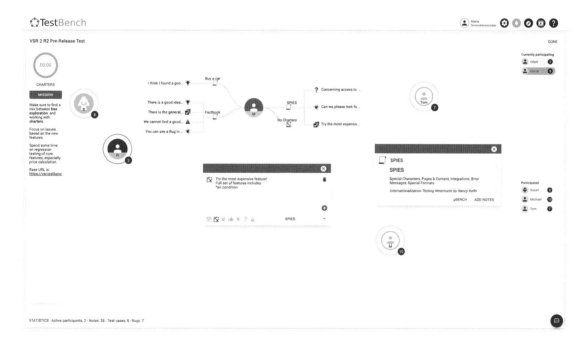

Fig. 5-12 *An Exploratory Test Session managed using TestBench CS*

Exploratory testing is closely interwoven with reactive testing strategies (see section 6.2.2), as all exploratory testing activities can only be undertaken once coding is complete.

Neither a white-box nor a black-box technique

Because neither the requirements nor the source code are the exclusive basis for testing, intuitive test case derivation techniques cannot be unambiguously assigned to either the white-box or the black-box technique. However, it is certainly a technique that is best suited to higher test levels, as there is usually sufficient information (such as source code or detailed specifications) available on lower levels.

Not to be used as the first or only testing technique

Intuitive testing shouldn't be used as your primary testing technique, but rather as a way to supplement your existing test cases and to support other, systematic testing techniques.

Test Cases

The experience that testers use to design additional test cases comes from a variety of sources.

Case Study: Intuitive test cases for VSR-II

The testers in our case study are fully familiar with the previous version, and many of them were involved in testing the original system *(VSR-I)*. They are aware of the system's weaknesses and, thanks to hotline queries and one-to-one conversations, they know about the issues faced by dealers when using the older software. People from the marketing department know from functional tests which vehicles and which configurations are sold most often, and which (combinations of) optional extras don't sell well or simply aren't deliverable. They use this knowledge to intuitively prioritize their systematically derived test cases and add supplementary test cases. The test manager knows which developer teams are under pressure and work long hours, and has the components they are working on tested more thoroughly as a result.

Use all available knowledge

A tester needs to use all of her knowledge to derive and design additional test cases. Pre- and postconditions, expected output, and expected test object behavior have to be predefined for intuitively derived test cases too.

- Because experience is usually only stored in a tester's head, it is a good idea to keep lists of known errors, faults, failures, and potentially buggy situations. A list can be used to record situations that repeatedly cause failures and make these available to all the testers who are working on a job. These special situations are then used to derive additional test cases.

- Such a list can also be extremely useful to programmers too, as it helps to identify potential issues before implementation takes place, thus reducing the number of faults that enter the code.

Our Tip

Defining Exit Criteria

Typical exit criteria like the ones defined for systematic testing techniques cannot be precisely defined, but lists (if they exist) can be used to check how many of the known issues have been tested.

Exit criteria cannot always be defined

Benefits and Limitations

Intuitive, checklist-based, and exploratory testing techniques are usually quite successful and are a great addition to other, systematic testing techniques. The degree of success they yield depends very much on the skills and intuition of the testers involved, and also on their previous experience of similar applications and technologies. These techniques can also help to identify gaps in risk analyses. Combining intuitive and systematic techniques can also help to reveal previously overlooked inconsistencies in the test specifications. However, it is extremely difficult to reliably measure testing completeness or thoroughness.

Mostly successful in detecting further failures

5.4 Selecting the Right Technique

This chapter has introduced a large number of testing techniques[32], and the obvious questions they raise are which to use and when. The following sections address these questions and offer help in deciding how to proceed. The general objective is to use as little effort as possible to generate a sufficient number of test cases so that existing failures will be revealed with

When to use which technique?

---

32. Techniques not covered by this book include those for dedicated integration testing, testing distributed systems, and testing real-time or embedded systems. The *Certified Tester* (Advanced Level) course covers some of these. For more detail on these topics, you need to investigate appropriate literature, for example [Bath 14]).

a predictable degree of certainty. To do this, you need to select the "right" technique for deriving your test cases.

Combining testing techniques

Some testing techniques are better suited for use on particular test levels (see section 3.4), while others can be used on all levels. To make efficient use of the available time and budget, testers usually use a combination of techniques to derive test cases.

Test analysis, design, and implementation techniques range from extremely informal to thoroughly formal, and the degree of formality depends on the individual situation. The influencing factors here are the maturity of the development and testing processes, time restrictions, data security and regulatory requirements, the knowledge and skills of those involved, and the software development model in use.

The following sections take a closer look at these and other factors that influence the process:

Factors that influence your choice of testing technique(s)

- **The type of test object (component or system)**
  If the test object is a component, in addition to functional black-box testing techniques such as using equivalence partition and boundary value analysis, you can use white-box techniques too. If you are testing a complete system, use-case or state transition testing are more appropriate. If the test object is part of the user interface of a system, the focus of testing is more likely to be non-functional—for example, to test usability.

- **The complexity of the component or system**
  The adequacy of the chosen testing technique depends on the complexity of the source code. For example, if decisions in the code depend on multiple conditions, simple decision testing won't suffice. The technique you choose to test compound decisions will also depend on the importance of the component and the risks involved if it fails.

- **Adherence to standards**
  Industry standards and legal regulations often define the testing techniques that have to be used and the required degree of coverage. Such standards usually apply for safety-critical applications or where reliability is key.

- **Customer or contractual requirements**
  The customer may stipulate which testing techniques to use and the degree of coverage required. This ensures that at least the prescribed tests are performed during development, which hopefully leads to fewer failures during acceptance testing.

- **Testing objectives**

  The objectives of the testing process vary a lot (see also section 2.1.2). The focus can be on functional quality characteristics such as completeness, correctness or appropriateness, or on verifying that the planned system/component architecture has been fully and correctly implemented and that it fulfills its specifications. Testing techniques need to be selected according to the specified objectives.

- **Risk analysis (levels and types of risks)**

  The expected risks determine more or less which testing activities take place (i.e., test type and thoroughness). High-risk components need to be tested more thoroughly and using different techniques form other components.

- **Planned software usage**

  Risk analysis includes the planned usage of the system/component and also influences the test procedure. For example, an application that evaluates participation in a further education course will be tested less thoroughly than one that controls power distribution in a hospital. One simple test is probably sufficient for the former, while the latter should be subject to a combination of testing techniques and a verifiably high degree of coverage.

- **Available documentation**

  If formally worded models or specifications are available, these can be directly imported into appropriate tools for deriving test cases. This significantly reduces the effort involved in designing and writing test cases. If the documentation is outdated or simply not available, exploratory testing can help you to gather information about the test object and design your initial tests.

- **Available tools**

  Testing without using dedicated tools is not recommended. From statistical analysis tools that investigate code for possible anomalies, via tools for designing and executing test cases, to defect management tools (see section 7.1.1), testers need a wide range of tools in order to do their job effectively and efficiently. Always select testing techniques that are tool-supported if you can.

- **Knowledge and skills**

  If testers have had positive experiences of early defect detection using a particular technique, they will probably use the same technique in subsequent projects. If testers don't have the required knowledge to effectively use a required technique, they need to be schooled. Exploratory testing is often the technique of choice for creative testers.

- **Types of faults**
  If you expect particular types of failures to occur in a component or system, this makes selecting the appropriate testing technique simpler. For example, if you expect range limits to be poorly adhered to, you need to test using boundary value analysis.

- **Software development model**
  The development model in use influences the choice of testing techniques too. Because they require tests to be repeated more often, agile development models require highly automated testing. In contrast, the clearly defined test development and test levels in the V-model mean you can select a specific set of dedicated testing techniques for each individual level.

- **Time and money**
  Time and money are factors that can have a strong influence on the testing techniques you choose. Both are usually limited, so you need to apply techniques that deliver satisfactory results in the shortest time possible. In this respect, the more you can automate the testing procedure the better.

The test techniques you use to derive your test cases cannot be specified by default, and require a carefully considered selection process.

5.5 Summary

- Correct functionality is of central importance to any software system, so thorough testing of the test object's functionality needs to be guaranteed. Because the expected reactions and output from the test object are defined for each test case whichever technique and technique you use, comparing test results and/or the object's behavior with those expected automatically tests the object's functionality. You can then easily decide whether a defect is present or the functionality has been correctly implemented.

    Testing functionality is key

- Using equivalence partitioning and boundary value analysis to derive test cases is recommended for every test object. We also recommend that you use appropriate tools to automatically measure the degree of code coverage achieved by these tests.

    Combining equivalence partitioning with boundary value analysis

- If different states influence the control flow within the test object, you need to perform state transition tests. This is the only type of test that satisfactorily evaluates the interaction between states, state transitions and the corresponding functional behavior.

    Consider the history of the system

- If dependencies between input values need to be tested, use decision tables to document the dependencies and derive appropriate test cases.

- If there are no dependencies between input values (i.e., they can be freely combined), pair-wise testing is the technique of choice for the systematic derivation of test cases. Different combinations (2s, 3s, and so on) provide a compromise in testing thoroughness while identifying most existing failures.

    Side Note

- On the system testing level, use cases (illustrated in a use-case diagram) can be used as the basis for deriving test cases.

- During component and integration testing, measurements of the degree of coverage achieved must also be carried out for black-box testing. Any parts of the test object that have not yet been tested are then subjected to white-box testing. The white-box technique you use will depend on the importance and nature of the test object.

- You should always aim to achieve 100% decision coverage. If the test object contains compound decisions, you will need to use modified condition decision coverage tests to identify erroneous decisions.

    Minimum criterion: 100% decision coverage

Side Note

- When measuring coverage, remember that loops are run multiple times. For critical components, you need to use specialist techniques, such as boundary interior testing.
- It is not usually possible to achieve 100% path coverage in a test object. Path coverage is regarded as a theoretical metric and, because of the excessively high effort involved, has little or no meaning in practice.

- White-box techniques are best applied to low-level tests, while black-box techniques can be applied on all test levels.

Always utilize experience

- It is always beneficial to supplement systematic testing techniques using intuitive, checklist-based and/or exploratory testing techniques that leverage your testers' experience. These kinds of tests usually reveal further defects that systematic tests overlook.

Our Tip

- Testing always involves a combination of techniques, as there is no single technique that covers all the required aspects equally thoroughly.
- Your choice of testing techniques will depend on the importance of the test object and the degree of risk involved if it should fail.
- The test object's structure should serve as the basis for your choice of white-box techniques. For example, if the test object contains no compound decisions, there is no need to apply modified condition-decision coverage testing.

6 Test Management

This chapter addresses how to organize test teams, which skills are important, a test manager's role, and which supporting processes help to make testing more efficient.

6.1 Test Organization

6.1.1 Independent Testing

A software product has to be tested throughout its lifecycle (see Chapter 3), so testing activities have to be well coordinated with all other development activities. The simplest and most obvious solution is to have the developers do their own testing. However, this approach typically leads to developers being "blind to their own mistakes", so it is usually beneficial and more efficient to have separate development and testing teams that are independently organized:

- Testing teams that carry the responsibility for their own actions are more objective (less biased and with other technical or specialist viewpoints) and are well qualified to find additional defects in a test object that developers overlook.
- Independent testers view assumptions that are implicit in the specifications or coding of a test object more critically, and are able to verify or disprove such assumptions from a neutral point of view.

Benefits of independent testing

Potential drawbacks of separate development and testing teams are:

Drawbacks of independent testing

- If the teams are too isolated from one another, this can hinder communication between them and, in extreme cases, cause unnecessary animosity.
- Independent testers might not have sufficient knowledge of the test object or might not have access to enough technical or specialist information to test efficiently and effectively.

- If there aren't enough dedicated resources, testing can become a bottleneck in the development process and delay planned releases. Even if this isn't the case, testing may be blamed for project delays.
- Developers' own feeling of responsibility for product quality may decline, as they simply assume that the test team will find any errors they make.

However, these potential disadvantages can be mitigated and the advantages retained by selecting a degree of independence between the teams that is suited to the project at hand and the test level concerned. The following options for increasing independence between developers and testers are all models that have been proven in everyday practice:

Independent testing models

1. **Developer testing**
   Testing is performed by the developers and no separate "tester" role is established within the team. Nevertheless, "blindness to your own mistakes" can be reduced and testing effectiveness increased using "buddy" or "pair testing"—i.e., developers only test code written by a colleague, never their own.

2. **Independent testers**
   There is a separate "tester" role. Team members who fulfill this role are assigned exclusively to testing and perform all testing activities within the team.

3. **Independent testing teams**
   There are dedicated testing teams within the company or the project with their own team leaders or sub-project leaders who report to company (department) management or project management. For extra support, members of other specialist or IT departments can be assigned to these teams on a case-based or temporary basis.

4. **Test specialists**
   There is a pool of colleagues with training and specialist knowledge of specific aspects of testing (industry, application, or departmental know-how) or test types (for example, non-functional characteristics such as performance, usability, security, or conformity with standards and regulations). These people can be assigned to a project temporarily or as needs be. They can then perform specialized test activities or support the team with training, coaching, or help with test automation and other, similar tasks.

5. **External service providers**
   An external service provider takes over all or much of the testing activity for a company or individual project (for example, system testing). Such work can be carried out in-house (insourcing) or at an external site of the provider's choice (outsourcing).

Which of the models listed above is most suitable depends largely on the test level in question:

Side Note:
When to use which model

■ **Component testing**
This needs to be done in close cooperation with development work, and is thus often covered using developer testing (see model 1 above). Buddy testing is usually possible and helps to increase product quality. Model 2 is useful if enough dedicated testers can be assigned to the task. Both models nonetheless carry the risk of those involved seeing themselves as developers who end up neglecting the testing activities assigned to them. There are two ways to mitigate this:

- Project or test management predefines a testing plan (see section 6.3) and demands appropriate test documentation from the developers.
- Test specialists are assigned (at least some of the time) as coaches to provide methodical support.

Our Tip
Define testing plans in advance and organize appropriate coaching

■ **Integration testing**
If components that were developed by the same team need to be integrated and tested, you can apply a technique that is analogous to conventional component testing (models 1 and 2). However, if you are integrating components built by separate teams, you need either a "mixed" integration team with members from both development teams, or an independent integration team. A single integration team would have a one-sided view of its own components and is therefore likely to overlook existing faults. Depending on the size of the project, models 3, 4, or 5 are better suited to a situation like this.

■ **System testing**
Here, the finished product has to be viewed from the customer and end-user points of view, so independence from the development team is essential. For this kind of situation, only models 3, 4, or 5 should be considered.

The development model used by the company or for the current project will of course influence the degree of independence of the testing process.

→

Independent testing in projects developed using the V-model

As detailed in Chapter 3, the V-model stipulates explicit and strong separation of development and testing. Models 3-5 listed above are typical testing methods used in projects developed according to the V-model.

Independent testing in agile projects

In contrast, agile projects emphasize close, cross-functional cooperation in small teams. Some agile teams interpret this to mean that independent testing is simply "not agile" or that it "hinders agility". These kinds of teams use only models 1 and 2 based on the assumption that only these methods are truly agile. However, this approach automatically excludes the potential benefits of independent testing performed according to models 3, 4, and 5 (see [Linz 14]).

Not only can models 3-5 be used successfully in an agile environment, they can even increase the agility of a team:

- The short-term iterations demanded by agile development processes require automated tests (see sections 3.2 and 7.1.4) that are continually maintained and expanded. Team members or service providers who specialize in test automation will be able to do this efficiently and professionally, and the same is true when you are setting up and maintaining tool-based support for continuous integration (see section 7.1). Model 2 or model 5 (together with an external service provider) provide the best support for this approach.

- You can increase the efficiency of large-scale projects by bundling test automation and integration tasks for multiple components, and assigning the resulting workload to a service team that works according to models 3 or 5.

- Agile teams can (and should) use in-house or external test specialists (models 4 and 5) to coach them and regularly check and improve their test techniques and test design skills. Many non-functional tests aren't executed for each iteration, and temporary test specialists can perform such tests faster, more professionally, and more cheaply.

- The product owner—perhaps supported by experts from the departments involved (model 4)—performs (exploratory) acceptance tests at the end of each iteration to validate the resulting increment compared with the original user stories.

Case Study: Test organization within the VSR-II project

Component testing for the *VSR-II* project is the responsibility of the development teams and is organized according to models 1 and 2 as described above. An independent testing team has been formed alongside the development teams, and is responsible for integration and system testing. Figure 6-1 illustrates the setup.

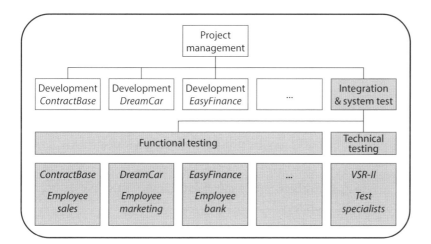

Fig. 6-1
How VSR-II testing is organized

Two or three members of each department (sales, marketing, etc.) are assigned to the task of functional testing for the corresponding modules (*ContractBase, DreamCar, etc.*). These people know all about the business processes implemented in "their" modules and know which requirements the end-users expect. They are all experienced computer users but are not IT experts. Their task here is to help the testing specialists specify functionally meaningful test cases and to execute the resulting tests. They have all been appropriately trained in the basics of testing (processes, specification, execution, documentation).

The testing team also includes three, four, or five additional IT and testing specialists who are responsible for integration, non-functional tests, test automation, and test tool support (see "technical tests" in the chart above).

The testing team is led by a test manager who is responsible for test planning and control. The test manager's other tasks include coaching members of the testing team, especially those testing the functional requirements.

6.1.2 Roles, Tasks, and Qualifications

In order to perform the testing process efficiently and professionally, a project requires staff with knowledge and experience in all aspects of the multi-facetted testing oeuvre. The following roles need to be filled, ideally with appropriately qualified personnel.

The test manager takes responsibility for all test activities in one or more development projects, and designs and leads these. The shape of the role and its integration in the organization varies from company to company and from project to project.

Test manager

A test manager is often a kind of sub-project manager assigned to the task by the overall project manager, and smaller teams are often led by a "lead tester" or "test coach". In larger companies (or projects) multiple test teams often answer to a single test leader, test coordinator, or head of testing.[1]

People who work in test management need experience in software testing, quality management, project management, and human resource management, and also require professional test management training. A test manager's typical tasks include:

- Contributing to the drafting and formulation of the test policy and company test strategy.
- Developing and sponsoring testers, the test team, and the overall image of testing work within the company.
- Supporting the function and organization within the testing team, and encouraging team members to develop their skills through training courses, performance reviews, coaching, and so on.
- Creation of the test plan (see section 6.2.1) and coordination with the project manager, the product owner, and other stakeholders.
- Preparing and setting up tests as defined in the test plan, especially planning and securing the required resources (budget, staff, tools, test environment, and so on).
- Creation and coordination of a test schedule and regular updates based on test progress and results.
- Implementation, monitoring, and control of planned test activities (see section 6.3.2) according to the specified objectives, exit criteria, risks, and the overall project context.
- Initiation and control of test case analysis, design, implementation, automation, and execution.
- Introducing the testing viewpoint into other project activities (for example, integration planning) and representing testing- and quality-related interests to management and other stakeholders.

---

1. These descriptions emphasize the different levels of responsibility for staff or line management that each embodies.

- Supporting the choice and implementation of test tools (see Chapter 7), including estimating and planning the budget, implementation (e.g., a pilot project), and operation/support.
- Introduction and optimization of supporting processes (including defect and configuration management) to ensure traceability of changes and reproducibility for individual tests.
- Introduction, application, and evaluation of the metrics defined in the test plan.
- Creation and communication of test progress and summary reports from the information collected during the testing process.

The term "tester" is used both as a generic term for people who are responsible for certain testing activities in an organization or in a project, and also to refer to "all-rounders" who perform (or are capable of performing) all testing activities.

Testers

The shape of this role and the required background and experience varies according to the test level concerned. In component and integration testing developers often assume this role (see section 3.4.1), whereas for functional acceptance testing, business analysts, application domain experts and employees from the affected business departments are delegated as "testers". For operational acceptance tests (which deal with the IT aspects of the system), the role is usually performed by employees from the IT department/IT operations or system administration.

Anyone who works as a tester (whether on a temporary or full-time basis) needs basic IT skills, as well as an understanding of and experience in operating the test object. They also need to have experience using the testing tools selected by test management. A *Certified Tester* certification is of course extremely useful. A tester's typical tasks include:

- Reviewing test plans, testing schedules and test cases with appropriate business domain and application expertise.
- Obtaining and preparing the required test data.
- Using the designated testing tools.
- Executing manual tests (according to the test specifications) and any necessary exploratory tests, plus the initiation and monitoring of existing automated tests.
- Execution of manual tests according to predefined test specifications and additional exploratory tests.

- Starting and monitoring of automated tests.
- Logging of tests and test results, and subsequent test result evaluation (see section 6.4.1).
- Creation and maintenance of defect reports (see section 6.4.2).

Side Note: Other roles and job profiles

Organizations that have an established testing culture often distinguish more precisely between individual testing roles. For example, between test analyst, test automation specialist, or test administrator. Where there is no precise differentiation between the roles, it is generally assumed that all respective tasks are included in the general role of „tester".

Test analyst

A test analyst or test designer is an expert in testing techniques and specifications (see Chapter 5) and will have software engineering experience. The *Certified Tester Test Analyst* certification [URL: ISTQB] is recommended for anyone filling this role. A test analyst's typical tasks include:

- Analyzing, checking and judging the testability of requirements (such as user stories and acceptance criteria), specifications, and system models (the test basis)
- Identifying and documenting test conditions and the traceability between test cases, test conditions and test basis
- Drafting test specifications
- Identification and preparation of test data

Test automation specialist

The test automation specialist is responsible for creating and maintaining automated tests and test automation solutions. This role requires basic testing skills, coding experience, and excellent knowledge of the test automation tools and scripting languages used in the project at hand. An automation expert's typical tasks include:

- Design or adaptation of test automation solutions in line with the current project's specific requirements
- Programming and maintenance of automated test cases within the project's existing tool environment

Test administrator

A test administrator is responsible for installing, maintaining, and operating the project test environment(s). This role requires system administrator know-how and excellent knowledge of the project hardware, software, and tool landscape. A test administrator's typical tasks include:[2]

- Design, set up, verify, deploy, and supervise operation of the test environment(s)
- Install and configure new versions of the test object
- Automate and optimize related processes—for example, using a "continuous integration toolchain" (see section 7.1)

→

---

2. Usually in close cooperation with company admins and network managers.

In addition to specialization in certain business-domain related topics (for example, specific industry, department, or application-level knowledge) the specialization in certain types of testing and, in particular, testing of non-functional properties is also important.

Test specialist

Such specialists generally work as consultants or trouble-shooters for many (or all) of a company's projects. It is assumed that they are able to quickly familiarize themselves with complex IT environments and issues, and that they can make the solutions they find usable and available for future projects. Testing specialists need to be mobile too, as they often have to work at multiple company or customer sites.

How does the ISTQB® *Certified Tester* certification help in this context? The *Foundation Level* certification takes participants to "tester" level (without teaching the related IT skills). In other words, a *Certified Tester* knows why structure and discipline are necessary in a testing environment, and can perform and document manual tests under the leadership of a qualified test manager. The certification also teaches knowledge of basic test specification and management skills. Every software developer needs basic testing skills in order to perform the tests described in models 1 and 2 (see section 6.1.1). However, to fill the role of a test designer or test manager, you first need to gain plenty of testing experience. The *Certified Tester – Advanced Level* certification provides training up to this level (see [URL: ISTQB], [Spillner 07]), while the *Certified Tester – Expert Level* certification expands on the *Advanced* syllabus to help you formalize your increased specialization and expertise. Developers and testers who work in an agile environment can take the ISTQB® *Agile Tester Foundation* and *Advanced Level* courses. There is also an ISTQB® *Automotive Software Tester* course available. For more details on all of the ISTQB® training courses, visit [URL: ISTQB].

Certified Tester

As well as technical and test-related skills, soft skills are also essential if testers want to succeed. These include:

Soft skills are important too

- The ability to work in a team
- Political and diplomatic skill
- Assertiveness and confidence
- Precision and creativity
- Willingness to question apparently objective facts
- The ability to quickly come to grips with complex situations and applications

It is often necessary to bring additional full- or part-time IT specialists into the team. These can be database specialists, database designers, or network experts. You will also often need sector specialists who work in the customer's industry. Managing such multidisciplinary teams isn't easy, even for experienced test managers.

Multidisciplinary teams

Specialized software testing service providers

If the required resources are not (or only partially) available in-house, you can always hire an external testing service provider, much as you would an external developer. These specialists have the experience to deliver ready-to-use solutions and are able to quickly set up and run highly optimized testing environments for customer projects. They can also provide experts with the specific skills required to fill any gaps in the job profiles listed above.

6.2 Testing Strategies

6.2.1 Test Planning

A task as complex as testing requires meticulous planning on an operational level (see section 6.3) and on a strategic level.

The starting points for strategic planning are provided by company testing policy and testing guidelines (if they exist), or by a generic company testing strategy. The test manager needs to transpose such generic guidelines to create a concrete testing strategy for the project at hand that fits the specific objectives, constraints, and risks of the project, the type, importance and risk level of the product being tested, and that conforms to any existing quality assurance plans[3]. A test manager's strategic planning involves the following tasks:

Tasks involved in strategic test planning

- **Specify the test object(s)**
  Identify which components, modules, neighboring systems, and interfaces (will) make up the system to be tested. Decide which of these objects need to be tested and which can or should be excluded from the testing process.

- **Draft the test objectives**
  Analyze, define and draft the specific testing objectives and the criteria you are testing against for each test object and the entire system (see section 2.2 and 6.3.1).

- **Customize the testing process**
  Customize the testing process foreseen by company policy or the project development model to suit the requirements of the project at hand.

---

3. Testing shouldn't be the only QA procedure, but rather part of a suite of measures. All such activities need to be documented in a comprehensive project QA plan (see also section 2.2.1).

Define which test levels are necessary (based on the nature of the test object and the test objectives you have defined). Discuss and define coordination and cooperation between testing and other project activities.

▪ **Select your testing methods and techniques**
Select and specify the overall testing approach and the testing techniques (see Chapter 5) that are suitable and/or necessary to achieve the defined test objectives for the individual test objects and the entire system. Determine and select the training courses necessary to implement or improve the operation of the selected testing techniques. Analyze the type and scope of potential test automation options.

▪ **Specify the required infrastructure**
Analyze which test environment(s) are required, which are already available, and which need to be extended or built from the ground up. Check which tools can or must be used to support the testing process (see Chapter 7). Document and acquire the stipulated tools and other resources required by the test team.

▪ **Define test metrics**
Select and describe the metrics you will use to control the testing process. Specify the measurement techniques, evaluation criteria, and limit values[4], as well as the required reactions to test results and test exit criteria.

▪ **Specify the reporting system**
Specify which documents and proofs are to be created and maintained (test schedule, test logs, defect reports, test reports, and so on). Specify who is responsible for creating, maintaining, publishing, presenting, and archiving reports. Provide templates and tool configurations that implement the required structure and degree of detail.

▪ **Plan costing and overall testing effort**
Provide an initial estimate of the overall testing effort and the corresponding resources (including personnel) required to execute the planned testing strategy. Calculate the overall cost of testing and secure the necessary budget. Update estimates and costs during the project.

---

4. These limit values determine the point at which specific responses kick in (for example, when a certain defect density is reached) or when a specific goal is achieved (for example, 80% decision coverage).

The result is your testing strategy

The result of all this strategic planning is a testing strategy.[5] The test manager uses the specified strategy to determine the testing objectives and constraints for the current project and documents them as part of the overall test plan. A well-formulated test strategy will include justification for the decisions it contains. It will usually also contain references to alternative approaches that were considered and could still be used if the decisions made (for example, regarding the available resources) should prove to be incorrect or unworkable.

Part 3 of the ISO 29119 standard [ISO 29119][6] provides a reference structure. A testing strategy can be worded generally so that it can be used for multiple members of a product family or for all test levels within a project (a "master test plan"). However, a test plan can also be drafted for a single test level (a "level test plan"), for individual test objects, or for concepts or strategies that apply to a specific type of test (for example, usability or performance tests). These kinds of strategies are optional and are usually used as an addition to the master test plan in critical projects.

Coordinating and adapting a strategy

Creating a strategy obviously requires comprehensive research, as well as intense discussion and negotiation between all parties to the project. In the course of this coordination process, the test manager will have to continually adapt, slim down, or refine the original test plan until a consensus is reached about how to proceed. This will sometimes require reducing the scope of useful measures, or even discarding them completely. Such decisions should always be based on systematic risk weighting and analysis (see section 6.2.4 for more details).

As a project progresses, the entire team will continually gain insight into and increasingly precise information about the product and its related technologies, and can then see whether these work well with the planned project strategy.[7] This is especially relevant to testing activities and the strengths and weaknesses of the testing strategy.

The results of tests that have already been executed and feedback from pilot customers help to identify the kinds of issues that testing has revealed

---

5. The word "strategy" comes from the Greek "stratégia", which means "general" or "troop leader". In the world of economics, "strategy" is used to mean the (usually long-term) planned behaviors of a company with a view to reaching its own predefined goals (see [URL: Strategy]).
6. IEEE 829-2008 was replaced by ISO 29119, Part 3 [ISO 29119]. [IEEE 1012] also provides a "Verification and validation plan" for more complex projects.
7. In agile projects, the short iteration cycles mean this kind of experience can be incorporated quickly and continuously into the overall test plan.

and which defects have slipped through the net. They can also be used to analyze which test levels or test types contribute most to testing effectiveness, and how much effort is involved.

Feature planning changes continuously too. Features are always being adapted or discarded, and new or changed requirements are constantly added during the course of a project. This makes it essential to regularly assess and update project and product risks.

Operative and strategic planning are continuous tasks that the test manager has to perform through every phase or iteration[8] of a project. A test manager has to remain critical and continuously update the testing process, the testing strategy, and the operative test plan whenever the situation changes.

Strategic test planning is a continuous task

6.2.2 Selecting a Testing Strategy

Selecting an overall testing strategy is one of the most important decisions that a test manger has to make. The overall objective is to establish a set of measures that maximize the effectiveness and efficiency of testing within the predefined project constraints. Or, viewed the other way around, the overall objective of testing is to minimize project and product risks (see section 6.2.4).

The previous section addressed the topics that need to be covered by strategic test planning (i.e., the "what"). This section addresses the "how" of selecting or developing appropriate measures. Test strategy development can be broadly divided into two basic avenues of thought:[9]

Developing a strategy

- Decision-making and design freedom
- Available knowledge of the project and the product

The moment at which testers first become involved in a project has a significant effect on whether certain elements of a testing strategy are actually workable and therefore whether they are to be seriously considered. There are two basic types of situation in which these kinds of decisions are made:

Preventative vs. reactive approach

---

8. This extends beyond the completion of the development project, as testing continues during product maintenance, update, and bug fixing.
9. We are talking here about approaches to selecting an overall testing strategy, not the individual testing methods and techniques that the overall strategy contains.

- **Preventative**

    Testers are involved from the very start of the project. The test manager can intervene and shape the testing strategy proactively with a view to optimizing the processes involved and reducing costs. Error mitigation measures (such as a design review), an early start for testing activities (such as specifying tests), and evaluating interim results (for example, using static analysis techniques) all contribute to avoiding faults, or at least discovering them as early as possible in the development process. This reduces defect density during dynamic testing, thus reducing costs and contributing to the stability and reliability of the product. A preventative testing strategy is often mandatory for safety-critical applications.

- **Reactive**

    If testers become involved later on it is usually too late to create a preventative strategy. They then have to react to the existing situation or unplanned situations and other unforeseen circumstances. One reactive technique that is often quite successful is exploratory testing. This is a heuristic approach to testing that involves "exploring" the test object and designing, executing, and evaluating the resulting tests on the fly (see section 5.3).

Our Tip
When should testing begin?

- You should take a preventative approach to testing whenever possible. Cost analysis clearly shows that testing and evaluation should begin as soon as possible within the project and continue throughout all phases of the project's lifespan.

Case Study: Test planning for the VSR-II project

For *VSR-II*, test planning and test specification begins immediately following release of the initial requirements document. At least one roughly worded test case is designed for each requirement, and the results are reviewed by representatives from the appropriate business departments, by the developers, and by the designated system testers. The review reveals that many of the requirements are vague or incomplete and that some of the test cases are faulty or inadequate.

Simply writing down and discussing meaningful test cases with the developers has helped to identify a whole raft of issues long before any tests are actually performed or any program code written.

On an additional level, the available knowledge of the project and the product affects which testing strategy elements you should consider. There are two very different approaches that we can consider here:

Analytical vs. heuristic approach

- **Analytical**
  The testing strategy is based on systematic data analysis. The factors that directly influence strategic decisions (in whole or in part) are determined and their mutual relationships are modeled mathematically.

- **Heuristic**
  The testing strategy is based on in-house or external expert experience and/or on "rules of thumb"—either because no data is available, modeling is too complex, or simply because the required know-how is not available.

6.2.3 Concrete Strategies

In practice, testing strategies are built up using a mixture of the various approaches described above. For example, you can combine risk-based testing (an analytical approach) with exploratory testing (a reactive strategy element). The following variants are often used in real-world situations:

- **Cost-based testing**
  The testing techniques you select (see section 6.2.1) should be driven mainly by the need to optimize the relationship between costs/time required and the number and complexity of the required test cases. Simple, broad-based tests are preferable to costly, in-depth tests, which should be avoided.

- **Risk-based testing**
  This approach (see section 6.2.4) analyzes data relating to project and product risks, and focuses testing on the highest-risk areas. Risk is the parameter that influences strategic decision the most.

- **Model-based approach**
  This approach uses abstract models of the test object to derive test cases, define exit criteria, and to measure test coverage. An example of this approach is state transition testing (see section 5.1.3) in which a state machine serves as the model. Other examples of models that can be used to draft a testing strategy are static models of fault distribution

within the test object, failure rates in use (reliability model), or the frequency of use cases (mission or usage profiles).

- **Methodical approach**
  This kind of strategy is based on the systematic use of predefined sets of tests or test conditions. For example, a set of common or probable defects, a list of important quality characteristics, or company-wide "look and feel" standards for mobile apps and websites.

- A **reuse-based approach** bases testing on existing tests and test environments from previous projects. The aim is to set up the testing process quickly and pragmatically.

- A **checklist-based approach** utilizes lists of defects from previous test cycles[10], lists of potential failures[11] and risks, prioritized quality characteristics, and other informal base materials.

- A **process- or standards-compliant approach** utilize guidelines or recommendations[12] that can be combined in testing "recipes". Sources can be generally accepted industry-wide or company-internal standards, or other legal stipulations and regulations.

- The **directed (or consultative) approach** leverages expertise and the "gut instincts" of testing experts, whose attitude to the technologies in use and/or the business domain influences and controls the choice of testing strategy. This kind of testing strategy is primarily determined by the advice, guidance, and instructions from stakeholders, experts and technologists external to the test team or even to the company itself.

- **Regression-averse approach**
  This kind of testing strategy is motivated by the desire to preserve product performance, and is based strongly on the reuse of existing test cases and test data, extensive test automation, and the repetition of these tests using regression test suites.

---

10. Where defects already exist you are likely to find more! Defects are a symptom of other, wider-ranging issues, so it makes sense to organize additional tests for parts of a project that are already buggy (see section 2.1.6, principle #4).
11. Failure Mode and Effects Analysis (FMEA) is a standardized analytical approach (FMEA, [URL: FMEA]).
12. These kinds of guidelines and recommendations also incorporate a lot of implicit knowledge and/or Heuristics.

6.2.4 Testing and Risk

"Risk" is one of the best criteria to use when selecting and prioritizing test objectives, testing techniques, and test cases.

Risk is defined as the product of the expected loss in the case of an accident and the probability of that accident occurring.

Risk = (expected loss in case of accident) x (the probability of the accident occurring)

The "loss" in this case is the consequence and cost of the product failing (see section 6.2.7). The probability of such a loss occurring depends on how the software product in question is used (i.e., its usage profile).

In practice, the parameters "loss" and "probability" can seldom be precisely defined and are usually estimated. A rough guess or screening using ranges or classes[13] is usually sufficient. When evaluating and handling risk, we need to distinguish between project and product risks.

Project risks can jeopardize the success of a project, or even kill it completely. Such risks include:

Project risks

- **Supplier issues** such as when a sub-contractor is unable to fulfill a contract. This can cause many types of delay, up to and including legal disputes.

- **Organizational issues.** One example is when required resources become scarce—for example, if there aren't enough people available with the skills required by the project, or if necessary training is planned but doesn't take place. Political or interpersonal issues can hamper your work too. Testers may not adequately communicate their needs and/or their test results, or a lack of cooperation between departments or competing projects creates conflict. Decisions regarding cost reductions can also represent a risk to a project.

- **Weaknesses in the development process** such as inefficient defect management or a lack of adequate configuration management can undermine a project.

- **Technical issues**
  Incorrect, incomplete, ambiguous, underrated, or unrealizable requirements, and late changes to requirements can easily cause the entire project to fail. If new technologies, tools, programming languages, or other methods are introduced without employing people with appropriate experience, they can be detrimental to the project rather than

---

13. A spreadsheet for classing risk according to loss and probability classes is available for download at [URL: imbus-downloads].

delivering the desired improvements. If interim results (such as design documentation, program code, or test cases) are of poor quality or contain defects that remain undiscovered, this too can put the project at risk. Testing itself involves technical risks, such as the late deployment of the test environment, non-functioning automation processes, or inadequate test data.

Product risks

Product risks are those that results from (or can result from) issues with the deliverable product. These include:

- The product doesn't perform its intended function or doesn't work at all.
- Features don't display the planned functionality, or non-functional characteristics are missing or incomplete (such as poor performance or usability). These kinds of risks are also referred to as quality risks.
- The system architecture is not scalable according to the growing needs of the application (for example, increasing number of users or connecting additional systems).
- Poor data quality, perhaps due to an earlier migration or conversion of system data.
- Use of the product causes physical damage or endangers human life.

Risk management

Project management needs to introduce systematic risk management[14] that identifies risks at an early stage and introduces appropriate countermeasures that either nullify the risk or at least reduce its effects to a controllable level. The following risk management steps need to be taken regularly:

- Risk analysis that anticipates potential risk factors
- Prioritize identified risks
- Plan and/or introduce measures that reduce or obviate identified risks
- Create contingency plans in case a (serious) risk occurs

Testing reduces risk

Testing is one of the most important anti-risk measures. Testing delivers data on existing, real-world issues and risks, as well as on troubleshooting success (or failure). Testing reduces the uncertainty inherent in risk factors, and helps you to estimate levels of risk and identify new risks.

---

14. The ISO 31000 standard [ISO 31000] defines terminology and provides predefined risk management requirements.

A test manager's job is therefore to minimize or eliminate product risks by identifying faulty product functionality as early as possible, and by ensuring that any corrective measures taken actually work[15].

Project risks (for example, sick leave) cannot be addressed directly by testing. However, testing can reduce the negative effects of project risks that are due to the occurrence of product risks (for example, an increased number of coding errors as a result of time pressures due to a developer sick leave).

A risk-based testing strategy reduces and combats product risks right from the start of the project. Such a strategy uses data on identified risks to plan, specify, prepare, and execute tests. In this case, all the most important elements of the testing strategy are risk-based:

Risk-based testing

- The techniques used to derive test cases, the test levels, and the types of test (for example, security or accessibility testing)
- The extent of testing—i.e., the number of test cases and the number of product configurations (variants or releases) to be tested
- Test case prioritization (see below)

If risk analysis hasn't already taken place as part of the general project risk management process, the test manager will need to analyze product risks and prioritize them according to the level of knowledge and insight of the project stakeholders.

Evaluation of the probability and effects of a particular risk has to take place in the context of how the product is to be used. In other words, the evaluation takes place from the end-user's viewpoint with a view to the product's potential usage scenarios.[16]

In addition to testing itself, other activities (such as additional training for inexperienced designers) can be employed to further reduce risk.

Risk-based testing involves prioritizing test objectives and test cases according to the assumed probability of a risk actually becoming an event. This ensures that high-risk components or features are tested earlier and more thoroughly than other parts of the system. Serious issues that require a high degree of remedial effort that is likely to delay the project are thus identified early on.

Risk-based test prioritization

---

15. To do the job properly, a test manager has to take full responsibility for any test-related project risks (for example, ensuring that the automated tests actually work).
16. Incorrect use or deliberate misuse are additional risks that also have to be considered here, especially for medical and other safety-critical systems.

If you distribute your testing resources evenly, critical and non-critical test objects will be tested equally thoroughly. This means that critical objects are not sufficiently tested while resources are wasted on non-critical objects. Risk-based testing prevents this from happening.

6.2.5 Testing Effort and Costs

The cost of implementing a testing strategy significantly influences the testing strategy itself. The test manager therefore has to estimate the effort involved in performing the planned testing activities and the costs this entails. The resulting cost forecast details either the budget that has to be applied for or the degree to which the planned testing activities under- or overrun the available budget.

The cost of testing always has to be balanced with the test objectives and the risks that testing is designed to reduce. For low-risk components, you can reduce the number of test cases or halt testing completely, while high-risk components usually imply the acceptance of greater costs.

Factors that influence testing effort

The factors that influence testing effort and therefore the cost of testing are varied and difficult to quantify. The most important factors are:

- The maturity[17] of the development process
  - The number and frequency of changes to the software, the complexity of changes and corrections, and the number, seriousness, and frequency of failures
  - The maturity of the testing process, configuration management, defect management and change management, and the degree of routine and discipline in complying with these
  - Time pressure due to unrealistic estimates or planning
  - The overall stability of the company
- Software quality and testability
  - The number, seriousness and distribution of faults within the software
  - The quality, conciseness, and up-to-dateness of project documentation and other information that is relevant to the testing process

---

17. "SPICE" [ISO/IEC 15504] and CMMI [URL: CMMI] are two commonly used methods for evaluating software development processes.

- The size, type, and complexity of the system and its environment
- The complexity of the application domain

▪ Test infrastructure
- The availability of testing tools
- The availability of the test environment and test infrastructure
- The availability and recognition of the testing process, testing standards, and testing techniques

▪ Team and co-workers
- Team experience and know-how with regard to testing knowledge, testing tools, the test environment, and the test object
- Team experience of similar product and projects
- Team cooperation and the quality of the relationships among testers, developers, management, and the customer

▪ Quality objectives
- Planned test coverage
- Planned reliability of the product in use
- Required test documentation[18] and its degree of detail
- Legal and regulatory conformity (for example, with regard to system security, access security, and reliability)

▪ Testing strategy
- Test objectives (derived from the quality objectives) and resources for achieving them, including the number and scope of the planned test levels
- Selecting appropriate testing techniques
- Test scheduling (start and finish, number of iterations)

---

18. Medical devices usually have to be approved by a government agency such as the FDA [URL: FDA] that demands specific documentation standards.

Side Note:
The test manager's
influenceprofiles

> The test manager cannot directly influence many of these factors. From a test manager's viewpoint, the situation usually looks like this:
>
> ■ The maturity of the software development process cannot be influenced in the short term, so you simply have to accept it as it is. This factor can only be changed in the longer term through an appropriate process improvement program.
>
> ■ The software's testability depends heavily on the system architecture. Improving testability usually requires comprehensive changes to the system architecture and is therefore difficult to achieve in the short term. In the medium and long term, a well-structured development process (with appropriate reviews) will lead to a better overall software structure that is easier to test.
>
> ■ The test infrastructure is often left over from previous or similar projects. Within the constraints of the testing budget, the test manager can certainly influence whether and how the test infrastructure can be developed to increase testing productivity. If the test environment has to be built from the ground up, be aware that this usually requires a lot of extra time.
>
> ■ The test manager can influence the short-term structure of his team and the level of qualification within it simply by selecting the right personnel. In the medium term, he can increase the team's know-how by offering appropriate training.
>
> ■ If the quality objectives have already been defined by the customer and/or other stakeholders the test manager may be able to exert some influence by consulting with the stakeholders and prioritizing the objectives. If the test manager is able to set his own objectives they will become part of the overall testing strategy.
>
> ■ The "test object" and "test objectives" elements of the testing strategy (see section 6.2.1) can be prioritized too, while "testing techniques" are generally freely selectable and scalable.
>
> ■ The most important variable that a test manger can adjust and control during test planning (see section 6.3.1) is the overall extent of test execution.

6.2.6 Estimating Testing Effort

The estimated testing effort for a project depends on the factors discussed in the previous section. Most of these factors exert mutual influence on each other and it is virtually impossible to analyze them all exhaustively.

Estimation techniques

There are two basics approaches you can take to better estimate testing effort and costs:

- **Expert-based estimation**
  The overall testing effort is estimated task by task. This is done either by the task owner(s) or by experts with appropriate experience.

6.2 Testing Strategies

- **Metrics-based estimation**
  The testing effort is estimated based on the known effort involved in previous or similar current projects, or based on key metrics (for example, the average number of test cases executed per hour).

Even if the test manager doesn't overlook a single task, an expert-based estimate will usually view the project too "optimistically" and ignore things that could go wrong, thus underestimating the effort required. An estimate based on experience and/or figures from similar projects will usually provide a more realistic assessment.

An estimate for a small project can be made "in one go", whereas larger projects require a separate estimate for each test level and/or test iteration.

If there are no references available, you should always reckon to use 25-50% of the entire development effort for testing (on all levels).

Rule of thumb

- The amount of testing that the team can perform for the next iteration can be estimated using metrics based on team productivity (also known as "team velocity") or using a kind of expert analysis known as "planning poker" (see [Linz 14]).

  The important thing is to plan testing and all other tasks in the course of the sprint planning—and don't forget to include test infrastructure maintenance and improvement.

Our Tip
Estimating testing effort for agile projects

6.2.7 The Cost of Testing vs. The Cost of Defects

If the scope of checks and tests is reduced (or some tests are simply dropped), the number of undiscovered defects will increase accordingly. These then become part of the shipped product and increase the level of product risk and the likelihood of incurring additional costs:

Cost-benefit relation

- **Direct costs**
  These are costs that arise from defects that occur when the software is in use (which the manufacturer may be liable for). These can be the cost of incorrect calculations (lost data, accounting errors, damage to hardware or other plant components, personal injury); the costs involved when software-driven machines fail; the cost of installing new product versions and staff training; and so on. These kinds of costs are easy to overlook but can be significant—for example, consider the time and effort involved in installing a new software version at all customer sites.

The cost of a flawed product

- **Indirect costs**
  These are costs to the manufacturer that occur when the customer is not happy with the product. These can be contractual penalties, reduced payments due to non-fulfillment, or increased hotline and support costs. These kinds of issues can damage a manufacturer's image and even lead to a loss of licensing for safety-critical products.

- **Cost of defect correction**
  These are the costs related to the effort involved in analyzing and correcting defects, regression testing, delivery and installation of the amended software product, re-training users, delays in releasing new products due to development staff involved in defect correction, and reduced competitiveness.

Risks due to product defects

The probability of these costs occurring and to what extent (i.e., the degree of risk involved in product defects) can be estimated using risk analysis. The level of risk depends on the type and scope of the product, the customer's industry (contractual and legal stipulations), the number and type of defects, and the number of affected installations/end-users. There are also significant differences between custom and off-the-shelf software.

Early defect detection cuts costs

However large (or small) the risks, it is essential to identify the defects that cause them as early as possible. The costs of correcting defects increases significantly with every stage of the development process:

- An undiscovered fault (such as a poorly defined requirement) that occurs early on can lead to after-effects in the development process that multiply with each development phase.

- The later a defect is discovered, the more corrections are required to mitigate it. You may have to rework parts of previous project phases (requirement definitions, product design, coding) or, in agile projects, repeat some already completed tasks (which delays progress and postpones some objectives until later iterations).

- If the software is already installed at the customer site, the risk of additional direct and indirect costs increases. The potential cost and consequences of failure in safety-critical software (plant control, traffic control, medical applications, and similar) can be catastrophic for a manufacturer.

6.3 Test Planning, Control, and Monitoring

The testing strategy that results from strategic test management considerations is just a piece of paper. This means that the test manager's main task and responsibility is to manage and guarantee the implementation of the testing strategy. To do so, he or she needs to follow four major steps[19] (see fig. 6-2):

- Define/adjust the testing strategy
- Plan test execution
- Initiate and monitor test execution
- Evaluate and report test results

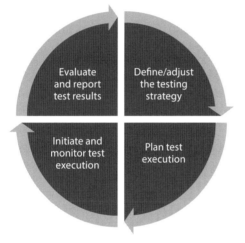

Fig. 6-2
Test management cycle

This process controls all testing activities (see section 2.3, figures 2-3, 2-4, and 2-5) and will be repeated many times during a software development project:

- For each new, altered, or corrected version of the test software
- On every planned test level (often in parallel)
- For every iteration in an agile project

---

19. These four steps are embodied in the PDCA cycle [URL: PDCA] for control and continuous improvement of products and processes. Applying the test management process improves and/or adjusts the overall testing strategy iteratively.

We have already discussed Step 1 (defining a testing strategy) in section 6.2.1. The other three steps constitute operative test management, and the following section goes in to more detail on these.

6.3.1 Test Execution Planning

Detail planning for each cycle

A testing strategy defines the testing framework (for example, which testing techniques to use), but doesn't define the details of the individual test cases. The test manager has to define test cases during the detail-planning phase that comes before the start of a new iteration or test cycle. The detail-planning phase defines which test cases need to be designed, which require automation, and which tests are to be performed by whom and in which order. The result of detail planning is a "test execution schedule" for the upcoming test cycle. Detail planning is always based on the current situation, which will definitely have changed since the previous iteration! The following factors are important when detail planning:

- **The current stage of development**
  The software under test that is actually available can have limited or altered functionality compared with what was initially planned, making changes to the test specifications and existing test case definitions necessary. Tests that are (currently) technically impossible to perform or that are not suitable to the current situation need to be postponed or discarded.

- **Test results**
  Issues identified by previous test cycles can make it necessary to change your testing priorities. Fixed defects require additional confirmation tests that have to be added to the test execution schedule. Additional tests can also be required for cases where issues have been identified but aren't sufficiently reproducible using the available tests. The opposite can also be true, and the number of regression tests (and therefore testing effort) can be reduced for an unchanged component that passed all its tests during the previous iteration.

- **Resources**
  Test cycle planning has to be coordinated with the current project or iteration plan and, more importantly, with the available resources. For example, you need to consider the current staffing and vacation plans, the availability of the test environment, the viability of automated tests and testing tools, and so on. If there aren't enough people available you

may have to cancel some manual tests or postpone further test automation. If time and money are limited, you may have to cut back some of the planned test activities or individual test cases.

If you can't requisition additional resources, you may have to adapt the test plan. Low-priority test cases can be canceled or tests with multiple variants can be pared down (for example, run a test on just one operating system instead of many). These kinds of adjustments mean some meaningful tests won't be executed, but the resources you save can be used to ensure that at least the higher-priority tests get done.

When planning test cycles, the test manager controls not only the selection of test cases, but also how he distributes the test effort within the current cycle between test design, test automation, the initial execution of newly specified tests, and the execution of regression tests.

Plan the test execution sequence

The weighting of all these activities has to be balanced according to the current situation and the factors detailed above. During the early phases of a project, test design and automation often require more effort than they do later on. For later iterations in which functionalities change only slightly, you will usually need to define and automate only a few new tests. The weighting can then be shifted toward test execution instead.

■ Newly specified system test cases should at first be executed manually. Only once you have gathered some experience of how the test object and the test environment react, and whether the new tests do what they are designed to do can you begin to automate them. Ideally, the newly automated tests will be available and fully functional for the next iteration.

Our Tip
"Definition of Ready" for system test automation

Test execution planning includes establishing or optimizing the sequence in which the planned tests are to be executed. Changes in the sequence can be due to tests or test objects that are either missing or that behave differently than they did during previous test cycles, or because a different sequence is simply more efficient.

If—due to any of the situations mentioned above—you need to discard test cases from the "complete" execution plan, you need to decide which these are. In spite of the resulting reduced set of test cases, the overarching objective is still to identify as many risks or potentially critical defects as possible—in other words, you need to concentrate on prioritizing the most important test cases.

Prioritizing tests

Side Note:
Prioritization criteria

The following criteria can be used to guide, objectivize, and formalize the prioritization process:

- The **frequency with which a function is called** when the software is in use. If a function is used frequently, it is highly likely that a fault witin the function will be triggered, thus causing a failure or system crash. Test cases that check these types of functions have a higher priority than ones that check less frequently used functions.

- **High-risk defects**
  A high-risk defect is one that can cause significant loss or damage to the customer—for example, if the software fails and costs the customer money. Tests that are aimed at identifying high-risk defects have a higher priority than ones that check low-risk defects (see also section 6.2.4).

- **Defects that are noticed by the end-user** offer another criterion for prioritizing test cases, especially for interactive systems. For example, the user of a web shop spots some faulty output in the user interface and is no longer convinced that the rest of the data presented by the system is correct.

- Test cases can be prioritized to correspond with the **prioritization of the requirements**. The various functions that a system provides are of differing importance to the customer. Some may be dispensable if they don't work properly, while others are essential to the system's basic functionality.

- As well as functional requirements, you need to consider **non-functional quality characteristics**, as these too can be of varying importance to the customer. More important characteristics have to be tested more thoroughly.

- Prioritization can also take place from a development or **system architecture** viewpoint. Components that can potentially cause a complete system failure need to be tested more thoroughly than other, less critical ones.

- The **complexity** of the individual components or modules can be used to prioritize test cases. Because they are more difficult to build (and are therefore more likely to contain errors), complex program parts need to be tested more thoroughly. However, you may find that apparently simple program parts contain a whole raft of errors, perhaps because they were developed with too little care. If figures based on experience are available, it will be easier to decide which option to take for the current project.

- Defects that require significant **correction effort** and take up valuable resources can delay project progress (see section 6.4.3) and contribute to project risk, so they have to be identified as early as possible (for example, components that significantly influence system performance). Correcting these types of faults usually requires major changes to the system architecture, so it is never too early to put these kinds of components through performance tests.

6.3 Test Planning, Control, and Monitoring

Priority criteria are defined by the test manager as part of the test plan. These criteria may already be defined on the test object or quality characteristic levels, but all test cases must have priorities assigned to them at the latest during planning for the first test cycle (either individually or in groups). The priorities thus defined are used in subsequent iterations to make rapid decisions if tests have to be discarded (for example, due to a lack of resources):

Define priority criteria in your test plan

- If a low-priority test case contains a precondition for a high-priority test case, the low-priority test case has to be executed first. The situation is similar where dependencies exist across multiple test cases—in this case, the test cases have to be arranged in a sequence that functions, regardless of the priorities assigned to the individual test cases.
- Sometimes, test case sequences can be arranged according to differing degrees of efficiency. In cases like this, you have to strike a compromise between testing efficiency and sticking to your prioritization strategy.

Prioritization only ever demonstrates the relative importance of test cases to one another within the context of the current project. Like all other aspects of test cycle planning, test case prioritization has to be checked regularly and, if necessary, adjusted to suit the current state of the overall testing strategy. The following rules of thumb apply when assigning or adjusting test case priorities:

- Test case prioritization should enable the best possible results regardless of whether testing is completed or terminated prematurely.
- Where many defects exist you are sure to find more (see also section 2.1.6, principle #4). Components (and their neighbors) that contain a large number of defects should be assigned a high priority for several iterations following defect correction.

Our Tip
Prioritization rules

Definition of entry and exit criteria is another important part of overall test planning. These criteria are part of the test plan and determine when particular test activities can begin and when they are considered to be finished. Separate entry and exit criteria can be defined for the entire project, each test level, or every different type of test, and can vary according to the test objectives you have defined.

Test entry and exit criteria

These criteria are measured and assessed regularly during testing to help test management plan test execution, and project management to decide when to approve a new release.

Entry criteria

Entry criteria (called "definition of ready" in agile projects) define the preconditions required to begin a specific test activity. If the entry criteria are not fulfilled, the activity will probably be more difficult to perform, take more time, cost more, and be more risky than planned. If this is the case, it probably makes little sense to begin the activity.

Typical entry criteria are:

- **The requirement** (i.e., the expected behavior) that is to be tested for is known and/or available in written form
- The **test environment** is available and ready to use
- The required **test tools** are ready for operation within the test environment
- **The test objects** are available within the test environment
- The necessary **test data are** available

These criteria are the precondition for starting the corresponding test activity, so checking them in a timely manner ensures that the test team doesn't waste time attempting to perform tests that are not yet fully executable.

Exit criteria

Exit criteria (called "definition of done" in agile projects) mitigate the risk of ending test activities randomly or for the wrong reasons. They serve to ensure that test activities are not terminated too early (for example due to a lack of resources or time pressure), but also that they don't get out of control. Typical exit criteria and their metrics are:

- All planned test cases defined in **the test execution schedule** have been completed
- The required **test coverage** has been achieved—for example, measured using the number of completed test cases (test coverage), requirement coverage, code coverage, or similar
- The target **product quality** is achieved—for example, measured by the number and seriousness of known but not yet corrected defects within a predefined range of tolerance, reliability, or other quality characteristics

- **Residual risks**

    A predefined degree of tolerable risk (i.e., a threshold) can also be used as an exit criterion. Examples are the number of executed tests, the number of lines of code not reached during testing, the estimated number and effects of undiscovered faults, and so on. If the threshold is crossed, the test can be considered successfully completed.

Every project is subject to economic restrictions. Testing may be halted before the originally planned exit criteria are met—perhaps because the budget has run out, time has run out, or simply because of pressure to get the product released. In such situations, the exit criteria and an estimate of how distant they still are can help stakeholders to objectively assess the risks involved in an early release.

Test results sampled during test execution help to determine testing progress and also to decide whether testing can be terminated[20] and the product released. Which criteria are appropriate for deciding whether to terminate testing depends on the quality characteristics that need to be fulfilled (i.e., the criticality of the software) and from the available resources (time, staff, tools).

Can we stop testing?

The project exit criteria, too, are defined as part of the test plan, and each exit criterion must be measurable using the metrics collected in the course of the project.

The *VSR-II* test cases are assigned one of three priorities:

Case Study:
Exit criteria for VSR-II
system testing

Priority	What it means
1	Test case must be executed
2	Test case should be executed
3	Test case can be executed

Based on these priorities, the test plan lists the following test case-based exit criteria for system testing *VSR-II*:

- All *Priority 1* test cases have run without failure
- At least 60% of *Priority 2* test cases have run without failure

Once these exit criteria are fulfilled, the project manager (assisted by the test manger) decides whether to release and deliver the test object. Within the context of component and integration testing, "delivery" means handing over the test object to the following test level.

---

20. Or the test activities on one level are complete and the next level can now be tackled.

6.3.2 Test Control

Test control comprises all leadership, initiatory, and corrective measures that are performed in order to put into practice all test activities defined in the test plan and the test execution schedule. Controlling measures can directly affect testing activity or any other type of development activity. We differentiate between the following types of situations:

- The initiation of planned measures—for example, assigning planned test activities to a certain team member, and ensuring that the activity begins and delivers results.
- Short-term reaction to changes or difficulties that arise—for example, you may have to apply for and assign additional test resources (staff, workstations, tools) to rein in an obvious backlog.
- Check whether corrective measures you have initiated are having the desired effect (for example, whether a previously unfulfilled exit criterion is now fulfilled).

React to deviations from plan

Short-term reactions to unexpected issues or changes can mean you may have to improvise rather than wait until the next test cycle.

If critical issues arise, you may have to plan additional test cycles, which in turn may delay the product release and extend the planned time to market.

Clear communication of issues and changes

If issues occur that affect project activities external to the testing environment, or that cannot be solved within the team, the test manager must communicate the situation to the appropriate stakeholders (see section 6.3.4). If following up on the test execution schedule leads to test cases being discarded, this usually implies increased risk. In turn, this means the situation must be documented and included in the next test summary report. The test manager is responsible for the clear communication to the project leader(s) of issues that increase risk.

6.3.3 Test Cycle Monitoring

Test cycle monitoring is all about collecting information and feedback relating to all test activities. Information can be collected manually or automatically and are then used to assess testing progress and evaluate whether the exit criteria or in agile projects the "definition of done" have been fulfilled. For example, these could be fulfillment of product risk coverage, requirements, or acceptance criteria.

Ideally, test activity and success monitoring is measured using the metrics defined in the test plan. The test manager can then use these metrics to assess testing progress in relation to the test execution schedule and the available budget, and to assess the appropriateness and effectiveness of the testing techniques in use. Test metrics are differentiated as follows:

Side Note:
Categories of test metrics

- **Defect-based metrics**
  The number of identified faults and/or defect reports (per test object) for each release, dependent on the class of defect (see section 6.4.3) and defect status (see section 6.4.4, table 6-4) and possibly in relation to the size of the test object (in lines of code) or test duration, or similar (see section 6.4)
- **Test case-based metrics**
  Number or percentage of test cases with a specific status—for example, specified, planned, blocked, run, passed/failed
- **Test object-based metrics**
  Covered requirements, code coverage, dialog coverage, covered installed versions, platforms, and so on
- **Cost-based metrics**
  Accumulated testing costs, the cost of the next test cycle in relation to the expected usefulness (prevented cost of failure and/or reduced product or project risk)
- **General progress**
  For example, the percentage of completed tasks in relation to those planned

Our Tip

- The test manager should only use metrics that can be regularly, reliably, and easily gathered and evaluated. This is always the case with test tools that gather metrics automatically. If a metric proves too difficult to gather or doesn't provide useful data, it should be removed from the testing strategy or replaced by a more appropriate one.

6.3.4 Test Reports

The objective of a test report is to summarize and communicate the current state of testing activity to the project manager and other stakeholders. This normally takes place routinely at the end of an iteration/test cycle or when a particular test activity (for example, performance testing) is completed. However, an interim test report can be initiated any time that unexpected issues occur.

Test progress and test summary reports

Test managers often differentiate between test progress reports and test summary reports.[21] A test progress report is usually more succinct and focuses on the state reached and the test results from the current (or last finished) iteration. In contrast, a test summary report serves as a basis for deciding whether to approve and release the current product version.

It summarizes all completed test activities from all iterations that lead up to a release, and provides an overview of all completed tests. In this case, what actually took place during which iteration is of secondary interest.

Product release

One important element of a test summary report is the test manager's (subjective) evaluation (i.e., an expert opinion) of whether the test object can be approved for release. However, "approval" does not necessarily mean "free of defects". The product is sure to contain a number of undiscovered faults, as well as known faults that are not considered critical to approval and are thus left unchanged. The latter are documented in a database and are often remedied later during routine software maintenance (see section 3.6.1).

The contents of a test report will vary according the nature of the project, the organizational requirements, and the development lifecycle. The following elements are usually included in most reports:

- **A list of the test object(s)**
  What was actually tested

- **Dates (from ... to ...)**
  When the tests were performed

- **A summary**
  Which types of tests were performed on which test levels, or the general testing focus

- **Test progress statistics measured against the predefined exit criteria**
  For example, planned/run/blocked tests, factors that prevent further progress, or other achieved objectives (such as further test automation)

- **Test object quality statistics, especially defect status reports**
  New defects, defects in progress, or corrected defects

- **Risks**
  New, changed, or known risks, and any other unusual events

---

21. Structures and examples of both types of report are provided in ISO 29119, Part 3 [ISO 29119].

- **Deviations from plan**
  Including changes in scheduling, test duration, planned testing effort, or deviations from the approved budget
- **Forecast**
  Tests and testing activities that are planned for the next reporting period
- **Overall assessment**
  A (subjective) evaluation of the achieved degree of confidence in the test object

For example, a complex project with multiple stakeholders or a project that is subject to regulatory scrutiny will require reports that are more detailed and precise than those required for updating a small, non-critical mobile app. Agile projects produce regular test progress reports in the form of task boards, defect backlogs, and burndown charts that are discussed in daily standup meetings (see [URL: ISTQB], Foundation Level Agile Tester).

The contents of test reports need to be tailored to the needs of their recipients. The amount and type of data a report contains can vary a lot depending on whether its readers have technical or financial backgrounds. A report for presentation to a project steering committee will be different from one that is presented to the development team. The latter is more likely to contain detailed information about types of defects or test content, whereas the former will contain more detail on budget usage, overall test progress, and the current product quality from the end-user's point of view.

Adapt test reports to the target group

6.4 Defect Management

If you want to correct defects reliably, you need a well-thought-out system for recording, communicating, and managing the defects, faults, and other issues that testing reveals. All the activities that this comprises make up the process known as defect management.[22]

A defect management process consists of agreements and rules that define exactly how each defect report is structured, and a workflow that determines who is responsible for dealing with them and when. The pro-

Define the workflow for registering and processing incidents and defects

---

22. The defect management process is often also referred to as the issue management process, as it is used to retain an overview of all open issues. However, not every issue is caused by a developer error. "Issue management" also sounds less like it is laying blame!

cess begins with the creation of a report and ends when the reported issue is solved.

The content, scope, and stringency of the process vary from company to company, but it is crucial that everyone involved (designers, developers, testers, product owner, and so on) all adhere strictly to the process once it has been defined.

A defect report should be created every time a new failure becomes known (for example, when a user calls the hotline with an issue) or a previously unknown fault is discovered (for example, a programmer discovers an inconsistency in a requirement). Usually though, the starting point is a test result originating from a planned test execution.

6.4.1 Evaluating Test Reports

The result of every systematically performed test run is a test (execution) log[23].

This documents (per test case and/or testing step) the actual behavior observed during the test, the expected behavior, and any deviations between the two[24].

Analyzing test reports

When analyzing a defect report[25], you have to decide which of the deviations between expected and actual behavior constitutes a defect. This is a yes/no classification, and you need to watch out for the following cases and potential misclassifications[26]:

- **True positive**
  The test object is faulty and the test case correctly reports a deviation between the expected and actual behaviors. The test result is classed as "failed"[27], or "red"[28].

---

23. Dynamic tests produce "test logs", whereas the outcomes produced by static tests (such as code analysis and reviews) are often called "analysis reports" or "review minutes". The issues revealed by static tests (and especially reviews) are usually only documented in the corresponding protocols (such as the minutes of a review meeting) and no separate defect reports are created for each issue.
24. For automated tests, the test tool makes this comparison and records the results automatically.
25. These analysis tasks apply to test reports and analysis reports.
26. The problem of misclassifications is well known in a medical context: When tested for a certain illness, a patient tests "positive" if the illness is confirmed or "negative" if the patient is healthy. Analogously, a software test case acts as a binary classifier that—relating to a specific feature—classes a test object as "failed" or "passed" (see [URL: binClassifiers]).
27. The test object itself "failed", but the test case produced a "positive" result (i.e., it detected a failure).
28. Test tools usually flag such test cases "red".

- **False negative**
The test object is faulty but none of the test cases reveals this. This may be because the corresponding test data combination was left out of the test case design or wasn't executed during the test run. It may also be because the corresponding test case doesn't exist, or the fault in question cannot be revealed on the current test level or using the current testing technique.

- **False positive**
Analysis reveals that the test object behaves correctly but the test case still flags a deviation between the expected and actual behaviors. This may be due to an outdated or badly designed test case, an incorrectly configured test object, badly implemented test automation, or incorrect test execution on the part of the tester.

- **True negative**
The test object behaves correctly with regard to the corresponding test case and the test case confirms that *expected = actual* behavior. The test case is classed as "passed" or "green".

Figure 6-3 illustrates these four cases:

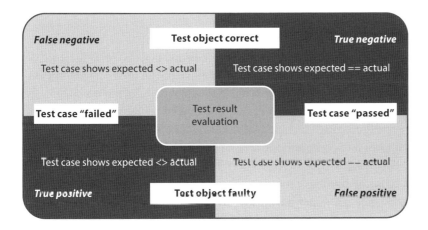

Fig. 6-3
True and false test results

If the issue is due to the test object[29] (i.e., a "true positive") a corresponding defect report is created. If the defect has already been reported, this may be a duplicate. You then have to check whether the new report provides new

---

29. If the issue is caused by the tester, a defect report can help to kick-start further analysis. Such a report is then addressed to the testers rather than the developers.

insights that enable you to further narrow down the issue and its causes. If this is the case the original report has to be updated accordingly and, to avoid multiple reports of a single defect, no new report is created.

In the case of a "false positive", this can be due to a defect in another part of the system or in the system environment. For example, a test case may fail because a network connection goes down or some other timeout kicks in. The resulting behavior is thus not due to the test object itself, even if the failure appears there. In cases like this the tester should, if possible, assign the issue to the causal component[30] in order to minimize the number of false positive findings.

If in doubt make a report

Time will often be too tight to decide which of the four cases listed above applies to each entry in a defect report, especially where you suspect "false negative" or "false positive" results. In these cases, you will often have to perform additional subsequent analysis, and it is often preferable to create a defect report in order to ensure that this analysis isn't overlooked.

This is also true for any other significant unexpected event that occurs during testing—for example, a symptom that infers a faulty test object but that isn't explicitly addressed by a test case.

6.4.2 Creating a Defect Report

A development project will usually have a central defect database for recording and managing all issues, incidents, defects, or failures that are discovered in the course of testing and use of the product. As previously mentioned, defect reports can relate to any kind of issue in a system or its components, as well as errors, faults, or gaps in the requirements, technical specifications, user manuals, or other documentation. Such reports serve to inform and communicate among all project participants.[31]

Report defects but don't attempt to analyze them

Creating a new defect report has nothing to do with establishing its cause or finding a solution. This happens later and is handled by the responsible developer who performs appropriate debugging.

A defect report has to describe the observed effect and its context, including any other side effects it has on the user or other parts of the

---

30. This component is then "true positive" and may require reworking. Alternatively, you can remedy the situation by adding appropriate exception handling to the test object.
31. The following explanations assume that defect reports and the defect management process serve internal project communication (unlike a user support ticket system). However, any data relevant to the development team that arises from user tickets needs to be appropriately linked to the projects defect database.

system. A defect report must be precise but brief so that the responsible developer can quickly understand and reproduce the situation with a minimum of effort[32] and find a solution as quickly as possible.

To keep these lines of communication running smoothly and to enable statistical report analysis, every report has to be made according to a strictly defined project-wide template.

Standardized reporting template

Alongside a description of the issue itself, a defect report typically contains additional information that identifies the software being tested, the test environment, the tester's name, some kind of defect classification, and any other information that helps to localize and reproduce the issue.

The *VSR-II* team decided to use the same basic defect reporting template workflow from the predecessor *VSR* project, as this proved useful and reliable. Table 6-1 illustrates the basic reporting template:

Case Study: The VSR-II defect reporting template

Table 6-1 Defect report template

Attribute	What it means
ID	Unique, sequential number
Title	Title and a short summary of the issue in question
Date	Date and (if necessary) the time of the initial report
Author	The person or organization issuing the report
References	
Test object	Name of the test object / test item / configuration item
Version	The exact version of the test object
Platform	Identifiers for the hardware and software and/or test environment in which the problem occurs
Test case	Reference to the test case that revealed the problem
Requirement	Reference to the (customer) requirement that is infringed or not fulfilled because of the defect
Cross references	Cross references to other related reports

→

---

32. Reproducing, localizing, and correcting a problem usually involves additional, unplanned work for a developer. In this kind of situation, developers tend to see vaguely worded defect reports as unwarranted and often simply reject or defer them.

Attribute	What it means
Classification	
Status	Processing progress[33], preferably with comments and the date of the change of status
Class	Classification of the problem's severity and/or its impact on stakeholder interests
Priority	Classification of correction urgency[34]
Root Cause	If possible, the project phase in which the original error or mistake was made (analysis, design, coding). This aids process improvement.
Discovery	The phase of the development lifecycle during which the defect was first observed
Problem description	
Test steps	Description of the (test) steps taken (or a reference to the corresponding test case) that trigger the defect
Expected behavior	Description of the expected component behavior
Actual behavior	Reproducible description of the observed behavior: The failure and fault (if known), including protocols, database dumps, screenshots, and so on (if available or to be produced if considered helpful)
History	
Measures taken	Correction measures taken, and other measures such as workarounds or actions that localize or isolate the issue
Comments	Comments from affected persons on report contents—for example, the extent to which other parts of the system are affected by the issue
Miscellaneous	Conclusions, recommendations
Approval	Completed approvals, if necessary with notes about limitations

ISO 29119, Part 3 contains another sample defect reporting template[35] [ISO 29119].

Tailoring

How a defect, issue, or incident reporting template actually looks will vary from project to project. The test manager or QA lead for the project has to create a template together with all those concerned. Some of the factors that influence the template are the lifecycle development model in use, the number and size of the team(s) involved, the context and criticality of the system being tested, the number and types of test levels, and the need for and purpose of any statistical evaluation. Smaller projects can do without many of the attributes listed above, and any attributes that are never evaluated should be left out anyway.

---

33. See section 6.4.4
34. See section 6.4.3
35. Further references to additional reporting attributes can be found in [IEEE 1044].

- When setting up or improving the testing process, one of the first things you should concentrate on is designing and implementing a disciplined defect management process. To do this, it is essential to select, install, and configure an appropriate defect management tool (see section 7.1.1). The configuration should give all project participants access rights appropriate to their roles within the team.

- Defect management tools can automatically set reporting attributes (for example, automatic numbering or author identification) or check their validity. Most tools also offer configurable user roles (such as tester, or test manager) and defect management workflows. Once configured, the tool can automatically check that the workflow is adhered to.

Our Tip
Using defect management tools

It is important to ensure that the recorded information enables fast reproduction of the failure and the localization of potential causative faults, as well as process status indicators and statistical metrics (see section 6.4.5).

Document all information relevant to reproducibility and fault correction

6.4.3 Classifying Failures and Defects

The correction of defects is managed via the reports in the defect database (see section 6.4.4). The urgency of correcting any particular fault depends on how seriously it affects the product's users. There is a big difference between unsolved failures that cause system crashes and defects that document simple visual issues in the interface layout. Defects that significantly impair (or even prevent) use of the product obviously have to be dealt with first.

The "degree of impairment of product use" can be quantified by labeling the defect with a severity class. Table 6-2 shows a sample:

Side Note:
Classing defects

Table 6-2
Defect severity

Class	What it means
1	System crash, possibly with a loss of data; test object is unusable in this state
2	Critical functionality or requirement ignored or incorrectly implemented; test object can only be used in severely limited form
3	Functional deviation or limitation (a "normal" defect); requirement incorrectly or only partially implemented; system can be used in restricted form
4	Minor deviations; system can be used normally
5	Visual defects (for example, spelling or layout error); system can be used without limitations

Prioritize fault correction

The severity of an issue alone does not determine the urgency of correcting the underlying fault. Factors affecting these kinds of decision include input from project or product management (for example, the estimated correction effort), test-related requirements (for example, whether the defect in question is blocking other tests), and release and update planning requirements.

The urgency attached to correcting a fault therefore has to be classified using an additional "priority" attribute.

Case Study:
The VSR-II fault correction priorities

Because the defect reporting template and the defect management tool introduced and used by the team for the original *VSR* project are the same as those in *VSR-II*, so they have been directly adopted in the new version. The defect priority scheme looks like this:

Table 6-3
Fault correction priority

Priority	What it means
1 – Patch	The problem has to be addressed immediately (if necessary temporarily) using a patch
2 – Next release	The correction will be implemented in the next regular release or the next (internal) test object version
3 – Non-urgent	The correction will take place when the affected system components are due for revision anyway
4 – Open	Correction not yet planned

6.4.4 Defect Status Tracking

Alongside effective defect management, the test manager also has to verify that any corrections made adequately remedy the faults that cause the recorded defects.

This requires continuous end-to-end monitoring of the defect analysis and correction process, from discovery and registration to the finished solution. An issue can also be "solved" by accepting the limitations that the fault causes, either until it is corrected or accepted permanently.

Monitoring is tracked using a "status" attribute and rules that determine which changes of status are possible and/or permissible. Table 6-4 shows a sample defect status template.

Status (set by)	What it means
New (Tester)	New defect report created. The author has provided a meaningful description and classification.
Open (Test manager)	New defect reports are regularly monitored by the test manager and checked for comprehensibility and complete allocation of attributes. Attributes are modified if necessary to comply with the project-wide workflow. Duplicate or unjustified reports are rejected. The defect is then flagged "open" and is assigned to a developer.
Rejected (Test manager)	A defect report is obviously incorrect, is a duplicate, or is classed as unwarranted (not a fault in the test object, but instead a request for change that is disregarded)
Analysis (Developer)	The responsible developer set this status once the issue has been analyzed. The results (the fault, its causes, proposed solutions, estimated correction effort, and so on) are documented in the comments.
Observation (Developer)	The issue can be neither reproduced nor dismissed. The defect remains open until further information/insights are available.
Correction (Project manager)	The analysis convinces the project manager to order a correction. The responsible developer performs the correction and documents the type of work done.
Test (Developer)	The developer sets the status to "test" once the problem is solved (from the developer's viewpoint). The status includes the product version number that contains the correction.
Done (Tester)	Issues with "test" status are tested during the next testing cycle. The test that revealed the fault is repeated alongside other tests if necessary. If the confirmation test verifies that the defect has been corrected, the tester sets the defect status to "done".
Flop (Tester)	If the confirmation test finds that the correction wasn't successful, the status changes to "flop". Further analysis is required.

Table 6-4
Defect status template

Figure 6-4 visualizes the potential changes in status and the corresponding workflow.

Fig. 6-4
Defect status model

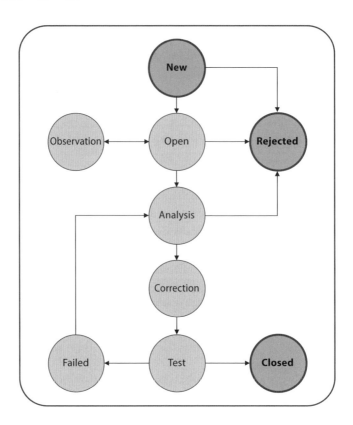

Our Tip
Only a tester can set status to "done"

■ It is essential that only the tester is allowed to set the defect status to "done", and only once a confirmation test has verified that the issue described in the defect report no longer occurs. If the correction causes new side effects, these have to be documented in new defect reports and are then handled separately.

Decision-making processes and bodies

The template shown above can be used for a wide range of projects, provided that the existing (or necessary) decision-making processes are adequately represented. This may require adjustments to the model. While the decisions made in the model described above all lie with individuals, in larger projects the same decisions are often made by panels or committees. This makes the decision-making process more complex as they involve representatives of multiple interests.

> A "Change Control Board" (or CCB) is a typical body that makes decisions regarding the implementation of corrections and changes to the product. The members of a CCB usually represent product management, project management, test management, and often the customer too.
>
> CCBs are necessary because decisions on whether a defect report is "warranted" or not and how much effort should be used to correct defects are usually discretionary. Every such decision has to be made from the point of view of "normal" product and feature planning.

Side Note: Change Control Board (CCB)

6.4.5 Evaluation and Reporting

Test and project management can evaluate the defect database to provide an overview of the current state of defect correction and the resulting product quality.[36]

Test management uses evaluation results and defect-based metrics to adapt the test plan (for example, to add tests for particularly fault-prone components, or for confirmation tests for corrected components), but also as a basis for conclusions and recommendations relating to product approval and release.

Input for test and project management

Project management uses correction progress reports to judge whether the planned release schedule is still valid or whether a release needs to be postponed. As well as localizing faults, determining how many failures have been found, checking how many of these have been corrected and how many issues are still open, trend analysis is an important part of the report evaluation process too. Trend analysis provides an estimate of how many defects are likely to be reported in future and helps to evaluate whether the number of defects is increasing or the incidence curve is flattening out.

Defect report data can also be used to improve test coverage. For example, a comparison of the data for different test objects may show a test object with relatively few defects—this could, however, be due not to more careful programing, but rather to missing test cases.

Tips for improving test coverage

This data can also provide input and ideas for general process improvement. For example, if it turns out that a large number of defects are caused by misunderstood requirements, you can use this finding as a good reason to initiate measures for improving the requirements engineering process.

Input for process improvement

---

36. The reports provided by defect management tools are usually configurable. This helps to focus reports on the needs of the project at hand and to filter out unnecessary data.

> *Case Study:*
> *Extended exit criteria for the VSR-II system test*
>
> The exit criteria for the V*SR-II* system test need to reflect testing progress and the current level of product quality. The test manager extends the exit criteria accordingly to include the following defect-based metrics:
>
> - All Class 1 defects are "done"
> - All defects with "patch" priority are "done"
> - The number of "new" defect reports per week is stagnating or decreasing

6.5 Configuration Management

A software system comprises a large number of individual components that have to work perfectly together if the complete system is to function properly. In the course of development, each of these components exists in new, corrected, or improved versions. For large projects, multiple development and testing teams work in parallel, making it difficult to retain an overview of the current version of each component and which versions belong together.

Typical symptoms of inadequate configuration management

If a project's configuration management (CM) is inadequately handled, the following issues can result:

- Because simultaneous access to the files is not managed, developers overwrite each other's changes to source code or other documents.
- Integration is hampered because multiple versions of components exist and it is not clear which versions work together and can be integrated to form larger modules. Similar issues can occur if developers use differing versions of compilers or other development tools.
- Defect analysis and correction or regression testing are hampered because it is not obvious where and why a component's source code has been modified, or which file is the source of a particular integrated component.
- Tests and test evaluation are impeded because it isn't clear which test cases relate to which version of a test object or which version of a test object produced which test results.

The test process requires CM

Inadequate configuration management can have various negative effects on the development and testing processes. For example, test results can quickly become meaningless if it isn't clear whether all the test objects on a particular test level are in the current version. Effective testing is impossible without reliable configuration management, so CM has to fulfill the following test-related requirements:

- Test objects, test cases, and test data must all be treated as configuration objects within the configuration management system.

- For every configuration object, you must be able to catalog, save, and retrieve all the available versions (1.0, 1.1, and so on). This version management data must also include documentation that details why any changes were made.

- Configuration management is based on effective version management. You have to be able to identify and retrieve the correct version of all the files that together make up a certain configuration.

- To support tracking of changes and corrections, defect reports should be linked to the configuration objects that are affected by the defect report.

CM requirements

To check the effectiveness of your configuration management it makes sense to perform occasional configuration audits. An audit checks that all relevant components are entered in the CM system and whether all configurations have been correctly identified.

The *VSR-II* user-interface modules are available in multiple languages (such as German, English, or French) and have to run on a variety of hardware and software platforms. Individual modules have to be compatible with specific versions of other components (for example, the *ConnectedCar* module has to be compatible with its opposite number in the vehicle, which can vary depending on the model and the year it was manufactured). Furthermore, data from various sources (such as product catalogs, price lists, and contract data) have to be imported at regular intervals, and their contents and formats can change during the system's lifecycle. The *VSR* configuration management must ensure that development and testing take place using consistently valid product configurations. The same is also true for productive use of the software by end-users

Case Study: Configuration Management for VSR-II

The CM process and the required CM tools will vary from project to project. In order to fulfill all the requirements listed above, you need to define a configuration management plan tailored to the project at hand. [IEEE 828] is one example of a widely used configuration management planning standard.

Side Note:
Standards and norms

6.6 Relevant Standards and Norms

These days there are a great number of standards in use in software development. These define various constraints as well as the technological "state of the art". The standards and norms mentioned in the course if this book demonstrate just how embedded such standards are, especially when it comes to software quality management and testing.

A quality or test manager's tasks therefore also include identifying the standards and legal guidelines that are relevant to the product (product norms) or the project (process norms), and making sure they are adhered to. Potential sources of standards include:

- **Company standards**
  Manufacturer's (and sometimes the customer's) internal guidelines and procedural directives, such as quality management manuals, test frameworks, or coding guidelines.
- **Best Practices**
  Non-standardized but proven techniques and procedures that reflect the technological state of the art in a particular field of application.
- **Quality management standards**
  Cross-industry standards that specify minimum process requirements without defining implementation guidelines. For example, [ISO 9000] suggests that appropriate (interim) checks are always performed during production processes (in this case software development) without actually stipulating when and how.
- **Industry-sector standards**
  Sector-specific standards (for example [EN 60601] for medical products, [RTC-DO 178B] for aeronautic software, or [EN 50128] for railroad signaling systems) that define a minimum scope for tests to be performed for a specific category of product or field of application.
- **Software testing standards**
  Product-independent process standards that define how to perform software testing professionally. The most important of these in the context of this book is [ISO 29119].

Alignment to such standards (see also the list of standards and norms in Appendix C.3) can be useful even in situations where it is not mandatory. If a project should ever find itself in legal difficulties, it can be very important to be able to prove that development was performed in compliance with appropriate standards.

6.7 Summary

- In principle, development and testing activities should remain separate with regard to staff and organization. The clearer this distinction, the more effective testing will be.
- In agile project environments, this separation of activities is relinquished in favor of close, cross-functional cooperation within the team. Test effectiveness then has to be retained through strict use of suitable testing techniques and test automation.
- Testing tasks and roles need to be assigned to people with appropriate specialist skills. As well as technical skills, testers should have comprehensive soft skills too.
- As well as overall strategic test planning, a test manager's tasks also include operational planning, monitoring, and control for each individual test cycles.
- The test manager describes the testing strategy (objectives, tasks, tools, and so on) in the test plan. The international [ISO 29119] standard provides a reference testing strategy template.
- Faults and defects overlooked by testing can cause significant additional costs. A testing strategy has to strike the best possible compromise between the cost of testing, the available resources, and the potential costs of insufficient testing.
- Tests are prioritized to ensure that less important tests are discarded in the case of a lack of appropriate testing resources.
- "Risk" is one of the best criteria to use to prioritize tests. Risk-based testing uses information about identified risks to plan and control all aspects of the testing process. All significant elements of the testing strategy are defined using a risk-related basis.
- Measurable exit criteria provide an objective way to judge when testing is complete. A lack of clear exit criteria increases the risk of testing being terminated randomly.
- The defect and configuration management processes form the bedrock of an efficient testing process.
- Defect reports have to be recorded using a unified, project-wide template and must be tracked through all stages of the subsequent analysis and correction processes.

Side Note ■ Standards and norms contain requirements and recommendations for the professional application of software testing procedures. Aligning your testing processes to these kinds of guidelines is a good idea, even if they are not mandatory for the current project.

7 Test Tools

This chapter provides an overview of the various types of tools that can be used to support software testing activities. We look at what these tools are capable of, and how to select and introduce the ones that are best suited to your particular project.

Test tools[1] are used to support single or multiple software testing activities (see section 2.3) and a wide range of purposes:

- **Increase testing efficiency** *Uses of test tools*
  Manual test activities, and especially those that have to be repeated regularly or are generally time-consuming, can benefit from the use of appropriate tools—for example, automated static code analysis or automated dynamic testing.
- **Increase test quality**
  Tool-based test case management helps you to manage large numbers of test cases and retain an overview of your work. Tools help to eliminate duplicate test cases and reveal gaps in the selected test case suites, which helps to keep your testing activities consistent.
- **Increase testing reliability**
  Automating manual test activities increases overall testing reliability—for example, when comparing the expected vs. actual values of large amounts of data or when repeating identical test sequences.
- **Make some tests possible**
  The use of tools makes it possible to perform tests that cannot be executed manually. These include performance and load tests, or testing real-time systems.

Some tools support only a single task while others cover multiple tasks. *Tool suites*
There are also complete tool suites that can be used to manage the entire testing process, from test management through test design to test auto-

---

1. Sometimes referred to as CAST (Computer Aided Software Testing) tools, similarly to CASE (Computer Aided Software Engineering) tools.

Test framework

mation, execution, documentation, and evaluation. Such suites are often marketed as "Application Lifecycle Management" (ALM) tools.

"Test framework" is another familiar term in the context of test tools, and is usually used to mean one of the following:

- Reusable and extensible program libraries that are used to build test tools or test environments
- The type of methodology used to automate testing (for example, data-driven or keyword-driven, see section 7.1.4)
- The entire test execution process

7.1 Types of Test Tools

Tool types

We can differentiate between various types (or classes) of test tools depending on the phase of the testing process you are involved in (see section 2.3) and the type of task you want to automate. Types of test tools are also subdivided into specialized categories[2] for use with specific platforms or fields of application (for example, performance testing tools for web applications).

You will rarely need to use the whole spectrum of test tools in the course of a single project, but it is nevertheless useful to know what is available so you can make informed decisions about what you need when the time comes.

The following sections describe the basic functionality of different types of test tools.

7.1.1 Test Management Tools

Test management

Test management tools offer ways to register, catalog, and manage test cases and their priorities. They also enable you to monitor the status of test cases—in other words, you can record and evaluate whether, when, or how often a test has been performed and the results it delivered (pass/fail).

They help test managers to plan and manage hundreds or thousands of test cases. Some tools also support project management tasks within the testing process (such as resource planning and scheduling).

Today's test management tools support requirements-based testing too, with requirements either entered directly or imported from a require-

---

2. A list of common test tools and providers organized according to tool types is available online at [URL: Tool List].

ments management tool. Once imported, every requirement can then be linked to the test cases that test whether it has been fully and correctly implemented. The following example illustrates the process.

The team working on the *VSR-II DreamCar* module uses epics to describe its functionality [URL: Epic]. The *vehicle configuration and price calculation* functionality is described by the following epic:

Case Study: Requirements-based testing for the VSR-II DreamCar module

- Epic: *DreamCar – Vehicle configuration and price calculation*

    The user can configure a vehicle (model, color, extras, and so on) on a screen. The system displays all available models and equipment variants and displays the corresponding list price in real time. This functionality is implemented in the *VSR-II DreamCar* module.

The detail of the epic is filled out with user stories. The following user stories are assigned to the *DreamCar* epic:

- User Story: Select vehicle model
    - The system displays all available base models
    - The user can select one of the displayed base models
- User Story: Configure vehicle
    - The system displays all available options for the selected base model (equipment options, special editions, extras)
    - The user can select the desired options (for example, *red pearl* effect paint, the *OutRun* sports package, the *OverDrive* music system, and the *Don'tCare* autopilot system). Options that are generally available but not for the current configuration are grayed out.
- User Story: Calculate vehicle price
    - The list price for the selected base model and configuration options is calculated and displayed

To check whether a user story has been correctly and fully implemented, the team defines corresponding test cases and links them to the corresponding user story using a test management tool. The test cases defined for the *configure vehicle* user story are as follows:

- *Test Case*: Base model with one option
- *Test Case*: Base model with multiple options
- *Test Case*: Base model with non-selectable option
- *Test Case*: Base model with equipment package option
- *Test Case*: Base model with no options

Requirements Management	Requirements management tools save and manage all kinds of data relating to requirements. They also enable you to prioritize requirements and track their implementation status.

These are not test tools in the narrow sense but are nevertheless very useful when it comes to deriving and planning requirements-based tests (see section 3.5.3)—for example, based on the implementation status of individual requirements. Most requirements management tools can swap data with test management tools, which can then create links between requirements, test cases, test results, and defect reports.

Traceability

This in turn enables full traceability (see section 2.3.8) for every defect or defect report (solved or unsolved), the relevant requirements, and with regard to which test cases have been executed. The verification and validation status for every requirement is then fully transparent, so requirements that have been incorrectly implemented or overlooked (i.e., not covered by any test cases), or those with gaps in their specifications can be easily identified.

Defect management

Defect management tools are a must for every test manager. As described in section 6.4, these tools register, manage, distribute, and statistically evaluate reported defects. High-end defect management tools include parameterizable defect status models and enable you to specify the entire process, from discovery of a defect through correction to regression testing. This way, the tool can guide everyone involved through the defect management process.

Configuration management

Configuration management tools too are not test tools in a strict sense (see section 6.5). What they do is enable you to manage multiple versions and configurations of the software being tested, including different version of test cases, test data, and other product and test documentation. This makes it easier to determine which results from a test sequence were produced by which version of a test object.

Continuous Integration

In agile and iterative/incremental projects, integration and integration testing of modified components are usually highly automated. As soon as a block of code is checked in to the integration environment, all of the necessary integration steps and test processes are performed completely automatically (see also [Linz 14, section 5.5]). This process is called continuous integration. Tools that control and perform this process are called continuous integration (CI) tools.

Tool integration

Test management tools require high-performance interfaces to a range of other tools. These include:

- A general export interface for converting data into a format that is generally readable for other teams and company departments (for example, in a spreadsheet).
- An interface to the requirements management tools for importing requirements or linking them bi-directionally. This enables requirements-based test planning and traceability of the relationships between requirements and test cases. Ideally, the test status of every requirement can then be tracked by the users of test management and requirements management tools (see section 2.3.8).
- An interface between test management and test execution tools (test robots) for the provision of scripts and starting automated testing. The results are automatically returned and archived.
- An interface between test management and defect management enables seamless confirmation test planning (i.e., a list of the tests that are necessary to verify which defects have been corrected in a specific version of a test object).
- Test management tools can be linked to continuous integration (CI) tools so that tests planned using the test management tool can be executed as part of the CI process.
- Code files can be flagged with version numbers in the configuration management tool. A test management tool that can read such data can then link test cases or defect reports to the corresponding files and file versions.

Test management and defect management tools usually offer comprehensive analysis and reporting functionality and can, to an extent, generate test documentation (test schedule, test specifications, test summary report, and so on). The format and content of such documentation is usually configurable.

Generating test summary reports and test documentation

Test data can be evaluated quantitatively in a variety of ways. For example, you can analyze how many test cases have been run and how many of those were successful, or the frequency with which a particular class of defect is identified (see section 6.4.3). These kinds of data help to judge and manage overall testing progress (see section 6.3).

7.1.2 Test Specification Tools

To ensure that a test case is reproducible, the individual testing steps, the test data, and the corresponding pre-and postconditions have to be defined and recorded (see section 2.3). Most test management tools offer templates or familiar notations to support the creation of consistently structured test cases. These include keyword- or interaction-based notations, as well as the generally accepted notations used in behavior-driven development (BDD, see [URL: BDD]) and acceptance test-driven development (ATDD, see [URL: ATDD]). While keyword-based testing using tables to list test cases, the BDD and ATDD methodologies use a text-based notation that is similar to natural language. These notations are explained in more detail in [Linz 14, section 6.4.3].

Test and test data generators

Regardless of the notation used to record a test case, the tester has to specify the test data it uses. Test (data) generators can be used to determine and generate appropriate test data. According to [Fewster 99] there are various approaches to test data generation that depend on the basis from which the test data are derived:

- **Database-based test data generators** use database structures or contents to generate or filter appropriate test data. The same approach can be applied to generating test data from files of various formats.

- **Code-based test data generators** analyze the test object's source code. The downside of this approach is that it cannot effectively derive expected behaviors (which requires a test oracle). As with all white-box testing techniques, only existing code can be used and defects caused by missing statements remain undiscovered. Logically, using code as a basis for generating test cases that are used to test the same code (i.e., the code "tests itself") doesn't make much sense and is not an effective testing technique.

- **Interface-based test data generators** analyze the test object's interface, identify its parameter range and use techniques such as boundary value analysis and equivalence partitioning (see sections 5.1.1 and 5.1.2) to derive test cases. These tools work with various types of interfaces, and can analyze application programming interfaces (APIs) or graphical user interfaces (GUIs). The tool identifies the types of data fields present in a mask (numerical date/time, or similar) and generates test data that cover the corresponding value ranges. These tools, too, cannot derive expected behaviors but are ideal for generating robustness tests (i.e., testing whether rather than how a test object reacts).

- **Specification-based test data generators** derive test data and the corresponding expected behaviors from project specifications, but only if the specifications are available in a formal notation. For example, a method call sequence specified using a UML sequence diagram. This approach is known as model-based testing (MBT). The UML model is created using an appropriate tool and is imported by the test generator, which then creates test scripts that are handed over to a test tool for execution.

However, don't expect miracles from these kinds of tools. Specifying tests is demanding work that requires comprehensive knowledge of the test object coupled with creativity and intuition. A test data generation tool can apply certain rules (such as boundary value analysis) to create tests systematically, but cannot judge which of those test cases is good or bad, important or irrelevant. This kind of creative/analytical work has to be done by a human tester, and the test object's expected behaviors usually have to be defined manually too.

A tester's creativity is irreplaceable

7.1.3 Static Test Tools

Static tests and analyses (such as reviews) can generally be performed on documents with any kind of structure, but tool-based static analysis relies on documents having as formal a structure as possible. For source code, the structure is prescribed by the syntax of the programming language, while formal specifications or models are governed by the syntax of the modeling language you use (UML, for example).

There are also tools designed to investigate informal documents written in natural language, which can, for example, check spelling, grammar, or readability. These, too, are classed as static analysis tools.

What all these tools have in common is that they do not analyze executable code. Static testing tools can therefore help to identify faults and inconsistencies at an early stage in a project (see the left-hand branch of the V-model in figure 3-2) or during early iterations in the development cycle. Identifying faults immediately or at least early on prevents the occurrence of follow-on defects and thus saves time and money overall.

Review support tools

Reviews are structured, manual checks performed according to the buddy principle ("two pairs of eyes are better than one"—see also section 4.3). Review support tools aid the planning, execution, and evaluation of reviews. They are used to manage information related to planned and past review meetings, participants, findings, and results. Verification aids such as checklists can be managed and provided online. Information collected during reviews can be evaluated and compared to estimate the overall effort involved and to plan subsequent reviews. Comparing review results also helps to bring weaknesses in the development process into the open, where they can be more effectively combated.

Review support tools are especially useful in projects being developed by multiple teams located in different countries or time zones. In such cases, online reviews are not only useful, but may also be the only really practicable solution.

Static analysis

Static analysis tools provide figures relating to various aspects of the code—for example, cyclomatic complexity[3] or other code metrics. This kind of data can be used to identify particularly complex, error-prone (i.e., risky) blocks of code that can then be reviewed in more detail separately and manually.

Such tools can also be used to check that coding guidelines are adhered to (for example guidelines that support code security or code portability aspects). Checking HTML code for broken or invalid links is also a form of static analysis.

Our Tip
Increase analytical detail step by step

■ Static analysis tools list all "suspicious" places in the code, and such lists of findings can quickly become very long indeed. Most tools offer functionality for defining the scope and detail of the analysis. We recommend using a setting that keeps the number of findings small for an initial analysis, and you can always refine your settings later. These kinds of tools are only accepted if they are set up specifically to suit the project at hand.

---

3. See [URL: McCabe].

Side Note:
Analyzing data use

Data flow analysis is a good example of a static analytical technique. The aim of the process is to analyze data usage along its path(s) through the program code. Findings detected by this kind of tool are called "data flow anomalies" (or just "anomalies"). An anomaly is an inconsistency that can but doesn't necessarily cause a failure. Anomalies need to be flagged as risks.

Examples for data flow anomalies are when a variable is referred to although it hasn't been initialized or a reference to a variable without a value. The following three states of a variable need to be distinguished here:

- **defined (d):** the variable is assigned a value
- **referenced (r):** the variable's value is referenced
- **undefined (u):** the variable has no defined value

Three types of data flow anomalies can be distinguished:

Data flow anomalies

- **ur anomaly**
  An undefined variable value (*u*) is read on a path (*r*)
- **du anomaly**
  The variable has a value (*d*) that becomes invalid (*u*) without having been used in the meantime
- **dd anomaly**
  The variable receives a second value (*d*) on a program path without having used the first value (*d*)

Example of anomalies

The following examples illustrate data flow anomalies using a C++ code fragment. The function in question is designed to swap the integer parameters Max and Min using the variable Help if the value of Min is greater than that of Max:

```
void Swap (int& Min, int& Max) {
    int Help;
    if (Min > Max) {
    Max = Help;
    Max = Min;
    Help = Min;
    }
}
```

Analyzing the variables' usage reveals the following anomalies:

- **ur anomaly** for the variable Help
  The variable is only valid within the function and is first used on the right-hand side of an assignment. At this point it is referenced although its value has not been defined. The variable wasn't initialized when it was declared (this kind of anomaly can be identified by most compilers if you set an appropriately high warning level).

- **dd anomaly** for the variable `Max`
  The variable is used twice consecutively on the left-hand side of an assignment, and is thus assigned two values. Either the first assignment can be ignored or use of the first value (before the second assignment) has been overlooked.
- **du anomaly** for the variable `Help`
  The final statement assigns a value to the variable Help that cannot be used because the variable is only valid within the function.

Data flow anomalies are not usually obvious

The anomalies in our examples are obvious. However, don't forget that—in "real-life code"—any number of other assignments using other variables could take place between the ones shown above, making the anomalies much more difficult to identify and easy to overlook during a review. Using a data flow analysis tool will give you a better chance of discovering anomalies like these.

Not every anomaly causes a failure. For example, a *du* anomaly won't always have a direct effect, and the program can continue to run. Nevertheless, we need to ask why the assignment occurs at this point before the variable's validity ends. It is always worth taking a closer look at the parts of a program that show anomalies, and you will usually find further inconsistencies if you do.

Model checkers

Like source code, specifications can be analyzed for certain attributes too, provided that they are written using some kind of formal modeling language or notation. Tools that do this job are called "model checkers". They "read" the structure of a model while checking static attributes such as missing states, missing state transitions, and other inconsistencies. The specification-based test generators discussed in section 7.1.2 are often add-ons to static model checkers. This type of tool is particularly useful for developer-side test case generation.

7.1.4 Tools for Automating Dynamic Tests

Tools take over repetitious testing tasks

People who refer to "test tools" are often actually referring to the tools used to automate dynamic testing. These are tools that relieve testers of repetitious "mechanical" testing tasks such as providing a test object with test data, recording the test object's reactions, and logging the test process.

Probe effects

In most cases, these tools run on the same hardware as the test object, what can definitely influence the test object's behavior. For example, the actual response times of the tested application or the overall memory usage may be different when executing the test object and the test tool in parallel, and therefore the test results may differ too. Accordingly, you need to take such interactions—often called "probe effects"—into account when evaluating your test results. Because they are connected to the test object's test interface, the nature of these types of tools varies a lot depending on the test level they are used on.

Tools that are designed to address test objects via their APIs are called unit test frameworks. They are used mainly for component and integration testing (see sections 3.4.1 and 3.4.2) or for a number of special system testing tasks (see section 3.4.3). A unit test framework is usually tailored to a specific programming language.

Unit test frameworks

JUnit is a good example of a unit test framework for use with the Java programming language, and many others are available online ([URL: xUnit]). Unit test frameworks are also the foundation of test-driven development (TDD, see section 3.4.1).

If the test object's user interface serves as the test interface, you can use so-called test robots. Which are also known as "capture and replay" tools (for obvious reasons!). During a session, the tool captures all manual user operations (keystrokes and mouse actions) that the tester performs and saves them in a script.

System testing using test robots

Running the script enables you to automatically repeat the same test as often as you like. This principle appears simple and extremely useful but does have some drawbacks, which we will go into in the next section.

How Capture/Replay Tools Work

In capture mode, the tool records all keystrokes and mouse actions, including the position and the operations it sets in motion (such as clicked buttons). It also records the attributes required to identify the object (name, type, color, label, x/y coordinates, and so on).

Capture

To check whether the program behaves correctly, you can record expected/actual behavior comparisons, either during capture or later during script post-processing. This enables you to verify the test object's functional characteristics (such as field values or the contents of a pop-up message) and also the layout-related characteristics of graphical elements (such as the color, position, or size of a button).

Expected/actual comparison

The resulting script can then be replayed as often as you like. If the values diverge during an expected/actual comparison, the test fails and the robot logs a corresponding message. This ability to automatically compare expected and actual behaviors makes capture/replay tools ideal for automating regression testing.

Replay

One common drawback occurs if extensions or alterations to the program alter the test object's GUI between tests. In this case, an older script will no longer match the current version of the GUI and may halt or abort unexpectedly. Today's capture/replay tools usually use attributes rather than x/y coordinates to identify objects, so they are quite good at recognizing objects in the GUI, even if buttons have been moved between versions. This capability is called "GUI object mapping" or "smart imaging technology" and test tool manufacturers are constantly improving it.

Test programming

Capture/replay scripts are usually recorded using scripting languages similar to or based on common programming languages (such as Java), and offer the same building blocks (statements, loops, procedures, and so on). This makes it possible to implement quite complex test sequences by coding new scripts or editing scripts you have already recorded. You will usually have to edit your scripts anyway, as even the most sophisticated GUI object mapping functionality rarely delivers a regression test-capable script at the first attempt. The following example illustrates the situation:

Case Study: Automated testing for the VSR-II ContractBase module

The tests for the *VSR-II ContractBase* module are designed to check whether vehicle purchase contracts are correctly saved and also retrievable. In the course of test automation, the tester records the following operating sequence:

```
Switch to the "contract data" form;
Enter customer data for person "Smith";
Set a checkpoint;
Save the "Smith" contract in the database;
Leave the "contract data" form;
Reenter the form and load the "Smith"
contract from the database;
Check the contents of the form against the checkpoint;
```

If the comparison delivers a match, we can assume that the system saves contracts correctly. However, the script stalls when the tester re-runs it. So what is the problem?

Is the script regression test-ready?

During the second run, the script stalls because the contract has already been saved in the database. A second attempt to save it then produces the following message:

```
"Contract already saved.
  Overwrite: Yes/No?"
```

The test object then waits for keyboard input but, because the script doesn't contain such a keystroke, the script halts.

The two test runs have different preconditions. The script assumes that the contract has not yet been saved to the database, so the captured script is not regression test-capable. To work around this issue, we either have to program multiple cases to cover the different states or simply delete the contract as a "cleanup" action for this particular test case.

The example illustrates a good example of the necessity to review and edit a script. You therefore need programming skills to create this kind of automated test. Furthermore, if you aim to produce automation solutions with a long lifecycle, you also need to use a suitable modular architecture for your test scripts.

Using a predefined structure for your scripts helps to save time and effort when it comes to automating and maintaining individual tests. A well-structured automation architecture also helps to divide the work reasonably between test automators and test specialists (see section 6.1.2) *Test automation architectures*

You will often find that a particular script is repeated regularly using varying test data sets. For instance, in the example above, the test needs to be run for other customers too, not just Ms. Smith.

One obvious way to produce a clear structure and reduce effort is to separate the test data from the scripts. Test data are usually saved in a spreadsheet that includes the expected results. The script reads a data set, runs the test, and repeats the cycle for each subsequent data set. If you require additional test cases, all you have to do is add a line to the spreadsheet while the script remains unchanged. Using this method—called "data-driven testing"—even testers with no programming skills can add and maintain test cases. *Data-driven test automation*

Comprehensive test automation often requires certain test procedures to be repeated multiple times. For example, if the *ContractBase* component needs to be tested for pre-owned vehicle purchases as well as new vehicle purchases, it would be ideal if the same script can be used for both scenarios. Such re-use is possible if you encapsulate the appropriate steps in a procedure (in our case, called something like *check_contract(customer)*). You can then call and re-use the procedure from within as many test sequences as you like.

If you apply an appropriate degree of granularity and choose your procedure names carefully, the set of names or keywords you choose reflect the actions and objects from your application domain (in our case, actions and objects such as *select(customer)*, *save(contract)*, or *submit_order(vehicle)*). This methodology is known as command-driven or keyword-driven testing. *Keyword-driven test automation*

As with data-driven testing, the test cases composed from the keywords and the test data are often saved in spreadsheets, so test specialists who have no programming skills can easily work on them.

To make such tests executable by a test automation robot, each keyword also has to be implemented by a corresponding script using the test robot's programming language. This type of programming is best performed by experienced testers, developers, or test automation specialists.

Keyword-driven testing isn't easily scalable, and long lists of keywords and complex test sequences quickly make the spreadsheet tables unwieldy. Dependencies between individual actions or actions and their parameters, are difficult to track and the effort involved in maintaining the tables quickly becomes disproportionate to the benefits they offer.

Side Note: tools supporting data-driven and keyword-driven testing

Advanced test management tools offer database-supported data-driven and keyword-driven testing. For example, test case definitions can include test data variables, while the corresponding test data values are stored and managed (as test data rows) within the tool's database. During test execution the tool automatically substitutes the test data variables with concrete test data values. In a similar way, keywords can be dragged and dropped from the tool's keyword repository to create new test sequences, and the corresponding test data are loaded automatically, regardless of their complexity. If a keyword is altered, all affected test cases are identified by the tool, which significantly reduces the effort involved in test maintenance.

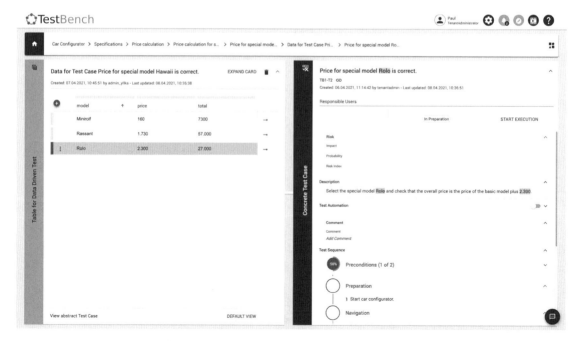

Fig. 7-1 *Data-driven testing using TestBench [URL: TestBench CS]*

Comparators Comparators are tools that compare expected and actual test results. They can process commonly used file and database formats and are designed to identify discrepancies between expected and actual data. Test robots usually have built-in comparison functionality that works with console content, GUI objects, or copies of screen contents. Such tools usually have filter functionality that enables you to bypass data that isn't relevant to the current comparison. This is necessary, for example, if the file or screen content being tested includes date or time data, as these vary from test run to test run. Comparing differing timestamps would, of course, raise an unwanted flag.

Dynamic analysis Dynamic analysis tools provide additional information on the software's internal state during dynamic testing—for example, memory allocation, memory leaks, pointer assignment, pointer arithmetic[4], and so on).

Coverage analysis Coverage (or "code coverage") tools provide metrics relating to structural coverage during testing (see section 5.2). To do this, a special "instrumentation" component in the code coverage tool inserts measuring instructions into the test object before testing begins. If an instruction is triggered during testing, the corresponding place in the code is marked as "covered". Once testing is completed, the log is analyzed to provide overall coverage statistics. Most coverage tools provide simple coverage metrics, such as statement or decision coverage (see sections 5.2.1 and 5.2.2). When interpreting coverage data, it is important to remember that different tools deliver differing results, or that a single metric can be defined differently from tool to tool.

Debuggers Although they are not strictly test tools, debuggers enable you to run through a program line by line, halt execution wherever you want, and set and read variables at will.

Debuggers are primarily analysis tools used by developers to reproduce failures and analyze their causes. Debuggers can be useful for forcing specific test situations that would otherwise be too complicated to reproduce. They can also be used as interfaces for component testing.

---

4. Many programming languages use "pointers" to enable direct access to specific memory addresses. Pointers are extremely error-prone and therefore play a significant role in dynamic testing.

7.1.5 Load and Performance Testing Tools

Load and performance tests are necessary when a system has to execute large numbers of parallel requests or transactions (load), whereby predefined maximum response times (performance) are not to be exceeded. Real-time systems, most client/server systems, and web-based or cloud-based systems have to fulfill these kinds of requirements.

Measuring response times

Performance tests verify how response times change with increasing load (for example, with increasing numbers of parallel user requests) and determine the point at which a system is overloaded and no longer responds quickly enough. Performance testing tools provide testers with comprehensive logs, reports, and graphs that illustrate the changing relationship between performance and load, and provide indications of where performance bottlenecks might occur. If it becomes apparent that the system is likely to underperform under everyday loads, you will need to tune the system accordingly (for example, by adding hardware or tweaking performance-critical software).

Load and performance testing tools have to perform two tasks: generating synthetic load (database queries, user transactions, or network traffic) and measuring, logging, and visualizing the test object's performance under these loads. Performance can be measured and evaluated in various ways, such as response times, storage requirements, network traffic, and similar. The corresponding "sensors" are called monitors.

The effects of intrusive measurement

The use of the load and performance test tool or the associated monitor can be "intrusive", i.e. the tool can influence the actual result of the test: The test object's (timing) behavior can vary depending on how measurements are taken and the type of monitor in use. In other words, the entire process is subject to a certain "examination effect"[5] that you have to take into account when interpreting the results. Experience is essential when using load and performance testing tools and evaluating the results.

---

5. Dynamic analysis tools can have intrusive effects too. For example, coverage metrics can be directly affected by the use of a code coverage tool.

7.1.6 Tool-Based Support for Other Kinds of Tests

Tools are also available to check for security vulnerabilities[6] that could be used to gain unauthorized access to a system. Anti-virus apps and firewalls belong to this category of tool, as they produce logs that can be used to identify security flaws. Tests that reveal such flaws or check whether they have been remedied are generally called (IT) security tests.

System access and data security

Projects that replace outdated systems with new ones usually involve the migration or conversion of large amounts of data. System testing then necessarily involves testing data integrity before and after conversion or migration. Tools supporting this kind of testing can check whether the data sets are correct and complete, or whether they satisfy certain syntactic or semantic rules or conditions.

Evaluating data quality

Various aspects of data quality are important to the *VSR-II* project:

Case Study: VSR-II data quality

- The *DreamCar* module displays various vehicle model and equipment variants. Even if the *DreamCar* module is working correctly, missing or incorrect data can produce failures from the user's point of view. For example, a particular model cannot be configured or non-deliverable combinations of options can be configured. In cases like this, a customer may look forward to purchasing a vehicle that isn't actually available.

- Dealers use the *NoRisk* module to provide appropriate insurance. If some of the data are outdated—such as the vehicle's collision damage rating—the system is likely to calculate an incorrect premium. If insurance is too expensive, the customer might opt to search for a cheaper policy online rather than buying insurance directly from the dealer.

- Dealers use the *ContractBase* module to manage all historical customer data, including purchase contracts and all repair work. For example, in Germany the sums involved are all displayed in Euros regardless of whether the invoice is dated before or after the currency switch from Deutschmarks to Euros in 2002. Were all the records converted correctly at the time, or did the customer really pay so little for a repair back then?

- As part of regular sales promotions, dealers send out special offers and promotions to regular customers. Customer addresses and data relating to the age and model of the customer's current vehicle are saved in the system. However, customers will only receive fully tailored advertising if all the data sets are correct and consistent. Does *VSR-II* prevent data collection errors such as zip

---

6. The *Open Web Application Security Project* (OWASP, [URL: OWASP]) publishes a catalog of potential security vulnerabilities that require security testing in web applications.

codes that don't match street names? Does the system automatically ensure that all marketing-related attributes are filled out (such as the purchase date and age of a pre-owned vehicle)? Does the system check that customers have agreed to receive advertising?

The customer records saved in the *ContractBase* module contain a lot of personal data. The *ConnectedCar* module's functions also enable the dealer or the manufacturer to look up private data, such as the vehicle's current position, routes taken, driver behavior, accidents, and so on. The collection, saving and use of such data is subject to appropriate data-protection regulations (such as the European DSGVO, [URL: DSGVO]). The system test therefore has to verify that *VSR-II* complies with all the relevant laws and other stipulations. Furthermore, these tests must not be performed using the original customer data! They can only be performed using anonymized or fictional data, which requires the use of specialist tools to generate appropriate test data sets.

These examples show that data quality is primarily the responsibility of the system operator and/or user. However, the system's manufacturer is definitely involved in supporting data quality—for example, by supplying fault-free data conversion software, meaningful input consistency and plausibility checks, legally watertight data usage, and other similar measures.

Other tools   In addition to the types of tools discussed above, there are also tools available for performing other, more specialized tasks—for example:

- **Usability** and general accessibility testing to make sure all users are catered for
- **Localization** tests check whether an application and its GUI have been translated completely and correctly into the local language
- **Portability** tests verify that an application or system runs properly on all its supported platforms

7.2 Benefits and Risks of Test Automation

Software automation tool selection, purchase, and maintenance costs money, while acquiring appropriate hardware and training staff to use them uses further resources. The cost of rolling out a complex tool to a large number of workstations can quickly run into six figures. As with any other investment, the planned amortization period of a new testing tool is a critical point when deciding whether to go ahead with a rollout.

7.2 Benefits and Risks of Test Automation

In the case of tools that automate test execution (test robots), it is relatively simple to estimate the savings compared with running tests manually. The effort involved in programing automated tests has to be subtracted from these savings, so a cost-benefit analysis usually delivers a negative result after a single test run. It is only once you have performed multiple automated regression test runs (see figure 7-2) that you really begin to save money with each test execution cycle.

Cost-benefit analysis

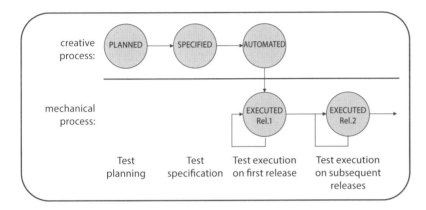

Fig. 7-2
Test case lifecycle

The balance becomes positive following a number of regression test runs, although it is still tricky to accurately estimate the amortization period. You will only effectively cover your costs if you can program test cases that are regression test-capable. If this is the case, a capture/replay tool can begin to make real savings after just three test cycles. However, this kind of calculation only makes sense if manual testing is a real alternative. Many tests (for example, performance tests) cannot be performed manually anyway.

However, evaluating testing effort only doesn't tell the whole story. You need to consider how a tool increases overall testing effectiveness too—for example, when more failures are revealed and thus corrected. In the medium term, this can reduce the development, support, and maintenance costs of a project, providing a much more attractive potential for overall cost savings.

Evaluate the influence on overall testing effectiveness

To summarize, the potential benefits are:

Potential benefits of introducing a test tool

- Tools cannot replace the creative side of testing, but they can support it. Using tools creates better test cases and test data, and increases the overall effectiveness of the testing process.

- Automation reduces testing effort (or increases the number of test cases that can be performed using the same amount of effort). However, using more test cases doesn't automatically equate to better testing.
- Tools simplify the collection, evaluation and communication of data relating to test progress, achieved coverage, and failures and their distribution among the test objects. These data help you to paint an objective picture of the quality of the software being tested.

Potential risks of introducing tools

Introducing new tools into the testing process also involves risks. These include:

- The expectations attached to a tool can be unrealistic.
- It is all too easy to underestimate the time it takes and the costs involved in introducing a tool. The effort involved in using the new tool can be underestimated too.
- A tool cannot be used effectively (or cannot be used at all) because a defined testing process is either not established or, if it exists, not well practiced.
- The improvements and changes in the testing process required to realize the tool's potential are more extensive than anticipated.
- The effort involved in maintenance and version control for test cases, test data, and other test documents is greater than expected.
- Using the tool in situations where manual testing is simpler and more economical.
- The new tool does not work well enough with existing tools.
- A tool's manufacturer goes out of business or no longer supports the product.
- The open source project developing the tool is discontinued.
- New versions of a tool no longer support older technology that is still used in the system being tested.
- Tool support is poor or is no longer provided.

7.3 Using Test Tools Effectively

7.3.1 Basic Considerations and Principles

Some of the tools listed above (such as comparators or coverage analyzers) are already built into several operating systems (Linux, for example), enabling testers to perform basic testing using "onboard" tools. However, built-in tools often have fairly limited functionality, so you will usually need additional, specialized tools to test effectively.

As described above, there is a broad range of tools available that support all testing activities—from the creative act of planning and specifying test cases to the test drivers and test robots that offer the purely mechanical assistance involved in automating testing processes.

If you are thinking about acquiring test tools, test drivers or test robots shouldn't be your first (or only) choice. The effectiveness of tool support depends a lot on the specific project environment and the maturity of the development and test processes. In poorly organized projects where "on-demand programming" is the order of the day, documentation is unheard of, and testing is either poorly structured or simply doesn't happen, there is no point in automating the testing process. Even the best tools cannot replace a non-existent or sloppy process. To quote [Fewster 99, p. 11]: "It is far better to improve the effectiveness of testing first than to improve the efficiency of poor testing. Automating chaos just gives faster chaos".

"Automating chaos just gives faster chaos"

In such situations, you need to sort out your manual testing processes first. In other words, you need to define, implement, and breathe life into a systematic testing process before you consider using tools to improve productivity or increase product quality.

Only automate well-organized test processes

- Try to stick to the following sequence of tool types when introducing test tools:
  - Defect management
  - Configuration management
  - Test planning
  - Test execution
  - Test specification

Our Tip
Introduce tools in sequence

Don't forget the learning curve

You also need to consider the time it takes for your team to learn how to use new tools. The learning curve involved can cause a drop in productivity in the initial transitional phase, making it extremely risky to introduce new tools in the hope of using "a little automation" to bridge staffing gaps in high-stress development phases.

7.3.2 Tool Selection

Once you have decided which test tasks you want to automate, you can begin the tool selection process. Because the cost of investing in a new tool can be very high (see above), you need to plan the process carefully. The tool selection process comprise five steps:

1. Specify the requirements for the planned usage
2. Research and creation of a list of suitable candidates
3. Demos and trials
4. Create a shortlist based on your requirements
5. Proof of Concept

Selection criteria

In *Step 1*, the following criteria influence requirements specification:

- Compatibility with the targeted test objects
- Tester know-how regarding the selected tool and/or the test task it supports
- Simplicity of integration into the existing development and test environment
- Potential integration with other existing (test) tools
- The platform the tool is due to run on
- Manufacturer support, reliability, and reputation
- Benefits and drawbacks of the available licensing options (for example, commercial vs. open-source, purchase vs. subscription)
- Price and cost of maintenance

These and other criteria need to be listed and prioritized. Deal-breaker (i.e., essential) criteria need to be flagged as such[7].

---

7. A sample catalog of selection criteria is available for download at [URL: imbus-downloads].

The next step is to compile a list of the available tools in each category that includes a description of each. You can then check out the best-sounding choices in-house or have the manufacturer demonstrate them. These experiments and demos usually make it fairly obvious which products work best for you and which manufacturers offer the best service. The most appropriate tools are then put on a shortlist and you need to answer the following questions for the shortlisted products:

Market research and shortlisting

- Is the tool compatible with your test objects and your existing development environment?
- Do the attributes that got the tool onto the shortlist function as required in real-world situations?
- Can the manufacturer provide professional-grade support for standard and non-standard queries?

7.3.3 Pilot Project

Once you have made a selection, you have to roll out your new tool. This is usually done within the context of a pilot project in order to verify the tool's usefulness in a real-world, project-based situation. A pilot project should be led and implemented by persons who were not involved in the tool selection and evaluation process, as this can lead to unintentional bias.

Pilot usage should provide additional technical data and practical experience in using the new tool in the planned environment. This should demonstrate where training is necessary and where you need to make changes to the testing process. You can also establish or update guidelines for a broader-based rollout (for example, naming conventions for files and test cases or test design rules). If you are rolling out test drivers or test robots, you should decide whether it makes sense to plan and build a library of test cases for re-use in different projects.

Pilot usage

If you are piloting tools that collect and evaluate metrics, you need to consider which metrics really are relevant to the project and to what extent the tool supports the collection of this kind of data. The tool may need to be configured appropriately to ensure that the desired metrics are captured, recorded, and processed correctly.

7.3.4 Success Factors During Rollout and Use

If the pilot project confirms your expectations, you can begin the project-wide and/or company-wide rollout. A rollout requires broad-based acceptance, as a new tool always generates extra work for its users. The following are factors that are important for a successful rollout:

- A large-scale rollout needs to be performed gradually
- Tool usage has to be firmly embedded in the relevant processes
- Make sure you offer relevant user training and coaching
- Always provide usage guidelines and recommendations for the new tool
- Collect user experience and make it available to everyone in the form of a FAQ or a "Tips and Tricks" document
- Offer support via in-house user groups, tool experts, and similar
- Continually track and evaluate the tool's acceptance levels and usefulness

Testing without tools is inefficient

This chapter has discussed the difficulties and additional effort involved in selecting and implementing tools that support various aspects of the testing process. We hope you are not now thinking that using additional tools is not worth the effort! In fact, the opposite is true—testing without tool-based support is basically impossible, especially in large-scale projects. However, you must always plan tool rollouts very carefully if you want to avoid your investment turning into a dud that just ends up gathering dust.

7.4 Summary

- For each phase in the testing process, tools are available to help testers perform their work more efficiently, reliably, or at a higher quality level. Some tasks, such as load and performance testing, can only be performed satisfactorily with tool-based support.
- Component and integration testing tools are squarely aimed at developers. These include unit test frameworks, test-driven development (TDD) frameworks, continuous integration (CI) tools, static analysis tools, and dynamic analysis (code coverage) tools.
- Test tools only provide benefits if the testing process itself is mastered and runs in a well-defined manner.
- The introduction of a new test tool can involve significant investment, so the tool selection process has to be conducted carefully and transparently.
- The potential benefits of tools are offset by risks that can cause tool usage to fail.
- A tool rollout must be appropriately supported, with training and information events for the future users. Information and trainings help to ensure acceptance and thus the regular use of the tool.
- The tool selection and implementation process consists of the following steps: tool selection, pilot project, rollout, permanent user support.

Appendices

A Important Notes on the Syllabus and the Certified Tester Exam

This is the fifth English-language edition of our reference book on Software Testing and is based on the sixth (2019) edition of our original German-language textbook. It thus covers the latest 2018 version of the ISTQB® *Certified Tester Foundation Level* syllabus.

The international English-language syllabi are published by the ISTQB® [URL: ISTQB]. Translations in other languages may be published additionally by ISTQB® national member boards.

Exams are based on the version of the corresponding national local-language syllabus that is current when the exam is taken. Exams are offered and monitored directly by each national board or by specially commissioned certification bodies. For a list of all national member boards and for more details on the current syllabus edition and exams, see [URL: ISTQB].

For didactical reasons, some of the contents of this book are arranged in a different order to the contents of the syllabus. The scope of the individual chapters does not provide an indication of the subject matter's relevance to the examination process. The book goes into plenty of detail and illustrates the subject matter with examples where necessary. Passages that go beyond the contents of the syllabus are marked as Side Notes. **The exams themselves are always based on the current version of the official syllabus.**

We recommend that readers who use this book to prepare for an ISTQB® exam study the syllabus and the official ISTQB® glossary, as these are the exclusive basis for the exam.

■ To help you prepare for the exam, the ISTQB® provides sample exam questions (including answers and explanations) and an Exam FAQ-list.

Our Tip
Sample exam questions

B Glossary

This glossary covers software testing terms as well as additional software engineering terms related to software testing. Terms not listed in the ISTQB® glossary are <u>underlined</u>, and additions to the ISTQB® definitions are printed in italics.

The definitions of most of the following terms are taken from the "Standard Glossary of Terms used in Software Testing" Version 3.5 (2020), produced by the International Software Testing Qualifications Board (ISTQB) Glossary Working Group. You can find the current version of the glossary here: [URL: ISTQB Glossary]. The ISTQB® glossary itself refers to further sources of definitions.

acceptance testing

A test level that focuses on determining whether to accept the system.

This test may be

1. *A test performed from the user's viewpoint*
2. *A partial set of an existing test, which must be passed, and an entry criterion (start criterion) for the test object to be accepted into a specific test level*

actual result

The behavior produced/observed when a component or system is tested.

alpha testing

A type of acceptance testing performed in the developer's test environment by staff with roles outside the development organization.

<u>analytical quality assurance</u>

Diagnostic based measures (for example, testing) to measure or evaluate the quality of a product.

anomaly

Any condition that deviates from expectations based on requirements specifications, design documents, user documents, standards, etc. or from someone's perception or experience. Anomalies may be found during review, testing, analysis, compilation, or use of software products or applicable documentation, and in other situations too.

[IEEE 1044] Also called bug, defect, deviation, error, fault, failure, incident, problem.

atomic condition

A condition that does not contain logical operators.

audit

An independent examination of a work product or process performed by a third party to assess whether it complies with specifications, standards, contractual agreements, or other criteria.

back-to-back testing

Testing to compare two or more variants of a test item or a simulation model of the same test item by executing the same test cases on all variants and comparing the results.

bespoke software

See *customer-specific software*.

beta testing

A type of acceptance testing performed at a site external to the developer's test environment by roles positioned outside the development organization.

With beta testing, a kind of external acceptance testing is executed in order to get feedback from the market and in order to create interest at potential customers. It is performed before the final release. Beta testing is often used when the number of potential production environments is large.

black-box test techniques

A test technique based on an analysis of the specification of a component or system.

blocked test case

A test case that cannot be executed because the preconditions for its execution cannot be fulfilled.

boundary value

A minimum or maximum value of an ordered equivalence partition.

boundary value analysis

A black-box test technique in which test cases are designed based on boundary values.

boundary value coverage

The coverage of boundary values.

branch

A transfer of control from a decision point.

The expression branch is used as follows:

- When a component uses a conditional change of the control flow from one statement to another (for example, in an IF statement)
- When a component uses a nonconditional change of the control flow from one statement to another, with the exception of the next statement (for example, using GOTO statements)
- When the change of control flow takes place through more than one entry point of a component. An entry point is either the first statement of a component or any statement that can be directly reached from outside of the component.

A branch corresponds to a directed connection (arrow) in the control flow graph.

branch condition combination testing / condition combination testing / multiple-condition testing

A white-box test technique in which test cases are designed to exercise outcome combinations of atomic conditions.

branch condition testing

See *decision condition testing*.

branch coverage

The coverage of branches.

branch testing

A control flow-based white box test technique that requires executing all branches of the control flow graph in the test object.

bug

See *defect*.

Business process-based testing

An approach to testing in which test cases are designed based on descriptions and/or knowledge of business processes.

capture/playback tool (capture-and-replay tool)

A type of test execution tool where inputs are recorded during manual testing in order to generate automated test scripts that can be executed later (i.e., replayed). These tools are often used to support automated regression testing.

cause-effect diagram

A graphical representation used to organize and display the interrelationships of various possible root causes of a problem. Possible causes of a real or potential defect or failure are organized in categories and subcategories in a horizontal tree structure, with the (potential) defect or failure as the root node.

cause-effect graph

A graphical representation of logical relationships between inputs (causes) and their associated outputs (effects).

cause-effect graphing

A black-box test technique in which test cases are designed from cause-effect graphs.

change

Rewrite or new development of a released development product (document, source code).

change order

Order or permission to perform a change in a development product.

change request

1. Written request or proposal to perform a specific change for a development product or to allow it to be implemented
2. A request to change a software artifact due to a change in requirements

class test

Test of one or several classes of an object-oriented system.

See also *component testing*.

code-based testing

See *structural test(ing)* and *white-box test technique*.

commercial off-the-shelf (COTS)

A type of product developed in an identical format for a large number of customers in the general market. *Also called standard software.*

comparator

A tool that performs automated comparisons of actual results with expected results.

complete testing

See *exhaustive testing*.

component

A part of a system that can be tested in isolation.

component integration testing

Testing in which the test items are interfaces and interactions between integrated components.

component testing

A test level that focuses on individual hardware or software components.

configuration

1. The composition of a component or system as defined by the number, nature, and interconnections of its constituent parts
2. State of the environment of a test object which must be fulfilled as a precondition for executing test cases.

configuration item

An aggregation of work products that is designated for configuration management and treated as a single entity in the configuration management process.

configuration management

A discipline applying technical and administrative direction and surveillance to identifying and documenting the functional and physical characteristics of a configuration item, controlling changes to those characteristics, recording and reporting change processing and implementation status, and verifying that it complies with the specified requirements.

constructive quality assurance

The use of methods, tools, and guidelines that contribute to making sure the following conditions are met:

- The product to be produced and/or the production process have certain a priori attributes
- Errors and mistakes are minimized or prevented

control flow

The sequence in which operations are performed by a business process, component, or system.

Often represented in graphical form, see control flow graph.

control flow anomaly

Statically detectable anomaly found during execution of a test object (for example, statements that aren't reachable).

control flow-based testing

A white-box test technique in which test cases are designed based on control flows.

control flow graph

- A graphical representation of all possible sequences of events (paths) through a component or system during execution
- A formal definition: A directed graph G = (N, E, nstart, nfinal). N is the finite set of nodes. E is the set of directed branches. nstart is the start node. nfinal is the end node. Control flow graphs are used to show the control flow in a component.

coverage

The degree to which specified coverage items have been determined or have been exercised by a test suite, expressed as a percentage. *Coverage can usually be found by using tools.*

customer-specific software

Also called *bespoke software*. Software developed specifically for a single customer or a group of customers. As opposed to standard or commercial off-the-shelf (COTS) software.

cyclomatic complexity

The maximum number of linear, independent paths through a program.

data flow analysis

A type of static analysis based on the lifecycle of variables.

data flow anomaly

Unintended or unexpected sequence of operations on a variable.

data flow coverage

The percentage of definition-use pairs that have been executed by a test suite.

data flow test techniques

White-box test techniques in which test cases are designed using data flow analysis and where test completeness is assessed using the achieved data flow coverage.

data quality

The degree to which data in an IT system is complete, up-to-date, consistent, and (syntactically and semantically) correct.

dead code

See *unreachable code*.

debugger tool

A tool used by programmers to reproduce failures, investigate the state of programs, and find the corresponding defect. Debuggers enable programmers to execute programs step by step, to halt a program at any program statement, and to set and examine program variables.

debugging

The process of finding, analyzing, and removing the causes of failures in software.

decision coverage

The coverage of decision outcomes.

decision table

A table showing rules that consist of combinations of inputs and/or stimuli (causes) with their associated outputs and/or actions (effects). These tables can be used to design test cases.

decision table testing

A black-box test technique in which test cases are designed to exercise the combinations of conditions and the resulting actions shown in a decision table.

decision testing / decision condition testing

A white-box test technique in which test cases are designed to execute condition outcomes and decision outcomes.

Control flow-based white box test technique requiring that each decision outcome (TRUE and FALSE) is used at least once for the test object. (An IF statement has two outcomes; a CASE or SWITCH statement has as many outcomes as given.)

defect

An imperfection or deficiency in a work product that does not meet its requirements or specifications.

defect database

1. List of all known defects in the system, a component, and their associated documents as well as their states
2. A current and complete list with information about known failures

Defect Detection Percentage (DDP) / Fault Detection Percentage (FDP)

The number of defects found by a test level, divided by the number found by that test level and any other means afterwards.

defect management

The process of recognizing, recording, classifying, investigating, resolving and disposing of defects.

defect masking

A situation in which one defect prevents the detection of another.

developer test

A test that is under the (sole) responsibility of the developer of the test object (or the development team). Often considered equivalent to a component test.

development model

See *software development model*.

driver

A temporary component or tool that replaces another component and controls or calls a test item in isolation.

dummy

A custom program, usually with restricted functionality, that replaces the real program during testing.

dynamic analysis

The process of evaluating a component or system based on its behavior during execution.

dynamic testing

Testing that involves the execution of the test item.

The opposite is static testing. Taken together, static and dynamic testing form the entire testing oeuvre.

efficiency

The degree to which resources are expended in relation to results achieved.

A set of software characteristics (for example, execution speed, response time) relating to performance of the software and use of resources (for example, memory) under stated conditions (normally increasing load).

equivalence class

See *equivalence partition*.

equivalence partition

A subset of the value domain of a variable within a component or system in which all values are expected to be treated the same based on the specification.

equivalence partition coverage

The coverage of equivalence partitions.

equivalence partitioning

A black-box test technique in which test cases are designed to exercise equivalence partitions by using one representative member of each partition.

error

A human action that produces an incorrect result.

Also a general, informally used term for terms like mistake, fault, defect, bug, failure.

error guessing

A test technique in which tests are derived on the basis of the tester's knowledge of past failures, or general knowledge of failure modes.

exception handling

Behavior of a component or system in response to incorrect input, either from a human user or another component or system, or due to an internal failure.

exhaustive testing

A test approach in which the test suite comprises all combinations of input values and preconditions.

Usually this is not practically achievable.

exit criteria

The set of conditions for officially completing a defined task.

The purpose of exit criteria is to prevent a task from being considered completed when there are still outstanding parts of the task that have not been finished. Achieving a certain degree of test coverage for a white-box test technique is an example of an exit criterion.

expected result

The observable predicted behavior of a test item under specified conditions based on its test basis.

exploratory testing

An approach to testing whereby the testers dynamically design and execute tests based on their knowledge, on exploration of the test item, and on the results of previous tests.

Extreme Programming (XP)

A software engineering methodology used within agile software development. Its core practices are: programming in pairs, doing extensive code review, unit testing of all code, and simplicity and clarity in code.

facilitator

see *moderator*.

failure

An event in which a component or system does not perform a required function within specified limits.

failure class / failure classification / failure taxonomy

Classification of found failures according to their severity from a user point of view (for example, the degree of impairment of product use).

failure priority

Determination of the urgency of correcting the cause of a failure by taking into account failure severity, necessary correction work, and the effects on the entire development and test process.

fault

An alternative term for *defect*.

fault masking

A fault in the test object is compensated by one or more faults in other parts of the test object in such a way that it does not cause a failure. (Note: Such faults may then cause failures after other faults have been corrected.)

fault-revealing test case

A test case that, when executed, leads to a different result than the specified or expected one.

fault tolerance

The degree to which a component or system operates as intended despite the presence of hardware or software faults.

field testing

A type of testing conducted to evaluate the system behavior under productive connectivity conditions in the field.

Also a test to check market acceptance.

See also *beta testing*.

finite state machine

A computation model consisting of a limited number of states and state transitions, usually with corresponding actions. Also known as *state machine*.

functional requirement

A requirement that specifies a function that a component or system must perform.

See also *functionality*.

functional testing

Testing performed to evaluate if a component or system satisfies functional requirements.

functionality

The capability of the software product to provide functions that meet stated and implied needs when the software is used under specified conditions. Functionality describes WHAT the system must do. Implementation of functionality is the precondition for the system to be usable in the first place.

GUI

Graphical User Interface.

incident database

A collection of information about incidents, usually implemented as a database. An incident database is designed to make it possible to follow up incidents and extract data about them.

informal review

A type of review that does not follow a defined process and has no formally documented output.

inspection

A type of formal review for identifying issues in a work product., Provides measures that help improve the review process and the software development process.

instruction

See *statement*.

instrumentation

The insertion of additional logging or counting code into the source code of a test object (by a tool) in order to collect information about program behavior during execution (e.g., for measuring code coverage).

integration

The process of combining components or systems into larger assemblies.

integration testing

A test level that focuses on interactions between components or systems.

high-level test case / logical test case

A test case with abstract preconditions, input data, expected results, postconditions, and actions (where applicable).

level test plan

A test plan that typically addresses one test level.

load testing

A type of performance testing conducted to evaluate the behavior of a component or system under varying loads, usually between anticipated conditions of low, typical, and peak usage.

low-level test case / concrete test case

A test case with concrete values for preconditions, input data, expected results and postconditions and detailed description of actions (where applicable).

maintainability

The degree to which a component or system can be modified by the intended maintainers.

maintenance / maintenance process

The process of modifying a component or system after delivery to correct defects, improve quality characteristics, or adapt to a changed environment.

management review

A systematic evaluation of software acquisition, supply, development, operation, or maintenance processes performed by or on behalf of management. A management review monitors progress, determines the status of plans and schedules, confirms requirements and their system allocation, or evaluates the effectiveness of management approaches to achieve fitness for purpose.

A review evaluating project plans and development processes.

master test plan

A test plan that is used to coordinate multiple test levels or test types.

A master test plan may comprise all testing activities on the project; further detail of particular test activities could be defined in one or more test sub-process plans.

metric

1. A measurement scale and the method used for measurement
2. A value gained from measuring a certain program or component attribute. Finding metrics is a task for static analysis.

milestone

Marks a point in time in a project or process at which a defined result should be ready.

mistake

See *error*.

mock-up / mock / mock object

A program in the test environment that takes the place of a stub or dummy but contains additional functionality. This makes it possible to trigger desired results or behavior.

moderator / facilitator

1. The person responsible for running review meetings
2. The person who conducts a usability test session

modified condition / decision coverage (MC/DC)

The coverage of all outcomes of the atomic conditions that independently affect the overall decision outcome.

modified condition / decision testing

A white-box test technique in which test cases are designed to exercise outcomes of atomic conditions that independently affect a decision outcome.

module testing

See *component testing*.

monitoring tool / monitor

A software tool or hardware device that runs concurrently with the component or system under test and supervises, records and/or analyzes the behavior of the component or system.

negative testing

1. Testing a component or system in a way it was not intended to be used.
2. *Usually a functional test case with inputs that are not allowed (according to the specification). The test object should react in a robust way—for example, by rejecting the values and executing appropriate exception handling.*
3. *Testing aimed at showing that a component or system does not work—for example, a test with incorrect input values. Negative testing is related to a tester's attitude rather than a specific test approach or test design technique.*

non-functional requirement

A requirement that does not directly relate to functionality but rather to how well or at what level of quality the system fulfills its function. Its implementation has significant influence on how satisfied the customer or user is with the system.

The corresponding attributes (from [ISO 25010]) are performance efficiency, compatibility, usability, reliability, security, maintainability, and portability.

non-functional testing

Testing performed to evaluate whether a component or system complies with non-functional requirements.

patch

1. A modification made directly to an object's code without modifying the source code or reassembling or recompiling the source program
2. A modification made to a source program as a last-minute fix or as an afterthought
3. Any modification to a source or object program
4. To perform a modification as described in the preceding three definitions
5. Unplanned release of a software product with corrected files to correct specific (often blocking) faults, often as a preliminary or "stop-gap" fix.

path

A sequence of consecutive edges in a directed graph.

path coverage

The coverage of paths.

path testing

A white-box test technique in which test cases are designed to execute paths in a control flow graph.

performance

The degree to which a system or component accomplishes its designated functions within given constraints regarding processing time and throughput rate. Called performance efficiency In [ISO 25010].

performance testing

Testing to determine the performance efficiency of a component or system.

performance testing tool

A test tool that generates load for a designated test item and that measures and records its performance during test execution.

Point of Control (PoC)

Interface used to send test data to the test object.

Point of Observation (PoO)

Interface used to observe and log the reactions and outputs of the test object.

postcondition

The expected state of a test item and its environment following test case execution.

precondition

The required state of a test item and its environment prior to test case execution.

preventive software quality assurance

Use of methods, tools, and procedures that contribute to designing quality into the product. As a result of their application, the product should then have certain desired characteristics, and faults are prevented or their effects minimized.

Note: Preventive (constructive) software quality assurance is often used in the early stages of software development. Many defects can be avoided if software is developed in a thorough and systematic manner.

probe effect

An unintended change in behavior of a component or system caused by measuring it.

process model

A framework in which processes of the same nature are classified into an overall model.

product risk

A risk impacting the quality of a product.

production environment

The hardware and software products, and software with data content (including operating systems, database management systems and other applications) that are in use at a specific user site.

This environment is the place where the test object will be operated or used.

project risk

A risk that impacts project success.

quality

The degree to which a component or system satisfies the stated and implied needs of its various stakeholders.

quality assurance (QA)

The degree to which a component or system satisfies the stated and implied needs of its various stakeholders.

quality characteristic

A category of quality attributes that bears on work product quality.

quality management

Coordinated activities to direct and control an organization with regard to quality that include establishing a quality policy and quality objectives, quality planning, quality control, quality assurance, and quality improvement.

random testing

A black-box test technique in which test cases are designed by generating random independent inputs to match an operational profile

regression testing

A type of change-related testing to detect whether defects have been introduced or uncovered in unchanged areas of the software.

release

A particular version of a configuration item that is made available for a specific purpose, such as a test release or a production release.

reliability

The degree to which a component or system performs specified functions under specified conditions for a specified period of time.

requirement

1. A provision that contains criteria to be fulfilled
2. *A condition or capability needed by a user to solve a problem or achieve an objective that must be met or possessed by a system or system component to satisfy a contract, standard, specification, or other formally imposed document*

requirements-based testing

An approach to testing in which test cases are designed based on requirements.

retesting

Testing that executes test cases that failed the last time they were run. Performed to verify the success of correcting faults.

review

A type of static testing in which a work product or process is evaluated by one or more individuals to detect defects or to provide improvements.

reviewable (testable)

A work product or document is reviewable or testable if the work is complete enough to enable it to be reviewed or tested.

risk

A factor that could result in future negative consequences
(often expressed as "risk = impact x likelihood").

risk-based testing

Testing in which the management, selection, prioritization, and use of testing activities and resources are based on corresponding risk types and risk levels.

robustness

The degree to which a component or system can function correctly in the presence of invalid inputs, or stressful or extreme environmental conditions.

robustness test(ing)

See *negative testing*.

role

Description of specific skills, qualifications and work profiles in software development. These should be filled by the persons (responsible for these roles) in the project.

root cause analysis

An analysis technique aimed at identifying the root causes of defects. By directing corrective measures at root causes, it is hoped that the likelihood of defect recurrence will be minimized.

safety-critical system

A system whose failure or malfunction may result in death or serious injury to people, loss or severe damage to equipment, or environmental harm.

security

The degree to which a component or system protects information and data so that persons or other components or systems have the degree of access appropriate to their types and levels of authorization.

security testing

Testing to determine the security of the software product.

severity

The degree of impact that a defect has on the development or operation of a component or system.

simulator

A device, computer program, or system used during testing which behaves or operates like a given system when provided with a set of controlled inputs.

smoke test

1. A test suite that covers the main functionality of a component or system to determine whether it works properly before planned testing begins
2. *A smoke test is often implemented without comparing the actual and the expected output. Instead, a smoke test tries to produce openly visible wrong results or crashes of the test object. It is mainly used to test robustness.*

software development lifecycle (SDLC) / software development model / software development process

1. The activities performed at each stage in software development, and how they relate to one another logically and chronologically

2. *Model or process that describes a defined organizational framework of software development. It defines which activities shall be executed by which roles in which order, which results will be produced, and how the results are checked by quality assurance*

software item

Identifiable (partial) result of the software development process (for example, a source code file, document, etc.).

software quality

The totality of functionality and features of a software product that bear on its ability to satisfy stated or implied needs.

specification

A document that specifies, ideally in a complete, precise, concrete and verifiable form, the requirements or other characteristics of a component or system. It serves developers as a basis for programming, and it serves testers as a basis for developing test cases with black-box test design techniques. (Often, a specification includes procedures for determining whether these requirements have been satisfied.)

state diagram

A diagram or model that describes the states that a component or system can assume and that shows the events or circumstances that cause and/or result from a change from one state to another.

state transition testing

A black box test design technique in which test cases are designed to exercise elements of a state transition model.

statement

An entity in a programming language that is typically the smallest indivisible unit of execution. Also referred to as an *instruction*.

statement coverage

1. The coverage of executable statements

2. *The percentage of executable statements that have been exercised by a test suite*

statement testing

1. A white-box test technique in which test cases are designed to execute statements.
2. *Control flow-based test design technique that requires that every executable statement of the program has been executed at least once.*

static analysis

The process of evaluating a component or system without executing it, based on its form, structure, content, or documentation.

static analyzer

A tool that carries out static analysis.

static testing

1. Testing a work product without the work product code being executed
2. *Testing of a component or system at the specification or implementation level without execution of any software (e.g., using reviews or static analysis)*

stress testing

A type of performance testing conducted to evaluate a system or component at or beyond the limits of its anticipated or specified workloads, or with reduced availability of resources such as access to memory or servers.

See also *robustness test(ing)*.

structural test(ing) / structure-based test(ing)

White-box test design technique in which the test cases are designed using the internal structure of the test object. Completeness of such a test is judged using coverage of structural elements (for example, branches, paths, data). General term for *control* or *data flow-based test*.

stub

A skeletal or special-purpose implementation of a software component, used to develop or test a component that calls or is otherwise dependent on it. It replaces a called component.

syntax testing

A test design technique in which test cases are designed based on a formal definition of the input syntax.

system integration testing

1. A test level that focuses on interactions between systems
2. *Testing the integration of systems (and packages); testing interfaces to external organizations (e.g., Electronic Data Interchange, Internet)*

system testing

1. A test level that focuses on verifying that a system as a whole meets specified requirements
2. *The process of testing a system to ensure that it meets specified requirements*

technical review

A type of formal review by a team of technically qualified personnel that examines the quality of a work product and identifies discrepancies from specifications and standards.

test

A set of one or more test cases.

test automation

1. The use of software to perform or support test activities
2. *The use of software tools to design or program test cases with the goal of being able to execute them repeatedly using the computer.*

test basis

1. The body of knowledge used as the basis for test analysis and design
2. *The documentation on which the design and choice of the test cases is based*

test bed

An environment containing hardware, instrumentation, simulators, software tools, and other support elements needed to conduct a test. Also called *test environment*. Also used as an alternative term for *test harness*.

test case

A set of preconditions, inputs, actions (where applicable), expected results and postconditions, developed based on test conditions.

test case explosion

The disproportionate growth of the number of test cases with growing size of the test basis or increasing number of parameters, when using a certain test design technique.

test case specification

Documentation of a set of test cases.

test condition

A testable aspect of a component or system identified as a basis for testing.

test coverage

See *coverage*.

test cycle

An instance of the test process performed against a single identifiable version of the test object.

test data

Data needed for test execution.

Data that exists (for example, in a database) before a test is executed and that affects or is affected by the component or system under test.

test design

The activity that derives and specifies test cases from test conditions.

test design specification

Documentation specifying the features to be tested and their corresponding test conditions.

test driver

See *driver*.

test effort

The resources required to perform the test process (can be estimated or analyzed).

test environment

An environment containing hardware, instrumentation, simulators, software tools, and other support elements needed to conduct a test.

test evaluation

Analysis of the test protocol or test log in order to determine if failures have occurred. If necessary, these are assigned a classification.

test execution

The activity that runs a test on a component or system and produces actual results

test harness

A collection of stubs and drivers needed to execute a test suite.

test infrastructure

The organizational artifacts needed to perform testing. Consists of test environments, test tools, office environment, and procedures.

testing

The process consisting of all lifecycle activities, both static and dynamic, concerned with planning, preparation and evaluation of a component or system and related work products to determine that they satisfy specified requirements, to demonstrate that they are fit for purpose, and to detect defects.

test interface

See *Point of Control (PoC)* and *Point of Observation (PoO)*.

test level

1. A specific instantiation of a test process
2. *A group of test activities that are executed and managed together. A test level is linked to the responsibilities in a project. Examples of test levels are component test, integration test, system test, or acceptance test (from the generic V-model).*

test log

A chronological record of relevant details about the execution of tests.

test logging

The activity of creating a test log.

test management

1. The planning, scheduling, estimating, monitoring, reporting, control, and completion of test activities
2. *Group of persons responsible for managing testing activities*

test manager

The person responsible for project management of testing activities, resources, and evaluation of a test object.

test method

See *test technique*.

test metric

A measurable attribute of a test case, test run, or test cycle, and the method used for measurement.

test object

1. The work product to be tested
2. *The component, integrated partial system, or system (in a certain version) that is to be tested*

test objective

The reason for or purpose of testing.

test oracle

A source that determines an expected result for comparison with the actual result of the system under test.

test phase

A distinct set of test activities collected into a manageable phase of a project—for exmple, the execution activities of a specific test level.

test plan

Documentation describing the test objectives to be achieved and the means and the schedule for achieving them, organized to coordinate testing activities.

The document can be divided into a master test plan or a level test plan.

test planning

The activity of establishing or updating a test plan.

test procedure

A sequence of test cases in execution order, and any associated actions that may be required to set up the initial preconditions and any wrap-up activities following execution.

test process

The set of interrelated activities comprising test planning, test monitoring and control, test analysis, test design, test implementation, test execution, and test completion.

test report

Documentation summarizing test activities and results.

test result

The consequence/outcome of the execution of a test.

test robot

A tool for executing tests that uses the open or accessible interfaces of the test objects (for example, the GUI) to provide input values and read their reactions.

test run

The execution of a test suite on a specific version of the test object.

test scenario

A set of test sequences.

test schedule

A list of activities, tasks or events that are part of the test process, and that identifies their intended start and finish dates and/or times, and interdependencies.

test script

A sequence of instructions for the (automated) execution of a test case or a test sequence.

test specification

1. The complete documentation of the test design, test cases, and test scripts for a specific test item
2. *The activity of specifying a test, typically part of the "test analysis and design" phase of the test life cycle.*

test strategy

Documentation aligned with the test policy that describes the generic requirements for testing and that details how to perform testing within an organization.

test suite

A set of test scripts or test procedures to be executed in a specific test run.

test summary report

A type of test report produced at a completion milestone that provides an evaluation of the corresponding test items against the specified exit criteria.

test technique

A procedure used to define test conditions, design test cases, and specify test data.

test tool

Software or hardware that supports one or more test activities.

testability

The degree to which test conditions can be established for a component or system, and to which tests can be performed to determine whether those test conditions have been met.

test-driven development (TDD)

A software development technique in which the test cases are developed (and often automated) before the software is developed incrementally to pass those test cases.

tester

1. A person who performs testing
2. *A general term for all people working in testing*

test-first approach

An approach to software development in which the test cases are designed and implemented before the associated component or system is developed.

See also *test-driven development.*

testing

The process consisting of all life cycle activities, both static and dynamic, concerned with planning, preparation and evaluation of software products and related work products to determine that they satisfy specified requirements, to demonstrate that they are fit for purpose, and to detect defects.

testware

Work products produced during the test process for use in planning, designing, executing, evaluating and reporting on testing.

traceability

The degree to which a relationship can be established between two or more work products.

tuning

Changing programs or program parameters and/or expanding hardware to optimize the time behavior of a hardware/software system.

unit testing

See *component testing*.

unnecessary test

A test that is redundant due to another test that is already present and thus does not lead to new results.

unreachable code

Code that cannot be reached and therefore is impossible to execute.

use case

A sequence of transactions in a dialogue between an actor and a component or system with a tangible result. An actor can be a user or anything that can exchange information with the system.

use case testing

A black-box test technique in which test cases are designed to exercise use case behaviors.

user acceptance testing (UAT)

A type of acceptance testing performed to determine whether the intended users accept the system.

validation

Confirmation by examination and through provision of objective evidence that the requirements for a specific intended use or application have been fulfilled.

verification

1. Confirmation by examination and through provision of objective evidence that specified requirements have been fulfilled
2. *Checking if the outputs from a development phase meet the requirements of the phase inputs*
3. *Mathematical proof of correctness of a (partial) program*

version

Development state of a software object at a certain point in time. Usually given by a number.

See also *configuration*.

V-model

A sequential development lifecycle model describing a one-for-one relationship between major phases of software development, from business requirements specification to delivery. The model also describes corresponding test levels from acceptance testing to component testing.

volume testing

Testing in which large amounts of data are manipulated or the system is subjected to the processing of large volumes of data.

See also *stress testing* and *load testing*.

walkthrough

A type of review in which an author leads members of the review through a work product and the members ask questions and make comments about possible issues.

white-box test technique

A test technique based exclusively on the internal structure of a component or system.

See also *structural test(ing)*.

C References

C.1 Literature

[**Bath 14**] Bath, G., McKay, J.: *The Software Test Engineer's Handbook: A Study Guide for the ISTQB® Test Analyst and Technical Test Analyst Advanced Level Certificates.* Rocky Nook; 2nd Edition, 2014.

[**Beck 04**] Beck, K.: *Extreme Programming Explained: Embrace Change.* Addison-Wesley Professional, 2nd Edition, 2004.

[**Beedle 02**] Beedle, M.; Schwaber, K.: *Agile Software Development with Scrum.* Prentice Hall, 2002.

[**Boehm 79**] Boehm, B. W.: *Guidelines for Verifying and Validating Software Requirements and Design Specification.* In: Proceedings of Euro IFIP 1979, pp. 711–719.

[**Boehm 86**] Boehm, B. W.: *A Spiral Model of Software Development and Enhancement.* ACM SIGSOFT, August 1986, pp. 14–24.

[**Bourne 97**] Bourne, K. C.: *Testing Client/Server Systems.* McGraw-Hill, 1997.

[**Crispin 08**] Crispin, L.; Gregory, J.: *Agile Testing: A practical Guide for Testers and Agile Teams.* Addison-Wesley Professional, 2008.

[**DeMarco 93**] DeMarco, T.: *Why Does Software Cost So Much?* IEEE Software, March 1993, pp. 89–90.

[**Fewster 99**] Fewster, M.; Graham, D.: *Software Automation: Effective use of test execution tools.* Addison-Wesley, 1999.

[**Gilb 93**] Gilb, T., Graham, D.: *Software Inspection.* Addison Wesley: Reading MA, 1993.

[**Gilb 05**] Gilb, T.: *Competitive Engineering: A Handbook for Systems Engineering, Requirements Engineering, and Software Engineering Using Planguage.* Butterworth-Heinemann, 2005.

[**Kruchten 03**] Kruchten, P.: *The Rational Unified Process: An Introduction.* Addison-Wesley Professional; 3rd Edition, 2003.

[**Linz 14**] Linz, T.: *Testing in Scrum, A Guide for Software Quality Assurance in the Agile World.* Rocky Nook, 2014.

[**Martin 91**] Martin, J.: *Rapid Application Development*. Macmillan, 1991.

[**Martin 08**] Martin, R. C.: *Clean Code: A Handbook of Agile Software Craftsmanship*. Prentice Hall; 2008.

[**Meyer 13**] Meyer, B.: *Touch of Class*. Springer Publishing, Heidelberg, Berlin, 2013.

[**Myers 12**] Myers, G. J.; Badgett, T.; Sandler, C.: *The Art of Software Testing*. 3rd Edition, John Wiley & Sons, Inc., 2012.

[**Pol 00**] Pol, M.; Koomen, T.; Spillner, A.: *Management und Optimierung des Testprozesses*. dpunkt.verlag, Heidelberg, 2000 (in German).

[**Royce 70**] Royce, W. W.: *Managing the development of large software systems*. In: IEEE WESCON, Aug. 1970, p. 1–9 (republished in *Proceedings of the 9th International Conference on Software Engineering*. 1987, Monterey, CA., pp. 328–338).

[**Sauer 00**] Sauer, C.: *The Effectiveness of Software Development Technical Reviews: A Behaviorally Motivated Program of Research*. IEEE Transactions on Software Engineering, Volume 26, Issue 1, pp. 1–14, 2000.

[**Shull 00**] Shull, F.; Rus, I.; Basili, V.: *How Perspective-Based Reading can Improve Requirement Inspections*. IEEE Computer, Volume 33, Issue 7, pp. 73–79, 2000.

[**Spillner 07**] Spillner, A.; Roßner, T.; Winter, M.; Linz, T.: *Software Testing Practice: Test Management: A Study Guide for the Certified Tester Exam ISTQB® Advanced Level*. Rocky Nook, 2007.

[**Wiegers 02**] Wiegers, K.: *Peer Reviews in Software*. Pearson Education: Boston MA, 2002.

C.2 Norms and Standards

[EN 50128] EN 50128:2001, Railway applications – Communication, signaling and processing systems – Software for railway control and protection systems.

[EN 60601] EN 60601-1:2013-12, Medical electrical equipment – Part 1: General requirements for basic safety and essential performance.

[IEEE 828] IEEE 828-2012 – IEEE Standard for Configuration Management in Systems and Software Engineering.

[IEEE 1012] IEEE 1012-2016 – IEEE Standard for System, Software, and Hardware Verification and Validation.

[IEEE 1044] IEEE 1044-2009 – IEEE Standard Classification for Software Anomalies.

[ISO 9000] ISO 9000:2015 Quality management systems, Series of standards.

[ISO 9001] ISO 9001:2015 Quality management systems – Requirements.

[ISO 20246] ISO/IEC 20246:2017 Software and systems engineering – Work product reviews.

[ISO 25010] ISO/IEC 25010, (2011) Systems and software engineering – Systems and software Quality Requirements and Evaluation (SQuaRE) System and software quality models.

[ISO 25012] ISO/IEC 25012, (2008) Software engineering – Software product Quality Requirements and Evaluation (SQuaRE) – Data quality model.

[ISO 29119] Software and systems engineering – Software testing. Consists of the following parts:

- ISO/IEC/IEEE 29119-1 (2013) Software and systems engineering – Software testing –
  Part 1: Concepts and definitions

- ISO/IEC/IEEE 29119-2 (2013) Software and systems engineering – Software testing –
  Part 2: Test processes

- ISO/IEC/IEEE 29119-3 (2013) Software and systems engineering – Software testing –
  Part 3: Test documentation

- ISO/IEC/IEEE 29119-4 (2015) Software and systems engineering – Software testing –
  Part 4: Test techniques

- ISO/IEC/IEEE 29119-5 (2016) Software and systems engineering – Software testing –
  Part 5: Keyword-Driven Testing

- ISO/IEC CD TR 29119-6 Software and systems engineering – Software testing –
  Part 6: Guidelines for the use of ISO/IEC/IEEE 29119 in Agile projects (Under development)

- ISO/IEC TR 29119-11 (2020) Software and systems engineering – Software testing –
  Part 11: Guidelines on the testing of AI-based systems

[ISO 31000] ISO 31000:2018 – Risk management – Guidelines.

[ISO 90003] ISO/IEC/IEEE 90003:2018, Software engineering – Guidelines for the application of ISO 9001:2015 to computer software.

[ISO/IEC 12207] ISO/IEC/IEEE 12207:2017 – Systems and software engineering – Software life cycle processes.

[ISO/IEC 15504] ISO/IEC 15504-6:2013 Information technology – Process assessment – Part 6: An exemplar system life cycle process assessment model.

[ISO/IEC 20246] ISO/IEC 20246:2017 Software and systems engineering – Work product reviews.

[ISO/IEC 24765] ISO/IEC/IEEE 24765:2017 – Systems and software engineering – Vocabulary.

[RTC-DO 178B] RTC-DO Std 178B, Radio Technical Commission for Aeronautics, Software Considerations in Airborne Systems and Equipment Certification, RTCA, Inc., 1992. RTC-DO Std 178C Software Considerations in Airborne Systems and Equipment Certification (new version "C" of the standard was released January 2012).

C.3 URLs[1]

[URL: ACTS] *http://csrc.nist.gov/groups/SNS/acts/download_tools.html*
Automated Combinatorial Testing for Software.[2]

[URL: ATDD] *https://en.wikipedia.org/wiki/Acceptance_test-driven_development*
Acceptance test–driven development.

[URL: BDD] *https://en.wikipedia.org/wiki/Behavior-driven_development*
Behavior-driven development.

[URL: binClassifiers] *https://en.wikipedia.org/wiki/Evaluation_of_binary_classifiers*
Evaluation of binary classifiers.

[URL: CMMI] *https://cmmiinstitute.com/*
CMMI Institute (Capability Maturity Model Integration (CMMI)).

[URL: DSGVO] *https://eur-lex.europa.eu/eli/reg/2016/679*
Regulation (EU) 2016/679 of the European Parliament and of the Council of 27 April 2016 on the protection of natural persons with regard to the processing of personal data and on the free movement of such data, and repealing Directive 95/46/EC (General Data Protection Regulation).

[URL: Epic] *https://en.wikipedia.org/wiki/User_story*
Epic.

[URL: ERM] *https://en.wikipedia.org/wiki/Entity-relationship_model*
Entity-Relationship-Model.

[URL: Error Costs] *https://www.nature.com/news/software-error-doomed-japanese-hitomi-spa- cecraft-1.19835*
Software error doomed Japanese Hitomi spacecraft.

[URL: FDA] *http://www.fda.com*
US Food and Drug Administration (FDA).

[URL: FMEA] *https://en.wikipedia.org/wiki/Failure_mode_and_effects_analysis*
Failure Mode and Effects Analysis.

[URL: imbus-downloads] *https://www.imbus.de/en/downloads*
Useful articles, documents, and templates from imbus AG for download.

[URL: ISTQB] *http://www.istqb.org*
International Software Testing Qualifications Board – ISTQB®.

---

1. All URLs were current at the time of going to press in May 2021.
2. This is not a direct download link. The linked page describes how to obtain the tool.

[URL: ISTQB Foundation Level Agile Tester] *https://www.istqb.org/certification-path-root/agile-tester.html*
ISTQB® Agile Tester – Foundation Level.

[URL: ISTQB Glossary] *https://glossary.istqb.org/en/search/*
ISTQB® Certified Tester Glossary.

[URL: Kanban] *https://en.wikipedia.org/wiki/Kanban_(development)*
Kanban (development methodology).

[URL: Mars Climate Orbiter] *https://en.wikipedia.org/wiki/Mars_Climate_Orbiter*
Mars climate orbiter cause of failure.

[URL: MAX-groundings] *https://en.wikipedia.org/wiki/Boeing_737_MAX_groundings*
Report about Boeing 737 MAX airplane groundings.

[URL: McCabe] *https://en.wikipedia.org/wiki/Cyclomatic_complexity*
Cyclomatic complexity.

[URL: OWASP] *https://www.owasp.org*
The OWASPTM Foundation – the free and open software security community.

[URL: PDCA] *https://en.wikipedia.org/wiki/PDCA*
PDCA (plan–do–check–act), Deming Circle or Deming Wheel.

[URL: Prototyping] *https://en.wikipedia.org/wiki/Software_prototyping*
Software prototyping.

[URL: Scrum Guide] *http://www.scrumguides.org*
The Scrum Guide, developed and sustained by Ken Schwaber and Jeff Sutherland.

[URL: Softwaretest Knowledge] *http://www.softwaretest-knowledge.de/en*
Book website.

[URL: Strategy] *https://en.wikipedia.org/wiki/Strategy*
General explanation.

[URL: SW-Dev-Process] *https://en.wikipedia.org/wiki/Software_development_process*
Software development processes.

[URL: TDD] *https://en.wikipedia.org/wiki/Test-driven_development*
Test-driven development.

[URL: TestBench CS] *http://www.testbench.com*
TestBench Cloud Testmanagement from imbus AG.

[URL: Tool-List] *https://www.testtoolreview.de/en*
Information portal coveringt the international market for software testing tools, compiled by imbus AG.

[**URL: UML**] *https://www.uml.org/*
Unified Modeling Language, Version: 2.5.1. A specification defining a graphical language for visualizing, specifying, constructing, and documenting the artifacts of distributed object systems, December 2017.

[**URL: xUnit**] *https://en.wikipedia.org/wiki/List_of_unit_testing_frameworks*
List of unit testing frameworks.

Index

A

acceptance testing 76, 281
actual result 281
ad hoc integration 73
ad hoc review 102
agile development 55
agile software development 54
agile testing technique 56
alpha test 79
alpha testing 281
analytical quality assurance 281
anomaly 282
anti-risk measures 218
atomic condition 282
audit 282
author 107
automating dynamic test 260

B

backbone integration 73
back-to-back testing 282
bespoke software 282
beta test 79
beta testing 282
big bang 73
black-box technique 85, 123
black-box testing 126
black-box test technique 126, 171, 282
blocked test case 282
bottom-up integration 73
boundary value 282
boundary value analysis 137, 283
boundary value coverage 283
branch 283
branch condition 283
branch condition combination testing 180
branch condition testing 179
branch coverage 283
branch testing 283
buddy check 109
buddy testing 62, 109
bug 9, 283
business process analysis 82
business process-based testing 283

C

capture and replay 261
capture/playback tool 284
capture/replay tool 261
cause-effect diagram 284
cause-effect graph 284
cause-effect graphing 153
certificate 2
certification program for software testers 2
Certified Tester 2, 5, 209, 279
Certified Tester certification 209
Certified Tester Foundation Level 279
change 284
change control board 245
change order 284
change request 284
checklist-based review 103
checklist-based testing 189
classifying defects 241
class test 284
code-based testing 284
code swapping 62, 109
commercial off-the-shelf (COTS) 284

communication 45
comparator 265, 285
complete testing 285
component 285
component integration testing 285
component testing 58, 59, 71, 203, 285
configuration 285
configuration item 285
configuration management 246, 285
confirmation bias 44
constructive quality assurance 285
continuous delivery 56
continuous deployment 56
continuous integration 55
continuous testing 56
control flow 286
control flow anomaly 286
control flow-based testing 286
control flow graph 286
cost-based testing 215
cost-benefit relation 223
cost of defect 223
cost of testing 220, 223
coverage 286
covering array 161
customer-specific software 286
cyclomatic complexity 286

D

data-driven testing 263, 264
data flow analysis 259, 286
data flow anomaly 286
data flow coverage 286
data flow testing 187
data flow test technique 287
data quality 75, 287
dead code 287
debugger 265
debugger tool 287
debugging 287
decision coverage 287
decision table 287
decision table structure 155

decision table testing 153, 287
decision testing / decision condition testing 175, 287
defect 9, 20, 241, 288
defect database 238, 245, 288
Defect Detection Percentage (DDP) 288
defect management 235, 288
defect masking 10, 288
defect report 236, 238
defect severity 241
defect status model 244
defect status tracking 242
definition of done 230
definition of ready 230
developer test 288
development model 288
  types 49
driver 288
dry run 103, 110
dummy 288
dynamic analysis 288
dynamic testing 117, 121, 288

E

efficiency 64, 289
entry criteria 230
equivalence class 289
equivalence partition 289
equivalence partition coverage 289
equivalence partitioning 126, 289
errare humanum est 43
error 10, 11, 289
error guessing 189, 289
estimation technique 222
exception handling 289
exit criteria 230, 290
expected result 290
experience-based testing 189
experience-based test technique 125, 189
exploratory testing 191, 290
Extreme Programming (XP) 290

F

facilitator 107, 290, 293
failure 9, 11, 38, 241, 290
failure class / failure classification / failure taxonomy 290
failure priority 290
fault 9, 11, 20, 290
Fault Detection Percentage (FDP) 288
fault masking 290
fault-revealing test case 291
fault tolerance 291
field test 79
field testing 291
finite state machine 291
formal review 102
functionality 291
functional requirement 81, 291
functional suitability 23, 81
functional test 62, 80
functional testing 291
function test 62

G

glass-box technique 123
guard conditions 145
GUI 150, 291

H

high-level test case / logical test case 292
hotfix 89

I

impact analysis 89
incident database 291
incremental development 54
independent testing 201
informal review 109, 291
inspection 111, 292
inspection meeting 112
inspector 107
instruction 292
instrumentation 292
integration 292

integration strategy 72
integration testing 66, 203, 292
integration testing in the large 68
internet of things 56
intrusive measurement 266
intuitive test case design 189
ISO 9000 26
ISO 25010 22
ISO 25012 22
ISO 29119 159, 212, 234, 240
ISO 31000 218
ISO/IEC 90003 26
ISTQB 2, 208, 279
iterative development 54
iterative-incremental development 54
iterative testing 28
iterative test process 29

J

JUnit 123, 261

K

keyword-driven testing 263

L

lead tester 206
level test plan 292
load and performance testing tool 266
load testing 292
load testing tool 266
low-level test case / concrete test case 292

M

maintainability 64, 292
maintenance / maintenance process 292
maintenance testing 88
management review 108, 293
master test plan 293
metric 293
milestone 293
mindset
    developers 46
    testers 46

mistake 11, 293
mock-up 293
model checker 260
moderator 107, 293
modified condition / decision coverage (MC/DC) 293
modified condition decision coverage testing 181
modified condition / decision testing 293
module testing 294
monitor 69
monitoring 30
monitoring tool 294
multidisciplinary team 209

N

negative testing 294
non-functional requirement 294
non-functional test 80, 83
non-functional testing 294
norms 248
n-switch coverage 150
n-wise testing 162

O

official syllabus 279
open-box technique 123
orthogonal array 161

P

pair programming 109
pair-wise testing 159
patch 294
path 294
path coverage 295
path testing 183, 295
peer review 109
performance 295
performance testing 295
performance testing tool 266, 295
pesticide paradox 21
pilot project 273

Point of Control (PoC) 124, 295
point of observation 124
postcondition 295
precondition 295
preventive software quality assurance 295
prioritization criteria 228
prioritizing 227
probe effect 296
process model 296
product backlog 40
production environment 296
product risk 218, 296
project risk 217, 296

Q

quality 296, 299
quality assurance (QA) 26, 296
quality characteristic 25, 296
quality in use model 23
quality management 26, 296
quality requirement 7

R

random testing 296
recorder 108
regression testing 91, 296
release 297
release development 90
reliability 23, 297
requirement 297
requirements-based testing 85, 297
retesting 38, 297
review 97, 297
　critical factors, benefits, limits 114
　success factors 115
reviewability 112
reviewable 297
reviewer 107
review leader 106
review meeting 101
review preparation 100

review process 97, 98
  responsibilities 106
  roles 106
review process activities 99
review rechnique
  scenario-based 103
review technique 102
  ad hoc 102
  checklist-based 103
  role-based 104
risk 217, 297
risk-based testing 215, 219, 297
risk classification 25
risk management 218
robustness 297
robustness test 298
role 298
role-based review 104
root cause analysis 298

S

safety-critical system 298
satisfaction 23
scenario-based review 103
scribe 108
Scrum 54, 57
security 298
security testing 298
sequential development model 49
session-based testing 192
severity 298
simulator 298
smoke test 171, 298
soft skill 44, 209
software development
  project and product contexts 56
software development lifecycle (SDLC) 49, 299
software development process 299
software item 299
software maintenance 88

software quality 7, 22
  functional suitability 23
  reliability 23
  satisfaction 23
specialist review 110
specification 299
specifications-based testing 85
standards 248
standards and legal guidelines 248
state diagram 299
statement 299
statement coverage 299
statement testing 173, 300
state transition testing 145, 299
static analysis 95, 300
static analyzer 300
static testing 95, 117, 300
static test technique 97
static test tool 257
static vs. dynamic tests 117
stress testing 300
structural test(ing) 86, 300
structure-based test 80
structure-based testing 86, 172
stub 300
syntax test 171
syntax testing 300
system integration testing 68, 301
system testing 74, 75, 203, 301

T

tailoring 57
technical review 110, 301
test 301
testability 305
test administrator 208
test analysis 31
test analyst 208
test automation 91, 268, 301
  benefits and risks 268
test automation specialist 208
test basis 14, 301
test bed 301

test case 14, 34, 37, 122, 131, 301
test case explosion 301
test case specification 123, 301
test coach 206
test completion 40
test condition 15, 36, 302
test control 232
test coverage 302
test cycle 302
test cycle monitoring 232
test data 302
test design 34, 302
test designer 208
test design specification 302
test-driven development (TDD) 66, 261, 306
test driver 302
test effort 302
test environment 36, 302
tester 207, 306
test evaluation 302
test execution 37, 38, 302
test execution planning 226
test execution schedule 15
test-first 66
test-first approach 306
test-first programming 66
test framework 121, 252
test harness 302
test implementation 36
test infrastructure 303
testing 12, 303, 306
  psychological factors 43
  risk 217
  roles, tasks, qualifications 205
  tool-based support 267
testing effort 16, 220
  estimation 222
  factors 220
testing infrastructure 36
testing levels 58
testing process 27, 42
  main activities 28

testing specialists 209
testing strategy 210, 213
  checklist-based approach 216
  cost-based 215
  directed approach 216
  implementation 225
  methodical approach 216
  model-based approach 215
  regression-averse approach 216
  reuse-based approach 216
  risk-based 215
  standards-compliant approach 216
testing techniques
  selecting 195
test interface 303
test item 15
test level 303
test log 15, 303
test logging 303
test management 201, 303
  evaluation results 245
test management cycle 225
test management tool 252
test manager 205, 206, 222, 303
test method 303
test metric 233, 303
test monitoring and control 30
test object 59, 304
test objective 304
test oracle 34, 304
test organization 201
test phase 304
test plan 15, 29, 304
test planning 29, 210, 304
test procedure 37, 304
test process 304
  influence of context 42
test report 233, 236, 304
test result 304
test robot 304
test run 14, 305
test scenario 305
test schedule 30, 305

test script 15, 37, 305
test specialist 209
test specification 305
test specification tool 256
test strategy 305
test suite 15, 37, 305
test summary report 40, 305
test technique 33, 305
test tool 251, 252, 305
test types 80
testware 40, 306
tool selection 272
top-down integration 72
traceability 33, 39, 41, 306
transition state test 151
transition tree 148
tuning 306
types of review 108
  selection 113
typical customer test 79

U

unit test framework 261
unit testing 306
unnecessary test 306
unreachable code 306
use case 307
use case testing 168, 307
user acceptance testing (UAT) 78, 307

V

validation 53, 307
verification 53, 307
version 307
V-model 51, 307
volume testing 307

W

walkthrough 103, 110, 308
waterfall model 50
white-box technique 86, 123
white-box testing technique 188
white-box test technique 172, 308

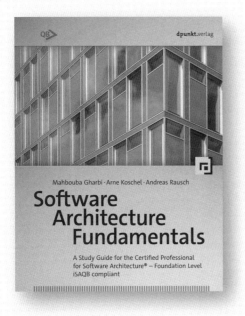

Mahbouba Gharbi · Arne Koschel · Andreas Rausch

Software Architecture Fundamentals

A Study Guide for the Certified Professional for Software Architecture® – Foundation Level iSAQB compliant

2019
232 pages, paperback
€ 36,90 (D)
US $ 39,95

ISBN:
Print   978-3-86490-625-1
PDF   978-3-96088-644-0
ePub   978-3-96088-645-7
mobi   978-3-96088-646-4

Software architecture is an important factor for the success of any software project. In the context of systematic design and construction, solid software architecture ensures the fulfilment of quality requirements such as expandability, flexibility, performance, and time-to-market.

This book gives you all the basic know-how you need to begin designing scalable system software architectures. It goes into detail on all the most important terms and concepts and how they relate to other IT practices.

Following on from the basics, it describes the techniques and methods required for the planning, documentation, and quality management of software architectures. It details the role, the tasks, and the work environment of a software architect, as well as looking at how the job itself is embedded in company and project structures.

The book is designed for self-study and covers the curriculum for the Certified Professional for Software Architecture – Foundation Level (CPSA-F) exam as defined by the International Software Architecture Qualification Board (iSAQB).

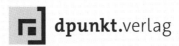

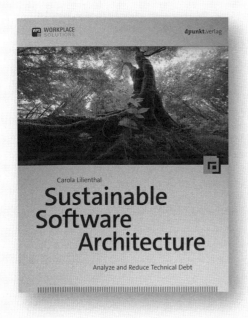

Carola Lilienthal

Sustainable Software Architecture

Analyze and Reduce Technical Debt

2019
310 pages, paperback
€ 36,90 (D)
US $ 46,90

ISBN:
Print (dt.)   978-3-86490-673-2
Print (engl.)   978-1-68198-569-5
PDF   978-3-96088-780-5
ePub   978-3-96088-781-2
mobi   978-3-96088-782-9

Today's programmers don't develop software systems from scratch. Instead, they spend their time fixing, extending, modifying, and enhancing existing software. Legacy systems often turn into an unwieldy mess that becomes increasingly difficult to modify, and with architecture that continually accumulates technical debt.

Carola Lilienthal has analyzed more than 300 software systems written in Java, C#, C++, PHP, ABAP, and TypeScript and, together with her teams, has successfully refactored them. This book condenses her experience with monolithic systems, architectural and design patterns, layered architectures, domain-driven design, and microservices.

With more than 200 color images from real-world systems, good and sub-optimal sample solutions are presented in a comprehensible and thorough way, while recommendations and suggestions based on practical projects allow the reader to directly apply the author's knowledge to their daily work.

"Throughout the book, Dr. Lilienthal has provided sound advice on diagnosing, understanding, disentangling, and ultimately preventing the issues that make software systems brittle and subject to breakage. In addition to the technical examples that you'd expect in a book on software architecture, she takes the time to dive into the behavioral and human aspects that impact sustainability and, in my experience, are inextricably linked to the health of a codebase."
　　　　　From the Foreword of Andrea Goulet
　　　　　CEO, Corgibytes, Founder, Legacy Code Rocks

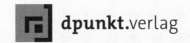